Teaching Politics and International Relati

Teaching Politics and International Relations

Edited by

Cathy Gormley-Heenan
Senior Lecturer
School of Criminology, Politics and Social Policy, University of Ulster, UK

and

Simon Lightfoot
Senior Lecturer
University of Leeds, UK

First published 2012 by
PALGRAVE MACMILLAN

Palgrave Macmillan in the UK is an imprint of Macmillan Publishers Limited, registered in England, company number 785998, of Houndmills, Basingstoke, Hampshire RG21 6XS.

Palgrave Macmillan in the US is a division of St Martin's Press LLC, 175 Fifth Avenue, New York, NY 10010.

Palgrave Macmillan is the global academic imprint of the above companies and has companies and representatives throughout the world.

Palgrave® and Macmillan® are registered trademarks in the United States, the United Kingdom, Europe and other countries.

ISBN 978–0–230–30001–9   hardback
ISBN 978–1–137–00339–3   paperback

This book is printed on paper suitable for recycling and made from fully managed and sustained forest sources. Logging, pulping and manufacturing processes are expected to conform to the environmental regulations of the country of origin.

A catalogue record for this book is available from the British Library.

A catalog record for this book is available from the Library of Congress.

10 9 8 7 6 5 4 3 2 1
21 20 19 18 17 16 15 14 13 12

Printed and bound in Great Britain by
CPI Antony Rowe, Chippenham and Eastbourne

Contents

List of Tables

List of Figures

List of Boxes

Acknowledgements

This book grew out of a number of learning- and teaching-related events that both editors attended. However, the main catalyst was the decision to co-organize the 2nd Political Studies Association Teaching and Learning Specialist Group Conference at the University of Leeds in 2009. We would like to thank the specialist group and C-SAP, the subject centre for Politics and international relations (IR), for their generous financial support of that event. The participants at the conference should be thanked for their contributions, as should Prof. Vivien Jones, the pro-dean for the student experience at the University of Leeds, who gave the welcoming address.

The contributors to the volume responded to our numerous requests for changes and editions to their chapters with good grace and best of all efficiency! Liz Holwell and everyone at Palgrave Macmillan deserve the usual praise for turning the draft manuscript into the book you hold in your hands. Our biggest debt at Palgrave Macmillan is to Amber Stone-Galilee, our editor, who took a gamble on this book and fought our corner. We believe this book will be useful for the profession, but without her support it would have remained just an idea.

Our families have been very supportive throughout, so thanks to Sam, Ronan, Hala and Ben. Finally, we would like to recognize all those people who have taken the time to discuss learning and teaching issues with us and to reflect upon the student experience. The growth in the activities of the PSA Teaching and Learning Group and the creation of the BISA Learning and Teaching Group (BLT) show the interest in the topic. In the modern academic world of 'small' research grants being less that £100K and the REF, learning and teaching can be overlooked as just part of what we do in the privacy of our own classroom. It is much, much more than that. Finally, the book is dedicated to the memory of Philippa Sherrington, a colleague who did much to raise the profile of teaching and learning in Politics and IR and who is greatly missed by many contributors to this book.

List of Contributors

Alasdair Blair is Professor of Politics and International Relations and National Teaching Fellow, Department of Historical and Social Studies, De Montfort University.

Jacqui Briggs is Principal Lecturer in Politics at the University of Lincoln and Associate Editor of *European Political Science*.

John Craig is a National Teaching Fellow and Assistant Dean, School of Social Sciences and Law, Teesside University.

Steven Curtis is Senior Lecturer in International Relations at London Metropolitan University and a National Teaching Fellow of the Higher Education Academy.

Cathy Gormley-Heenan is Director of the Institute for Research in Social Sciences (IRiSS) and Senior Lecturer, School of Criminology, Politics & Social Policy, University of Ulster.

Lisa Harrison is Head of Department, History, Philosophy and Politics, University of the West of England.

Jon Herbert is Lecturer in American Studies, University of Keele.

Jennifer Lees-Marshment is Senior Lecturer in Political Studies, Department of Political Studies, University of Auckland.

Cristina Leston-Bandeira is Senior Lecturer in Legislative Studies, Department of Politics and International Studies, University of Hull.

Simon Lightfoot is Senior Lecturer in European Politics, School of Politics and International studies, University of Leeds.

Samantha McGinty is Research Assistant on an NTFS project looking at assessment and feedback, De Montfort University.

Lee Marsden is Senior Lecturer in International Relations, Political, Social and International Studies, University of East Anglia.

Dave Middleton is Senior Lecturer in Politics and International Studies, Open University.

Knut Roder is Professor of Politics and Political Economy, Department of Business and Social Sciences, Saint Louis University – Madrid Campus.

Carmel Roulston is Senior Lecturer in Politics, School of Criminology, Politics & Social Policy, University of Ulster.

Christina Rowley is Lecturer in American Studies at Swansea University.

Heather Savigny is Senior Lecturer in Politics, Political, Social and International Studies, University of East Anglia.

Laura J. Shepherd is Senior Lecturer in International Relations, School of Social Sciences and International Studies, University of New South Wales.

Steve Spencer is Senior Lecturer in Sociology, Faculty of Development and Society Sheffield Hallam University.

Stephen Thornton is Lecturer in Comparative Politics, School of European Studies, Cardiff University.

Matthew Wyman is Senior Teaching Fellow, Politics, International Relations & Philosophy, Keele University.

Penny Welch, Learning and Teaching Co-ordinator, School of Law, Social Sciences and Communications, University of Wolverhampton.

Introduction

Simon Lightfoot and Cathy Gormley-Heenan

Why might we need a book on teaching, learning and assessment in politics and international relations? When we first proposed the idea of a book to Palgrave Macmillan in 2009, we wrote that 'teaching and learning issues are central to the student experience and increasingly assessed by a range of different external bodies (for example, through the National Student Survey (NSS), the *Times Higher* University League Tables and World Rankings)'. Since then, of course, there have been further developments, which illustrate the necessity of subject-specific teaching and learning support and guidance, such as this book.

Firstly, the Browne Review has been published, and from 2012 the majority of university students in the UK will pay £9000 annual tuition fees. Along with addressing issues of widening access, a key implication of this rise in fees will be to refocus attention on the student experience more generally. Secondly, the Higher Education Funding Council for England (HEFCE) has introduced a compulsory Key Information Set (KIS) for every undergraduate course of more than one year's duration which will come on stream in September 2012. The KIS will bring together a range of existing data sets that relate to the individual courses that institutions provide and will include details on overall student satisfaction, the particulars of the programme of study such as the range of assessments and the methods of learning and teaching used within the course and the employment and salary data of those who have graduated from the course. And so, for the first time, information on our courses and programmes will be presented by all institutions in a simple but consistent format. A key implication of the introduction of KIS will be to refocus attention on the student experience within individual programmes (such as politics), more specifically because of concerns that KIS will increasingly drive league tables and thereby students' choice of university. The need for an excellent student experience will require academic colleagues to ensure their teaching is of the highest possible quality.

This book, however, is not a call to 'bring teaching and learning back in', as we firmly believe that within politics and international relations (IR) there is considerable evidence of excellent teaching and learning across the sector. However the post-Browne environment means there is little room for complacency, and it will be increasingly common for all staff to be expected to demonstrate ever-increasing excellence in the field of learning and teaching as well as research. This is important, not least because of the seemingly traditional divide within the profession between teaching and research. In the past, departments had been accused of focusing solely on the Research Excellence Framework (REF) at the expense of the student experience. Anecdotally, colleagues would proclaim that the sure-fire way to promotion was to land a major research grant or 4* publications; not by delivering excellent teaching and learning. Non research-active staff were occasionally put on 'teaching only' contracts with a perceived reduction in status. Consequently, the student body felt that they were not getting value for money in terms of contact time, feedback and access to academic staff and were willing to complain about it. NSS comments such as 'they only care about their research' are, apparently, all too common.

Of course, the issues raised above are generic issues and will apply to every discipline in the higher education sector and so generic advice and guidance on issues of teaching and learning will be useful in this context. It begs the question again: why do we need a book dedicated to the *specificities* of teaching and learning in politics and IR? In libraries across the UK and beyond, there are already a myriad of book on politics and IR. Every conceivable subset of the genres are covered and yet there are hardly any books that focus on teaching and learning within the discipline.[1] This is something of an oddity not least because teaching politics and IR offers challenges that many other disciplines do not face. First, as a discipline, we are forced to confront the reality that our subject matter changes more rapidly than many other subjects. For example, the collapse of Communism in 1989 meant that an entire subdiscipline had to reinvent itself, while the attacks on September 11 led to radical changes in the direction of US Foreign Policy research. Second, the nature of academic publishing can mean that these changes will not be analysed in books or journal articles very quickly, yet staff are expected to teach these topics as they happen. Third, the discipline must also contend with the realities of political activism (among staff and students) and reflect on how do/should we teach those subjects to which we are ideologically opposed? By extension, we must consider to what extent should our own political views be common knowledge, if at all?

Notwithstanding these important questions, the perception remains of a lack of engagement with teaching and learning issues in politics and IR, despite all new programmes needing validation, while each existing programme at either undergraduate or postgraduate level has to undergo periodic review (revalidation) and Quality Assurance Agency (QAA) review. As part of such reviews, it should be standard practice to examine the awareness of staff understanding of current developments in teaching and learning, both at a generic and a subject-specific level. With the notable exception of journals such as *International Studies Perspectives*, *PS: Political Science & Politics*, *Politics* and *European Political Science*, which cover teaching and learning issues as part of a wider portfolio of articles, teaching and learning issues are still not given the prominence they merit.[2] We suspect that with the aforementioned changes to the higher education sector in terms of KIS and higher fees, degree programmes will have to be more explicit in their demonstrable knowledge of teaching and learning at a subject-specific level. This knowledge does exist, as is aptly demonstrated by the contributions to this volume.

This brings us to the real purpose of this book. It is a book that seeks to fill that gap in relation to teaching and learning in politics and IR. It takes a state-of-the-discipline approach to the topic by bringing together a range of contributions that promote a greater understanding of the most cutting-edge approaches, techniques and methodologies for politics and IR tutors. It also discusses the broader themes and challenges in teaching and learning but firmly places and highlights the peculiarities of these themes in the specific context of political science.

The book has been designed to appeal to anyone who teaches politics and IR in a higher-education establishment. The majority of the contributors work within the UK's higher-education sector but we believe that the examples they offer will speak across borders to colleagues in the USA, Canada, Australia and New Zealand. Of course, some of the chapters will be more relevant to specific groups of academics at specific times in their careers. For example, the full volume will have high appeal to early career scholars who are obliged to undertake some form of professional training and accreditation upon securing their first academic post in the area of higher-education practice and/or teaching and learning. Also, given the requirement (or CV building or financial necessity) to teach as part of a graduate teaching assistant (GTAs)/scholarship and the importance placed upon ensuring these GTAs have the necessary skills to teach, we also believe that GTAs will find plenty of tips and reassurance within the chapters as they start to balance their PhD research plans with their teaching duties. Yet despite these more obvious audiences, we have consciously designed the book to also be of value to more established academics within the discipline that are keen to adapt their teaching to reflect the changing landscape that is UK higher education. The insights we offer about the nature of the UK's higher-education system would also be relevant to anyone moving to the UK to take up a post from another country, keen to understand the similarities and differences of the teaching and learning agenda and the various assessments of this. As a guide to teaching and learning in politics and IR, it provides more than just academic analysis of the state of the discipline, by also including practical advice and a wide range of resource materials that colleagues and graduate students can draw upon on a regular basis.

The first Part of the book (Chapters 1–3) reflects on the changing context of teaching politics and IR in the UK and beyond. Things have changed remarkably in the higher education over the last 10–20 years and will continue to do so as a consequence of the new fee structure being introduced. We are delighted that our opening chapter looks at both the old and the new. In this first chapter, Penny Welch revisits the seminal paper she wrote for *Politics* ten years ago. Back then she argued that politics tutors needed to give more attention to teaching and assessment methods and to the learning needs of students. Ten years on, she argues that many more colleagues are taking learning and teaching seriously, in part due to QAA Subject Reviews, the establishment of the Fund for the Development of Teaching and Learning (FDTL) and the Higher Education Academy's (HEA) Subject Centres. Despite this, Welch raises concerns about the nature of higher education in the UK, especially relating to the pressures on teaching and suggests three strategies to defend creativity in politics teaching based on scholarship, collegiality and student-centredness. John Craig, Head of Social Sciences in the HEA, then examines the crucial issue for this book – 'what (if anything) is different about teaching and learning in politics?' This chapter reviews what we already know about teaching and learning in politics, in terms of both the cognitive nature of the discipline and the pedagogic practice of the discipline. It looks at Johnson's (1989) 'Limits of Political Science' which rejects politics as a numerate science and politics as simply the study of current affairs and promotes 'pure politics' based on historical and philosophical studies and 'applied politics' based on public administration. Craig argues that a more plural pedagogy can and should be developed along four core strands – history and philosophy (through lectures, seminars, texts); political science (through computer labs and problem solving); applied politics (through placements and simulations); and contemporary politics (through research skills and training). This analysis allows Lisa Harrison to examine what we teach via the current benchmarking statements for the discipline. She asks: what is it that we think should be part of a politics or IR degree? The chapter therefore examines who decides what is taught on (a) a politics programme as a whole; (b) the specific modules therein? As a composite, these chapters provide the reader with a solid grounding in terms of the context that the study of politics and IR operates within, both generally and pedagogically.

The second part of the book (Chapters 4–8) shifts from this macro-level overview towards some of the day-to-day realities of teaching and learning in the politics classroom. Beginning with the most common forms of teaching delivery in our subject area, Cristina Leston-Bandeira examines the challenges associated with large-group teaching, by presenting best practice in relation to lectures. Jacqui Briggs then explores the other common form of teaching within the discipline – small group teaching in seminars and tutorials – and outlines some specific seminar techniques to engage students with their learning (through the use of buzz groups, debates and posters). Steven Curtis and Stephen Thornton, in their respective chapters, move away from the traditional to an examination of alternative ways to learn about politics and IR. These alternatives range from group discussions that replicate real-world political situations such as role plays and simulations to the use of new technologies and new social media, especially the politics-specific forms of content such as political blogs, podcasts and even Twitter feeds. The final chapter in Part II outlines current modes of assessment in politics and IR and tackles the vexed question of the assessment feedback link or loop. Alasdair Blair and Samantha McGinty begin with an overview of the different types of assessment used in politics and IR; they show that up until the early 1990s the traditional approach to teaching and learning in politics was to use examinations and essays as the primary method of assessment and argue that a central feature of any method of assessment should be the objective of developing student engagement in 'deep' rather than 'surface' learning, a lesson too often forgotten by those of us who cling to the essay and exam format or assessment! Together, these chapters offer a series of helpful tips and suggestions for those new to the classroom environment as a lecturer as well as to those seeking to reinvigorate their teaching practices.

Part III of the book (Chapters 9–13) considers what we have broadly termed 'teaching the curriculum'. Teaching politics and IR can force staff and students to critically examine their own strongly held beliefs as well as those of other people and, quite rightly, this is something that needs to be handled with care. Issues of gender, race and political beliefs appear in almost every politics module. Grounding some of these issues in political theory can give lecturers a strong starting point but as Heather Savigny and Lee Marsden note from their own experiences of trying to engage students with an understanding of the need for theory in their work, this can be, just sometimes, a thankless experience. While remaining cognisant that there are different ways in which students can 'do' political analysis, these contributors focus upon the application of theoretical frameworks as a mechanism to understand, or attempt to explain, 'real world' events or phenomena. A key issue that often arises in the review of 'real world politics' is one's political beliefs and because of this Cathy Gormley-Heenan reflects on the extent to which lecturers should, if ever, admit their own political viewpoints in the classroom. She engages with the vexed question of whether a lecturer can or should ever be 'neutral' in the classroom and whether a position of 'neutrality' can affect one's capacity to develop a/the critical student. The next three chapters (11, 12 and 13) examine the teaching of three specific topics: gender, terrorism and race. Laura Shepherd and Christina Rowley argue that scheduling a 'week on gender' when teaching politics and IR, although common practice, is problematic. It offers two sets of strategies for gendering teaching; one strategy premised on retaining a 'week on gender' and one that encourages the viewing of politics and IR through a gendered lens throughout. Drawing on contemporary feminist literature as well as personal experience, the chapter concludes that teaching is a practice of disciplinary politics and a process that demands critical reflection on the politics of our own representations of the discipline. Knut Roeder then considers the growing popularity of subjects such as 'terrorism' with students. While such topics may pose additional pedagogical challenges to teachers, they also offer great potential for enhancing and facilitating student learning and for the development of critical thinking skills due to controversial nature of topic. The chapter argues that teaching such 'sensitive topics' calls for a more carefully planned (not to say controlled) classroom environment whereby even greater effort has to be made to carefully and consciously optimize a positive and tolerant learning atmosphere and provides those interested in teaching in these areas with a series of strategies to use in the classroom. In Steve Spencer's chapter on 'race' and ethnicity, the author suggest that the discipline faces two key challenges: first, how to interpret the meanings of 'race' and ethnicity in ways that do not simply reproduce a narrowly ethnocentric value system, in ways which expose the mythical nature of race and move towards a position which is positive and anti-racist; and second, how to engage and work with students in a way which avoids delivering some worthy 'sermon on the mount' but instead fosters an atmosphere of mutual learning. In short, this section raises the awareness of the reader to some of less commonly discussed aspects of our curriculum and encourages us to engage with these in our future curriculum developments.

Part IV (Chapter 14–17) picks up again the perennial tension between teaching and research within higher education. As identified earlier, this is an increasing perception gap among some students in terms of the relationship between teaching and research. While they are well versed in the strap lines of 'research-led teaching' and 'research-informed teaching', they often see the teaching and researching aspects of an academic's job as both distinct and separate. Therefore, Simon Lightfoot's chapter explores different ways to make the links between research and teaching more explicit to students in politics and argues that developing the research literacy of our students will not only bridge that perception gap but is key to student employability. This research literacy is, of course, best developed through many of the fine dissertations produced by our undergraduate and postgraduate students of politics and IR. Yet supervising undergraduate and MA dissertations as well as doctoral work often presents huge concerns to new lecturers, especially in relation to developing the research skills of those students whom you rarely see, as pointed out in Dave Middleton's chapter. This chapter presents the readers with a range of e-learning tools and techniques, more traditionally associated with 'taught modules', than can be adapted and used to enhance you supervision of undergraduate and graduate dissertations. Carmel Roulston's chapter moves away from technology to look at the other practicalities of supervising a doctoral student, from ensuring that the new lecturer him/herself has had adequate training in 'effective supervision' to building and sustaining a research relationship with you student. In all chapters within this section, the point is clear: teaching and research are inextricably linked and we should spend more time evidencing this to our student body.

Finally, in a nod to the government's employability agenda, the book ends with an exploration of what a professional politics curriculum might look like in the future. Matthew Wyman, Jennifer Lees-Marshment and Jon Herbert explore the study of politics as 'Applied Politics' and more particularly consider the academic priorities, student preferences and the public interest in relation to the professionalization of politics as a discipline. Increasingly, it seems, students are most interested in current affairs dimensions of their degree programmes and in the practical and vocational elements of their chosen subjects. With the introduction of KIS, we can be sure that these practical and vocational elements and employability statistics for specific subject, such as politics and IR, will remain in the spotlight. Shining the spotlight on what our politics curriculum needs to look like, to help us deliver on the employability agenda, is critical.

To conclude then, we have tried to present this volume as something of a 'how to' guide to teaching and learning in politics and IR. It is not meant to be prescriptive in any way but we hope that readers will be able to tailor some of the ideas, tips and suggestions to their own courses and curriculum. In short, this is the book that we wish we had had when we undertook our formal training in teaching and learning in higher education as newly minted, early career academics; this is the book that we know we will still need when we mentor current colleagues who are now taking the qualification of postgraduate level certificates in higher-education practice; and this is the book that we believe we should have to hand when asked to contribute to a programme or module review within the discipline and when we try to explain to our PhD students what it means to be at the cutting edge of teaching and learning within the discipline of politics and IR. These are some of the obvious ways in which this book can be used by academics, departments and institutions. In a scholarly environment which increasingly values 'research impact' it is easy for us to forget the impact that we, as lecturers, can have on the lives of our students. Great teaching can inspire students to engage with the discipline further (and we both speak from personal experience on this one), to go out and shape society *via* the jobs they do after graduation or just to have their assumptions challenged and tested. Now that really is impact!

Notes

1. There are, of course, journal articles. *The International Politics Education Database* (IPED) includes more than 800 papers on teaching and learning in Politics, International Relations, Public Administration and other related fields, more than 100 of which are by UK authors. We believe that IPED will be the most comprehensive bibliographic database of teaching and learning resources for Politics available. http://sites.google.com/site/psatlg/Home/resources. Date of access: 4 January 2012.
2. *Journal of Political Science Education* provides a much-needed forum for papers on learning and teaching.

1

Teaching and Learning in Politics: Thinking about Teaching Politics Revisited

Penny Welch

Just over ten years ago, I wrote a short piece for the Political Studies Association journal *Politics* in which I argued that Politics tutors should give more attention to teaching and assessment methods and to the learning needs of students (Welch, 2000). I was aware at that time that there were many reasons why colleagues might be reluctant to do this. The material conditions in which we worked – underfunded expansion of student numbers in many institutions, declining enrolments and threats of redundancy in others, pressures to do well in the Research Assessment Exercise (RAE), increased government intervention and managerial control across the higher education system – made our jobs even more demanding than they had been five or ten years earlier. The lives of many students had also got harder in the 1990s, particularly with the introduction of tuition fees for full-time undergraduates from the UK and the European Union in 1998 and the complete replacement of maintenance grants by loans in 1999. The pace and nature of these changes led me to suggest that setting our reflection on learning and teaching within the context of our understanding of national higher policy could reveal more clearly the scope we had to make changes in our professional practice.

Writing in 2011, I believe it is even more important for teachers of Politics and International Relations to understand the politics of higher education and to consider how they might influence policymaking and implementation at departmental, institutional and national levels. The next two sections of this chapter set out the recent history of government policy on higher education and outline the current situation. The two sections that follow show that many academics in Politics and International Relations are committed to innovation and creativity in their teaching and support of students' learning. The final section explores how we might continue to be innovative in what is likely to be a less favourable environment.

Key aspects of national higher education policy 1985–2009

From 1985, governments' use of their legislative and funding powers to reshape higher education in the UK were accompanied by pronouncements stressing the economic purposes of higher education and the need for institutions and staff to serve more closely the needs of employers and of students as future employees. The theme that higher education institutions and academic staff were deficient in certain respects continued throughout the period. Expansion of student numbers without commensurate increases in funding from the mid-1980s onwards reduced the average cost of student places but created major financial problems for higher education institutions. As a result, the National Committee of Inquiry into Higher Education (NCIHE) (the Dearing Committee) was established by the Conservative government in 1996 to 'make recommendations on how the purposes, shape, structure, size and funding of higher education, including support for students, should develop to meet the needs of the United Kingdom over the next 20 years' (NCIHE, 1997, Terms of Reference).

Although the incoming Labour government modified the Dearing proposals before implementation (see Box 1.1), in that tuition fees were means-tested and all maintenance grants abolished, it used the same arguments about the increased earning power of graduates and the likely attitudes of fee-paying students. The Green Paper of 1998 stated: 'Our new funding system gives students the right to demand better quality of teaching and greater attention to their needs' (DfEE, 1998, Chapter 5, Section 6). The subsequent Teaching and Higher Education Act of 1998 enabled the government to set the level of tuition fees for full-time home and EU undergraduates. At the time, independently minded academics in the UK could easily have concluded that giving more attention to their teaching and being innovative in their approaches was colluding with the construction of knowledge as a commodity and of students as consumers. The emphasis on the benefit of higher education to individuals became stronger with the publication in 2003 of the White Paper *The Future of Higher Education* (DfES, 2003). By this time, powers over higher education in Scotland, Northern Ireland and Wales had been devolved, so the White Paper's proposals applied to England

Box 1.1 Main conclusions of the Dearing Committee 1997

'The costs of higher education should be shared among those who benefit from it' (NCIHE 1997, Paragraph 90 of Summary).

Graduates in work were identified as the main beneficiaries.

Students 'are likely to be more demanding of institutions if they are contributing' (NCIHE 1997, Paragraph 111 of Summary).

These conclusions constructed students explicitly, and for the first time in the history of UK higher education policy, as consumers.

only. The government proposed to permit English higher education institutions to raise tuition fees for full-time UK and EU undergraduates from the existing level of £1100 a year to a maximum of £3000. The higher earnings of graduates were again used as a justification, but this time those with sub-degree higher education qualifications were also deemed to benefit from increased salaries (DfES, 2003, Chapter 5, p. 59). The proposed shift in the balance between private and public sources of funding for higher education was directly linked to notions of institutional freedom. Increased income from the private source of students and their families was identified towards the end of the White Paper as having 'the benefit of enhancing the independence of universities by making them less reliant on government funding' (DfES, 2003, Chapter 7, p. 83).

As the higher education system has expanded and government intervention in it has intensified, the salience of higher education as a national policy issue has increased. Public interest in and media coverage of higher education has been more widespread since 2000 than they were in the previous decade. In 2000, the government committed itself to a target of 50 per cent of 18 to 30 year olds experiencing higher education by 2010 (Blunkett, 2000) and in the academic year 2001–2, the total number of students in UK higher education crossed the two million mark (Ramsden, 2004). The proposal for variable top-up fees in the 2003 White Paper was opposed vigorously by the National Union of Students (NUS) and the higher education staff unions. When the Higher Education Bill, based on the 2003 White Paper, was introduced in the House of Commons in January 2004, it was opposed by a significant number of backbench Labour MPs, as well as by the opposition parties. In response, the government made a number of concessions, including increasing the value of the proposed means-tested maintenance grants, remitting the first £1200 of tuition fees for low-income students and writing off all student debt after 25 years. As the date of the second reading approached, the government promised an independent review of top-up fees in 2009 and no subsequent increase in the maximum fee without new legislation. The bill passed its second reading by a narrow margin of five votes and top-up fees were charged for the first time in the academic year 2006–7. In due course, the independent review of top-up fees took the form of the Browne Review, set up in November 2009 and scheduled to publish its report in the autumn of 2010. Like the Dearing Committee, it was established a few months before a General Election had to be held and asked to report back after that election had taken place.

The Browne report, the comprehensive spending review and the future

By the time the report was published on 12 October 2010, a Conservative–Liberal Democrat Coalition Government, committed to severe cuts in public services, had been formed.

Box 1.2   Main conclusions of the Browne Review 2010

All English higher education institutions should be permitted to set their own tuition fees for home and EU undergraduates.

The government to pay the full amount of the fees for both full-time and part-time students up to a maximum of £6000 a year for full-time study. Beyond this level, only a proportion of the extra costs to be paid by the government.

Graduates to repay the cost, plus interest, once they earn £21,000 a year.

'The rationale for seeking private contributions to the cost of higher education is strong and widely accepted. Previous reforms failed to deliver a real increase in private contributions for higher education. Especially with public resources now limited, new investment will have to come from those who directly benefit from higher education' (Browne, 2010, p. 25).

Greater competition between institutions for students is necessary in order to improve the quality of teaching and the student experience. The Higher Education Funding Council for England (HEFCE) block grant discourages competition and should be withdrawn from all undergraduate course except for science, technology, medicine, nursing, healthcare degrees and certain languages (Browne, 2010, p. 47).

The outcome of the Comprehensive Spending Review was announced on 20 October 2010 (see Box 1.2). By 2014–15, the higher education budget (excluding research) will have been cut by 40 per cent and the further education budget by 25 per cent (BIS, 2010). Current spending levels on research will be maintained, but inflation will reduce their value. On 3 November 2010, David Willetts, Minister of State for Universities and Science, announced the government's response to the Browne report in the House of Commons. He endorsed the system of graduate contributions for both full-and part-time students but proposed a cap of £9000 per annum on the fees charged by institutions. Repayment of fees would start when graduates earned £21,000 a year and would include interest. He stated that 'The bulk of universities' money will not come through the block grant but instead follow the choices of students' and that institutions would be obliged to publish information on 'contact hours, teaching patterns and employment outcomes'. He reported that the government proposed to 'open up higher education provision to new providers, including Further Education Colleges'. He anticipated that the government would bring its proposals on graduate contributions before both Houses of Parliament in December 2010 so that they could be implemented for the academic year 2012–13 (Willetts, 2010).

Extensive resistance to the government's intention to remove public funding from undergraduate education in most subjects and to pass on the whole costs to graduates has begun. The national protest in London on 10 November 2010, organized by the NUS and the University and College Union (UCU), was the biggest student demonstration for many years. Intensive lobbying of MPs, particularly of Liberal Democrat MPs who had pledged their opposition to tuition fees before the election, local demonstrations by school, college and university students and occupations of university buildings are all part of the ongoing campaign of protest against the proposed fees and the abolition of the Educational Maintenance Allowance (EMA) that has assisted young people from low-income households to undertake qualifications leading to university entrance.

The government was successful in obtaining parliamentary approval for annual tuition fees of between £6,000 and £9,000 for full-time home and EU undergraduates and for the abolition of the EMA. A White Paper, *Students at the Heart of the System*, was published in June 2011 and consultation on its main provisions is closed in September 2011 (BIS, 2011).

The government's proposals can be characterized as wholesale marketization of the higher education system in England and the end of any commitment to higher education as a public good. The traditional role of higher education in promoting critical enquiry, individual and societal enlightenment and the preservation and extension of knowledge for the benefit of humanity in general seems to be more at threat now than at any time in the last 25 years. Requiring students to repay between £6000 and £9000 for each year of their degree programme could have far-reaching effects on the composition of the student population and the relationships between students and academic staff. Reduced participation rates in public institutions by students who fear incurring such a large burden of debt would reverse what progress has been made to date towards equity of access, as well as leading to a significant reduction of provision in many parts of the sector. Private companies that can offer cheaper and/or quicker degree qualifications outside a university setting could prosper instead. It is hard to avoid the conclusion that the relationship between academics and those students who are prepared to mortgage their future and embark on undergraduate programmes will be more profoundly changed than after the initial introduction of tuition fees in 1998 or top-up fees in 2006.

It is possible that the government has calculated that proposing such a dramatic change to the way in which higher education is funded and then backing down slightly on the proposals which attract the most opposition is an effective way of pleasing its supporters and appeasing public opinion. Nonetheless, even if some of the details change, the government's overriding commitment to reducing the size of the public sector and thoroughly marketizing what is left threatens an extended period of turbulence for higher education. There are good grounds for fearing that government-imposed market disciplines will damage students, staff, academic values and the everyday life of universities and colleges in far-reaching ways. On the other hand, there are limits on the extent to which teaching and research can operate according to a purely market model without undermining the integrity, and therefore the value, of the qualification obtained or the knowledge created. In a similar manner, any further restriction on the academic freedom or professional autonomy of higher education teachers runs the risk of removing the professional element that gives their work its additional value.

2000–10: A decade of innovations in learning and teaching in politics

In 2000, I argued that tutors did have and should use their remaining pro-fessional autonomy to design teaching methods, materials and assessment tasks that were congruent with the educational values they wished to pro-mote (for example, the importance of deep knowledge and critical thinking) and/or directed at solving the pedagogic problems that they encountered (for example, students who want to be spoon-fed just enough information to pass the exam).

A decade later, it is clear that many teachers of Politics have paid a great deal of attention to learning and teaching and have been extremely crea-tive in their approaches (see Box 1.3). Evidence for this includes the range of papers offered at the 2008, 2009 and 2010 conferences of the Political Studies Association (PSA) Teaching and Learning Specialist Group and at the panels put on by this group at PSA annual conferences. Curriculum innovation, assess-ment and feedback, active learning, teaching democracy, teaching sensitive topics, citizenship and politics placements, skills development for students and staff, the student voice, information literacy and many forms of technology-enhanced learning have all been addressed. More detail can be found on the Teaching and Learning Specialist Group website http://sites.google.com/site/psatlg/Home/resources. The Specialist Group has also compiled a list of journal articles on learning and teaching in Politics called IPED – the International Political Education Database. It shows significant growth in publications since 2000 and it is now possible for Politics and International Relations teachers in the UK to find subject-specific literature on virtually any pedagogic topic they wish to investigate. IPED can be found at http://sites.google.com/site/psatlg/Home/resources/journal-articles.

Sarah Hale, in her introduction to the Symposium on Innovations in Learning and Teaching Politics in *European Political Science*, describes this growth as 'an explosion of innovations in teaching and learning' (Hale, 2008, p. 7). She iden-tifies it as both a response to the challenges faced by the higher education sector in the UK and an example of the collective commitment to improving students' experiences. Among the influences stimulating innovation are renewed interest

Box 1.3   Evidence of innovation in Politics teaching between 1995 and 2001

1995: A survey of teaching practices in Politics across the UK came to the conclusion that 'Politics departments were struggling to cope with increased student numbers and resource constraints, while using broadly traditionalist approaches to teaching and learning in terms of course delivery, assessment patterns and the development of student skills' (Stammers, Dittmar and Henney, 1999, p. 124).

2001: The overview report for Politics, following Subject Review in England and Northern Ireland in 2000–1, found that 'Examples of innovation are widespread, and include computer-assisted learning, Internet-based discussion groups, role-play and simulation exercises, case studies, data analysis workshops and student-led group work' (Quality Assurance Agency (QAA), 2001).

in citizenship, both a topic in Politics and as an educational objective through community involvement and volunteering, the introduction of vocational Foundation degrees and increased emphasis on employment-related skills in general, greater diversity among students as a result of widening participation and the availability of information and communication-technologies that can be used for learning and teaching (Hale, 2008).

Two snapshots of the state of learning and teaching in Politics, although based on different types of evidence and written for different purposes, indicate that changes in classroom practice began in the 1990s, even if their dissemination came later.

Initiatives that have supported innovation

The Teaching and Learning Specialist group of the PSA, particularly since its relaunch in the latter part of the decade with John Craig as convenor, has been an important catalyst in the changes in professional practice outlined above and has provided a supportive framework in which teachers of Politics can explore the ways they might respond to new challenges in teaching. There have also been official, sector-wide initiatives that have, to a greater or lesser extent, provided further encouragement for academics to consider ways of being more creative in their teaching, to put their ideas into practice and to publish the results of their innovations.

Subject Review was a system of quality monitoring, based on teams of academics inspecting all departments in each subject and reporting to the QAA. It was a continuation of the teaching quality assessments that had been started by the higher education funding councils shortly after the 1992 Further and Higher Education Act that gave degree-awarding powers to the polytechnics and permitted them to use the title of university. The amount of paperwork and pressure generated by the visits of Subject Review teams was often resented by academics in departments, but preparation for these inspections did provide a focus for collective and systematic consideration of what was taught and the resources and support that were offered to students.

Following the Dearing report of 1997, a number of other national initiatives were launched by the government and its agencies, all intended to focus more attention on learning and teaching. The Institute for Learning and Teaching was set up in 1999 to support the professional development of higher education teachers. In the same year, the QAA initiated the Subject benchmarking process. Subject benchmark statements were drawn up by groups of academics from each discipline and described the main characteristics of undergraduate programmes in their subject and the skills that graduates of those courses would be able to demonstrate (see QAA, 2000, 2007 for the original and the updated Politics and International Relations benchmark statements). Another 1999 initiative was creation of the Teaching Quality Enhancement Fund (TQEF) by HEFCE. The TQEF programme funded activities at institutional, discipline and individual levels (HEFCE, 1999). Institutions were given funds to develop learning and teaching strategies, disciplines had access to resources through the Fund for the Development of Teaching and Learning (FDTL) and through a network of 24 Subject Centres and individuals could compete to become a National Teaching Fellow.

After the 2003 White Paper, there was a substantial new initiative and some tweaking of existing arrangements for improving the quality of learning and teaching. In January 2004, institutions were invited to bid for a Centre for Excellence in Teaching and Learning and 74 institutions were funded. In June 2004, the Subject Centres were merged with the Institute for Learning and Teaching to form the Higher Education Academy. In 2009, some of the TQEF money was diverted to the Teaching Enhancement and Student Success funding stream, leaving the last year of the Centres for Excellence in Teaching and Learning (CETLs), The Higher Education Academy and the National Teaching Fellowship Scheme as the remaining parts of this programme.

Politics departments had the opportunity to bid for FDTL projects once subject review was completed. A number of Politics projects were funded and have produced stimulating conferences and useful resources. One important example is the book that resulted from the Scholarship of Engagement project (Curtis and Blair, 2010). Some academics in Politics have won National Teaching Fellowships and been involved in CETLs and many have had opportunities in their own institutions to undertake projects funded out of TQEF money. However, I believe that the Subject Centre for Sociology, Anthropology and Politics (C-SAP) has been particularly important for teachers of Politics. The ethos of C-SAP right from the beginning was to be responsive to the expressed needs of academics within their subject communities, to provide funding for the projects that the disciplines wanted to initiate and to provide a collective space for purposeful innovation and discipline-specific pedagogic research. Many Politics academics have participated in C-SAP conferences, served on its committees, received funding for projects and been seconded to leadership roles within the organization. Indeed, three of the six C-SAP Directors/Co-Directors to date have been from Politics! The range of activities sponsored by C-SAP and the other Subject Centres has stimulated creativity and the accompanying funding for individuals and teams has conferred legitimacy on endeavour that some still do not consider to be central to the work of academics.

Unfortunately, the Higher Education Academy (HEA) has chosen to respond to cuts in its budget by closing down what many see as the most effective part of its operation – the network of 24 Subject Centres. Instead, the HEA states that

> [k]ey services such as the provision of subject-level support to new teachers and graduate teaching assistants, and consultancy support at departmental level will be provided and delivered by subject specialists and a network of academic associates. The HEA will provide online materials, events and subject-specific resources to academics in different discipline areas.
>
> (HEA, 2010.)

Even if the HEA has the staff and resources to deliver on these undertakings, it remains to be seen if it has the structures to enable academic staff in their disciplines to set the agendas according to which it works.

What can we do next?

In September 2009, I gave a conference presentation reviewing some of these changes. I asked: What is going to happen when the earmarked money runs out, when the teaching economy of our departments is subject to year-on-year 'efficiency gains', when the institutional spotlight switches to 'business-facing' activities? What will happen if there is downward pressure on class contact hours, if the cap on home and EU undergraduate numbers continues and if the cap on tuition fees, on the other hand, comes off and the inequalities between high-prestige and low-prestige universities become greater and more obvious? What happens if the Research Excellence Framework is less favourable to pedagogic research than the RAE was? Is this well of creativity in teaching going to dry up?

In response to my own questions, I can now say that most of the earmarked money will run out very soon and the model of higher education funding proposed by the current government will not lend itself to the ring-fencing of funds by HEFCE or its successor. Moreover, if the government's funding model is implemented, efficiency gains and business-facing activities might look like relatively benign policies in comparison. On contact hours, institutions may increase them rather than reduce them in order to compete for students. Unless they are challenged, institutional managements will allocate the extra hours to hourly paid lecturers on term-time contracts or expect existing staff to teach them on top of current workloads. The government has the power to replace the cap on student numbers with new mechanisms that restrict student places, but the size of the planned fee increases may reduce student demand without the need for additional government intervention. Further stratification of the higher education sector, in terms of prestige, facilities, career outcomes for graduates and research funding, is likely to occur.

These structural constraints make the task of maintaining creativity in Politics/International Relations teaching extremely daunting. Nevertheless, for those of us who enjoy being imaginative in our teaching, who find that it makes the classroom experience more satisfying for us and for the students, to give up on giving attention to learning and teaching is a worse alternative. So we need to develop individual and collective strategies that defend what we have achieved so far and allow us to continue to be innovative in our teaching. I think there are four principles that could usefully feature in our strategies.

The first principle is to think politically. We need to make connections between the politics *of* higher education and Politics *in* higher education and to conceive of ourselves as having political, as well as professional, agency. Whatever our specialism within the discipline, we have knowledge, skills and insights that enable us to understand and act upon the situation in which we find ourselves.

The second principle is scholarship. We need to apply the same type of systematic investigation to our teaching approaches and methods as we do to our preparation of course content and our subject-specific research. A scholarly orientation will help us to more effectively evaluate, use and contribute to the expanding body of pedagogic and policy literature about higher education. Scholarship not only gives us a firm intellectual basis for our practice as teachers, but provides us with evidence and argument for our resistance to, or endorsement of, government and institutional policies.

The third principle is collegiality. This used to mean that academic institutions were and should be run by academics collectively. But over the last 30 years of government intervention in higher education and the growth of hierarchical systems of institutional management, collegiality has come to have the more restricted meaning of co-operation and solidarity between academics. Co-operation and solidarity need cultivating even more in the current context to counter the individualistic and competitive climate already found in many universities, to offer undergraduates and postgraduates an alternative model

Box 1.4 Strategies for maintaining creativity in Politics teaching

1. Find out where there is still money for learning and teaching projects in your own institution or from outside bodies such as the HEA, the Staff and Educational Development Association (SEDA), research councils and charities and the European Union.
2. Look out for collaborative opportunities for learning and teaching projects, either with other departments in the same institution or with other Politics/International Relations departments in the UK and internationally. Collaboration is valuable in its own right and can also lead to better access to funding.
3. Study your own institution's mission statement, strategic plan, targets and key performance indicators. Link the projects you want to undertake with one of the stated educational aims of the organization – for example, student satisfaction, widening participation or graduate employment. Such an approach could lead to official endorsement of your project and the allocation of time, if not additional funding.
4. Another way to official endorsement is to follow the evolution of national policy on issues like quality enhancement or teacher professionalization in the sector. Use this knowledge to persuade key decision-makers in your institution to sponsor a departmental initiative on a relevant topic.
5. Make contact with colleagues who do pedagogic research across the university. There may or may not be scope for research into higher education teaching to be entered in the Education Unit of Assessment. If there is not, lobby professors of Politics and the PSA to use their influence to persuade the Politics sub-panel in the Research Excellence Framework (REF) to give due recognition to research into Politics teaching in higher education.
6. Recognize that many students are concerned about the planned changes in higher education and find ways of including the topic on the curriculum. The issue of tuition fees in England could make an excellent case study in public policy or in the politics of protest. Higher education reform through the Bologna process could feature on EU courses and the marketization of higher education could be included on political economy modules. The differences between higher education in England, Scotland, Northern Ireland and Wales could illustrate aspects of devolution in the UK and debates about citizenship could be enriched by consideration of whether (or how much) students should pay back the costs of their higher education.
7. Most importantly, defend course provision and jobs in your department and institution through political, trades union and professional body activity.

of professional behaviour and to strengthen the ability of academic groups to achieve their legitimate aims.

The fourth principle is student-centredness. By this, I mean consideration of the needs of students as learners, understanding the pressures on them and helping all of them to achieve their potential. Student-centredness involves creating plenty of opportunities for staff-student dialogue inside and outside the classroom and treating students as partners in the pursuit of knowledge, rather than as passive consumers or as customers who are always right.

Guided by these principles, what might be the content of our strategies? All the suggestions in Box 1.4 are about getting involved in the politics of the academy in the interests of the department and the students.

In summary, I am advocating that we keep on innovating and researching and publishing, that we are clear about our educational values and the value of what we do, and that we equip ourselves intellectually and politically to navigate our way through the turbulence and uncertainty of the next few years.

Further reading

The website of the PSA Teaching and Learning Specialist Group (http://sites.google.com/site/psatlg/Home/resources) is the place to start if you want to find out what learning and teaching issues have been addressed and what innovations have been tried out by colleagues in Politics.

For me, the 1994 article by Bruce Wood and Michael Moran, titled 'The Engine Room of Instruction: Small Group Teaching' and published in *Politics*, 14(2), 83–90, remains very relevant today. It would be interesting to read it side by side with the 2005 article by Amy Bogaard, Sabine Carey, Gwilym Dodd, Ian Repath and Richard Whitaker titled 'Small Group Teaching: Perceptions and Problems', *Politics*, 25(2), 116–25.

Not all the innovations in Politics teaching have been written up for journals and at http://www.c-sap.bham.ac.uk/browse-projects you can find reports from all the C-SAP funded projects.

For an overview of higher education policy in England since 1979, I recommend my own article 'The evolution of Government Policy Towards English Higher Education 1979–2007', published in 2009 in *Learning and Teaching: The International Journal of Higher Education in the Social Sciences*, 2(2), 96–122. It presents a chronological account, an analysis and a long list of references to official documents and academic writings.

References

Blunkett, D. (2000), 'Modernising Higher Education: Facing the Global Challenge', speech at University of Greenwich, 15 February, http://cms1.gre.ac.uk/dfee/#speech (accessed 26 November 2010).

Browne, Lord (Independent Review of Higher Education Funding & Student Finance in England) (2010), *Securing a Sustainable Future for Higher Education* (London: Central Office for Information), http://www.bis.gov.uk/assets/biscore/corporate/docs/s/10-1208-securing-sustainable-higher-education-browne-report.pdf (accessed 25 November 2010).

Curtis, S. and Blair, A. (eds) (2010), *The Scholarship of Engagement for Politics: Placement Learning, Citizenship and Employability*, Birmingham: Sociology, Anthropology, Politics (C-SAP), The Higher Education Academy Network, http://www.lulu.com/product/file-download/the-scholarship-of-engagement-for-politics/6427740 (accessed 25 November 2010).

Department for Business Innovation and Skills (BIS) (2010), Spending Review Settlement Press release, 20 October, http://nds.coi.gov.uk/content/Detail.aspx?ReleaseID=416110&NewsAreaID=2

Department for Business, Innovation and Skills (BIS) (2011), *Students at the Heart of the System* CM 8122, June, London: HMSO, http://c561635.r35.cf2.rackcdn.com/11-944-WP-students-at-heart.pdf (accessed 10 September 2011).

Department for Education and Employment (DfEE) (1998), *The Learning Age: A Renaissance for a New Britain*, http://www.lifelonglearning.co.uk/greenpaper/ch5006.htm (accessed 26 November 2010).

Department for Education and Skills (DfES) (2003), *The Future of Higher Education*, Cm 5735, January, http://www.bis.gov.uk/assets/biscore/corporate/migratedd/publications/f/future_of_he.pdf (accessed 26 November 2010).

Hale, S. (2008), 'Innovations in Learning and Teaching Politics', *European Political Science*, 7(2), 133–4.

Higher Education Academy (HEA) (2010), 'Academy Plans from 2011', 17 November, http://www.heacademy.ac.uk/aboutus/plans (accessed 25 November 2010).

Higher Education Funding Council for England (HEFCE) (1999), Learning and Teaching: Strategy and Funding, Report 99/26, April, Bristol: HEFCE, http://www.hefce.ac.uk/pubs/hefce/1999/99_26.htm (accessed 27 November 2010).

National Committee of Inquiry into Higher Education (NCIHE) (1997) *Higher Education in the Learning Society* (summary), http://www.leeds.ac.uk/educol/ncihe/sumrep.htm (accessed 26 November 2010).

Quality Assurance Agency (QAA) (2000) *Politics and International Relations Benchmark Statement*, Gloucester: QAA, http://www.qaa.ac.uk/academicinfrastructure/benchmark/honours/politics.pdf (accessed 25 November 2010).

QAA (2001) *Subject Overview Report 2000 to 2001, Politics*, QO7/2001, Gloucester: QAA, paragraph 20, http://www.qaa.ac.uk/reviews/reports/subjectlevel/qo7_01_textonly.htm (accessed 25 November 2010).

QAA (2007) Politics and International Relations Benchmark Statement, Gloucester: QAA, http://www.qaa.ac.uk/academicinfrastructure/benchmark/statements/Politics.pdf (accessed 25 November 2010).

Ramsden, B. (2004) *Patterns of Higher Education Institutions in the UK: Fourth Report*, (London: Universities UK and Standing Conference of Principals).

Stammers, N., Dittmar, H. and Henney, J. (1999), 'Teaching and Learning Politics: A Survey of Practices and Change in UK Universities', *Political Studies*, 47(1), 114–26.

Welch, P. (2000), 'Thinking about Teaching Politics', *Politics*, 20(2), 99–104.

Willetts, D. (2010), Statement on higher education funding and student finance, Houses of Parliament, 3 November, http://bis.gov.uk/news/speeches/david-willetts-statement-on-HE-funding-and-student-finance (accessed 25 November 2010).

2
What (if Anything) is Different about Teaching and Learning in Politics?

John Craig

As a subject taught within higher education, Politics is as healthy today as it has ever been. Having emerged as a distinct area of academic enquiry during the course of the twentieth century, it is now a well-established element of higher education. In the UK, for example, there are currently over 60 universities offering undergraduate degrees with nearly 25,000 students enrolled on a full or part-time basis (HESA, 2009). In the United States, the number of students graduating as majors in Political Science, Public Administration, Public Policy and International Relations had risen to over 50,000 per year in 2006 (APSA, 2010). There are Politics departments in universities and colleges in virtually every other country of the world providing opportunities for students to study the discipline. Whichever way you choose to look at this, there is an awful lot of Politics teaching and learning going on.

The question that this chapter aims to explore is whether there is anything that is different or distinctive about the way in which teaching and learning is undertaken on a Politics course and indeed, should there be? This question is not raised in a vacuum. In recent decades there has been a growing interest in the practice of university education. A transnational movement for the scholarship of teaching and learning has grown out of the desire of many academics to re-examine their practice as teachers and consider how they might promote student learning more effectively (Murray, 2008). Ernest Boyer's (1990) *Scholarship Reconsidered: Priorities of the Professoriate* is widely regarded as a landmark publication in this field, placing the scholarship of teaching alongside that of discovery, integration and application as valuable academic activities. There has developed a large research literature in books and journals exploring the aspects of theory and practice and organizations such as the International Society for the Scholarship of Teaching and Learning (ISSOTL) providing global networks to support research collaboration and dissemination. As Johnston, McDonald and Williams (2001, p. 195) put it, 'research into university teaching is becoming recognized as a legitimate research activity of all academics, not just those in the area of education'.

The growing interest from within the academic community to improve teaching and learning coincided with a growing public and governmental interest. Within the UK, an infrastructure was established in the late 1990s consisting of the Institute for Teaching and Learning and Learning, Teaching Support Networks and Teaching Quality Enhancement Fund, which were subsequently brought together in the Higher Education Academy (HEA). Schemes such as the Fund for the Development of Teaching and Learning (FDTL) and Centres for Excellence in Teaching and Learning (CETLs) provided large grants for projects designed to develop good and innovative practice. The Quality Assurance Agency (QAA), albeit with a more regulatory remit, has regularly reported on the quality of teaching and management of learning opportunities at higher education institutions for over a decade. As such, there has been a sustained focus on developing teaching and learning in higher education that has been supported from both within and without the academy.

Yet, within these movements, institutions and literature, there has been a tension between the generic and the discipline-based approaches.[1] Many of the standard works, such as Light and Cox (2001), Ramsden (2003), Biggs and Tang (2007) consider the teaching and learning practices generically and refer to disciplinary examples only in passing. Fry, Ketteridge and Marshall (2009) aim to cover both aspects; with the first half of their book devoted to generic issues and the second to the teaching of particular disciplinary groupings. Interestingly, Politics is included within a single chapter covering the entire field of Arts, Humanities and the Social Sciences. The present volume, in exploring the issues of academic practice relevant to one particular subject area, is in the distinct minority. The focus of journal articles is more evenly spread, with journals such as *Learning and Teaching: The International Journal of Higher Education in the Social Sciences* (LATISS) and the *Journal of Political Science Education* focusing, as the names imply, on the Social Sciences and Politics respectively. In addition, some general disciplinary journals, such as *Politics, European Political Science* and *PS: Politics and Policy* regularly carry pedagogical articles alongside a range of other articles. Within the American Political Science Association, UK Political Studies Association and the British International Studies Association there are specialist groups or sections focused on researching and developing teaching and learning in the discipline. The HEA was established with a central unit which focused on cross-cutting thematic areas, such as employability and assessment, and a network of 24 Subject Centres, with the Centre for Sociology, Anthropology and Politics (C-SAP) providing specialist support for academics within these three disciplinary areas. Following the closure of the subject centres in the HEA's 2011 restructuring, the balance between the generic and the disciplinary focus is yet to become clear and, at the time of writing, is a contentious issue.

Such duality begs a serious question as to how the generic and the subject-specific are related. Is the scholarship of Politics teaching and learning simply concerned with applying the generic theories and practices to our teaching or is it about us developing our own understanding of the types of teaching and learning that are best suited to our subject? To put it another way, who should determine what is good practice in Politics teaching? Is it educationalists or Politics academics? And should the answers be derived from educational or political literature? Students of Chemistry, Politics and Aeronautics will typically attend lectures as part of their learning experiences, but are the features of a good lecture the same in each?

To answer all these questions is beyond the scope of this chapter, but they do underlie that which is addressed: what, if anything, is different about teaching and learning in Politics? We will begin by considering the relationship between disciplines and teaching and learning practice in general, before turning to consider the nature of Politics as a subject in higher education. We will then consider patterns in the current teaching and learning of Politics, before considering how this might be further enhanced.

Disciplines, teaching and learning

Within the educational research literature there are two main strands of thought on the relationship between the nature of academic disciplines and their practices of teaching and learning. The first position treats teaching and learning practices of a discipline as a reflection of their epistemology. The starting point for much of this work is a four-fold classification of disciplines which Becher (1994) derived from the work of Biglen (1973). The classification is based on variation in two dimensions. The first is the extent to which a discipline generates hard or soft knowledge, a distinction which broadly reflects that which can be made between the arts and sciences. Hard knowledge consists of objective laws, regular relationships of cause and effects that can be replicated and quantified. Soft knowledge, by contrast, is more subjective and value laden, with a greater emphasis on interpretation and the contestability of core concepts. The second dimension through which disciplines can be distinguished is the extent to which they are either pure or applied. Those disciplines with a stronger emphasis on the generation of pure knowledge have a greater orientation towards the production of abstract knowledge, while those that are applied place a greater emphasis on the processes through which knowledge can be applied and generated though such applications. On this basis, four disciplinary groupings are derived: hard–pure disciplines; soft–pure disciplines; hard-applied disciplines and soft-applied disciplines. The characteristics of each of these are set out in Table 2.1.

Neumann, Parry and Becher (2002) argue that the different types of knowledge developed by each of these discipline types has led to the development of distinctive practices with regard to curriculum, teaching methods and assessment

Table 2.1 The Biglen–Becher typology of disciplines

Category	Nature of knowledge	Examples of disciplines
Hard–pure	Cumulative, atomistic (crystalline/ tree-like); concerned with universals, quantities, simplification, resulting in discovery explanation.	Biology, Chemistry, Geology, Mathematics, Physics
Soft–pure	Reiterative; holistic (organic/river-like); concerned with particulars, qualities, complication, resulting in understanding/ interpretation.	History, Sociology, Music, Languages, Philosophy
Hard-applied	Purposive; pragmatic (know-how via hard knowledge); concerned with mastery of physical environment; resulting in products/techniques.	Medicine, Dentistry, Agriculture, Engineering
Soft-applied	Functional; utilitarian (know-how via soft knowledge); concerned with enhancement of (semi-) professional practice; resulting in protocols/ procedures.	Accounting, Business, Education, Social work, Urban Planning

Source: Adapted from Becher (1994, p. 154), and Nelson Laird et al. (2008, p. 475).

between the different groups. Hard–pure subjects are identified as having a linear and hierarchical curriculum in which certain elements of learning must be securely in place before others can be progressed. A student studying Physics, for example, must gain a secure understanding of certain mathematical principles before being able to progress their learning. By contrast, they argue the curriculum of the soft–pure subjects is more open and flexible, with learners encouraged at an earlier stage to grapple with the uncertain and contested nature of knowledge. As such, the teaching of English Literature will encourage the student to explore the multiple ways in which a particular text can be read. The types of teaching methods used to facilitate this will also vary. Students in hard–pure areas such as the natural sciences may undertake some of their learning in lectures, but will also spend a significant period of time in laboratories, while those in applied disciplines often undertake extended periods of placement. Likewise, with regard to assessment, the hard- and soft–pure disciplines will seek to examine the extent to which students have gained a knowledge and understanding of a set of ideas and propositions, while the soft- and hard-applied disciplines place a greater emphasis on the competent application of knowledge in practice. In addition, the greater quantitative focus of both the pure- and hard-applied discipline will lend itself to forms of objective testing, such as multiple-choice examinations, whereas the pure- and soft-applied disciplines place a greater emphasis on assessment techniques such as essays which will be qualitatively evaluated.

While apparently abstract in nature, the analysis of Neumann, Parry and Becher (2002) aimed to address a very practical issue. If, as they suggested, different types of discipline properly have different practices of teaching and learning, then the development of generic university policies and regulations which did not take account of this could be detrimental to student learning. However, their approach has been criticized for epistemological essentialism by Trowler (2008) on the grounds that it overemphasizes the extent to which the knowledge structures of the discipline determine the practices of teaching and learning. Kreber (2008a) has also identified a number of criticisms of their approach. It is based on too fixed a conceptualization of disciplinary identities and does not take sufficient account of the way in which they are shaped by the academics and students who engage with them. In addition, it tends to over-generalize the differences between disciplines while underemphasizing those within them. Finally, it de-emphasizes the extent to which undergraduate education is nowadays expected to develop transferable skills and attributes of 'graduateness' in graduates regardless of the subject studied (Fallows and Stevens, 2000).

Others have sought to develop models that capture a wider range of the variables that might impact upon teaching and learning practices. Berthiaume (2009), for example, identifies nine factors that influence teaching and learning practices. While these include the epistemological structure of the field of study, they also take account of the socio-cultural aspects of a subject such as its norms and conventions. In addition, there are a range of factors that relate to the teacher's generic understanding of the nature of the learning which will implicitly or explicitly inform their teaching style. Finally, there are various issues relating to what is referred to as the teacher's personal epistemology which encompasses their own beliefs about the practice of teaching. To these factors could be added a range of other influences that are also likely to affect teaching and learning practices. These include the physical architecture of the university and resource issues such as staff-student ratios. Whatever the discipline and the pedagogic perspectives of the academic staff, it will be difficult to teach through small-group discussions if resource constraints require classes of 60 or 70 students which are timetabled in lecture theatres.

There are a number of relevant points that I would like to draw out from these debates for the purpose of the argument that I am pursuing in this chapter. The first picks up on the point made previously with regard to the positive and normative elements of the relationship between disciplines and teaching and learning practice. While it may be the case that influences such as the availability of teaching rooms and staff-student ratios may effect the types of teaching that do occur, we can nevertheless continue to consider the question of how it should be structured and the extent to which the epistemological structure of the discipline should influence this. In considering this, the model developed by Neumann, Parry and Becher (2002) can provide only a partial solution, as in grouping all disciplines within one of four over-arching categories, it does not provide the tools to consider the differences that might exist between subjects such as Politics, Sociology, History and Languages all of which have tended to be placed within a soft–pure category. To take this further we need to consider the nature, history and development of Politics as a subject in higher education.

The discipline of Politics

It was not until after the Second World War that Politics became established as a distinct area of study within UK higher education.[2] Kavanagh (2003) identifies the inter-war period as one in which there were few academics who specialized in Politics, few students who studied it, few places in which it was studied and little development of a distinctive method or approach to its study. At the University of Oxford, Politics was taught within Modern Greats (later renamed as Philosophy, Politics and Economics or PPE) and was grounded within Moral Philosophy, while at the University of Cambridge it was more closely aligned to the study of History. At the London School of Economics and Political Science, the approach was somewhat different. Having been founded by Sidney and Beatrice Webb in 1885 to develop education that would serve the purposes of social reform, the steer was towards the development of Politics more strongly tied to Law, Economics and Public Administration. As Kenny (2004, p. 572) writes of this period, it was 'largely conducted by scholars trained to regard themselves as "generalists" who ranged across the disciplines of History, Philosophy and Law, the teaching of Politics still reflected the ideas of classical education that was intended to provide a liberal-humanist preparation for those likely to assume prominent positions in public life', or as Haywood (1991, p. 1301) puts it, the 'belief that a liberal elite education could best be acquired through acquaintance with the political philosophies of Plato and Aristotle, coupled with a knowledge of the history of the political systems of Athens and Rome, survived the Second World War'.

A collection of articles published in the early 1950s under the collective title 'The Teaching of Politics in the Universities' in the journal *Universities Quarterly* (now *Higher Education Quarterly*) well illustrates these points. Smellie (1953, p. 14) identified a 'variety of good and bad fad [*sic*] fairies [that] visited the cradle of political science' whose influences were shaping the course of her subsequent development. Reflecting the influences identified above, it is perhaps not surprising that the 'good fairies' were identified as utility, History, Classics, English Empiricism and German Idealism.[3] Cole (1953) recalled his own experiences as a student of politics at Oxford almost 50 years before, stating '[I] learnt my "Politics", as an academic study, largely out of Plato and

Aristotle and essentially as a branch of Philosophy', while Hanson (1953, p. 40) observed that 'having been trained as a historian, I am so used to thinking historically that I cannot imagine myself with the vaguest idea of what politics is "about" if deprived of the historical knowledge I had acquired'. Yet both Cole and Hanson also made the case for developing stronger links with discipline such as Sociology and Economics. It was the contribution by Finer (1953) which made the strongest case for Politics as a distinct area of study related to problems of collective choice and power, although he too was to stress its close links to other more established disciplines.

It is important to recognize that these considerations of the role of politics in higher education were taking place at an important watershed in its development. In 1950, the UK Political Studies Association, the professional association for Politics academics, was founded with its journal *Political Studies* beginning publication three year later. As Kenny (2004, p. 569) states, it was in the 1950s and 1960s that 'political studies was transformed from being a loosely constituted intellectual community into an institutionally accepted academic discipline'. During these years the numbers of staff and students studying Politics increased as did the number of books and journals devoted to the field. The first single honours Politics degree emerged during this period and the traditional focus on History and Philosophy as the basis of Politics was steadily eroded particularly in newer universities and the polytechnics (Haywood, 1991, p. 313; Grant, 2010, p. 6).

The development of these trends was not without tensions, debate and resistance. Preece (1969, p. 472), for example, identified a discipline split between traditionalists who looked to 'institutions, normative theory, the Great Books, and history' as the basis for the subject and 'modernists' whose focus was upon 'social forces, empirical theory, "hard" data and scientific method'. In this context, he pleaded the case for students whose work might become the battleground of the two opposed camps. Chester (1975, p. 163) expressed concern that there was no core curriculum and that 'three first-class graduates in Politics from say, Essex, London and Oxford are unlikely to have covered the same reading'. This situation reflected not just methodological differences but also the emergence of subfields and specialism within the subject.

As a result of these developments, Politics could, by the turn of the century, be seen to have become a diverse or even a divided discipline. Almond (1988) characterized the profession as consisting of groups that sat at separate tables with little to say to one another. These groups were identified by their combination of a particular methodological perspective and political viewpoint. The soft-left academic group combined a left-of-centre approach to politics with methods of analysis drawn from History and Philosophy and tended towards the view that academics should engage beyond the university with the wider community. Those identified in the hard-right group, by contrast, relied on deductive, statistical and experimental methods and took a right of centre approach to Politics. Smaller groups of soft-right and hard-left academics were also identified. Almond's analysis was the inspiration for King and Marian (2008), who conducted a cross-national survey of Politics academics to explore their understanding of the discipline. They were able to identify three group-ings of Politics academics: one drawing on a humanistic conceptualization of Politics; a second focused on a scientific approach; and a third valuing a meth-odological pluralism. In addition, they were also concerned with the apparent absence of a common core of literature even within subfields, commenting that 'there is a fine line between diversity and disorganization' (King and Marian, 2008, p. 215).

While Almond (1988) and King and Marian (2008) were primarily focused on the research methodologies and identities of Politics academics, Johnson (1989), in contrast, focused on the development of the taught discipline within higher education. He identified four versions of Politics as a taught subject that have developed within UK higher education. What he referred to as pure Politics and applied Politics, he believed had a proper place within academic Politics. By contrast, politics as a science and politics as the analysis of current affairs, while significant parts of the offerings of the courses that he observed in higher education at that time, were dismissed as being of little value. For the purposes of this chapter, it is necessary to briefly explore each of these four variants before considering if they provide a useful and valid basis for exploring the diversity of Politics within higher education.

Politics as an analysis of current affairs had become, by the late 1980s, by Johnson's (1989, p. 36) reckoning, the dominant type of Politics studied in UK higher education institutions, accounting for 'at least half of the Politics taught and examined' in the majority of institutions. It formed the basis of many mod-ules on domestic, international and comparative Politics that considered recent or contemporary issues and often asking students to deploy various conceptual tools to analyse them. Johnson criticized this approach on a number of counts. The content of such courses would tend to be determined by transitory events and issues that were prominent in the media, rather than topics that are derived from developments within the academic literature. In addition, any analysis of these events could only be speculative and subjective in nature, since the observer could not know the outcome of processes that were ongo-ing. Neither the student nor the lecturer could enjoy the full view of events that are 'completed and settled' afforded by historical studies.[4] Such analysis would also tend to focus on the peculiarities of personalities and particular office holders, for example Barack Obama's presidency or Manmohan Singh's premiership, rather than the nature of the office itself. Johnson's (1989) second category is that of Political Science, which is broadly constructed to include work from behaviouralist and rational-choice methodological approaches, statistical and quantitative analysis and some other aspects of empirical work. As Johnson observes, this variant of Politics has become more entrenched within the US than the UK, although he identifies certain fields within the latter, such as election studies, where such work is well established. In comparison with Economics, he argues, Political Science has achieved little. It has not successfully identified and isolated aspects of recurrent behaviour, as Economics has with market transactions. Much of the data that is captured and analysed, such as voting patterns, provides just a momentary snapshot of behaviour which provides a weak basis for developing models. As such, knowledge is not cumulative in nature and does not provide a robust basis for professional action that Economics might provide to those in business.

With these two defective versions of Politics in a dominant position, Johnson (1989) argued for a reconstruction of the subject in two forms. Pure Politics was to draw on the historical and philosophical roots of the subject. This is an approach that places Politics firmly in the field of the Humanities and points the student towards the study of the development of institutional forms over time and the critical assessment of these based on a knowledge of the course of political ideas and argument. Johnson emphasizes that this is essentially an abstract study that makes no claim to utility. Alongside this, Johnson argues that there is scope for Applied Politics, a vocational route for those intending to pursue careers in public administration. This variant would be more closely aligned to disciplines such as Economics, Management and Law and be focused on the study of the governmental processes. It should, he emphasized, be an unpretentious and practical approach to the subject. Neither Pure nor Applied Politics, he argues, is new. Rather they are both elements within the heritage that should come to the fore.

The validity of the typology offered by Johnson (1989) can be considered independently of the relative value he places upon them. The identification of a variant of the subject that draws on the historical and philosophical tradition of the discipline and another that draws upon a more scientific approach is reflected in the work of others that we have considered earlier in the chapter. The relative merits of each approach has been a subject of debate for many decades and most Politics academics would regard each as having a valid place within the discipline. Many would agree with Stoker and Marsh (2010) that such methodological diversity should be celebrated as strength of the discipline. The identification of Politics as current affairs, which might be retermed contemporary politics, and Applied Politics, is by contrast a relatively distinctive element of Johnson's typology. However, both find echoes in the wider literature that confirm the validity of both variants within the discipline.

Applied Politics can, on the one hand, be seen as a continuation of the public administration tradition (Chandler, 2002; Craig, 2010). However, it can also be broadened to embrace the idea that Politics should address learners not just as students, but also as active citizens (Smith et al., 2008). This aspect of political education is perhaps more established within the US than the UK, and literature there has emphasized both the intrinsic merit of the approach and the contribution that it can make to a deeper understanding of other aspects of the subject (Snyder, 2001). In addition, it also finds its parallel in arguments that the discipline as a whole should be more engaged with the professional political and governmental communities (Donovan and Larkin, 2006).

The centrality of contemporary politics to most higher education courses is such that it almost goes unnoticed as the distinctive feature of the discipline which it is. However, it is difficult to think of other disciplines in which the object of study can change so dramatically in a short period of time. Unexpected events such as the rise of the Ayatollah Khomeini, the fall of the Berlin Wall or the September 11 attacks can transform the political world and challenge our understanding of it. I experienced this myself as an undergraduate student sitting for my final exams in 1989. We sat the Government and Politics of China paper within two days of the suppression of protests in Tiananmen Square, at which point it was unclear who was in power in Beijing or elsewhere in China. Such questions as the role of the armed forces, the prospects for democratization and the relationship between China's leaders and youth acquired a significance that they were unlikely to have had when the exam was set.

For Blondel (1981, p. 13) such occurrences reflect a fundamental uncertainty attached to the process by which political 'trends become outcomes'. While it may be possible to identify the growing strength or weakness of particular social groups or political parties over a period of time, the transformation of this into one political outcome rather than another has an essential unpredictability. Kuran (1991), seeking to explain the unexpected nature of revolutions and the collapse of Communist regimes in Eastern Europe, focuses on the often hidden nature of political preferences and the dynamic of bandwagon effects. Lebow (2010) argues more generally that there is a tendency to overemphasize the inevitability of past events and underestimate the extent to which the particular outcome that did occur was the result of a wide range of contingent factors. As such, the political world is often likely to surprise those who study it as it develops in unforeseen ways. As the authors of the QAA (2007, p. 4) Benchmark statement put it, 'perhaps in no other academic discipline are the subject matter and approaches so much in flux. This contributes to the challenging yet captivating nature of the discipline'. This, it seems to me, is the particularly distinctive aspect of the discipline of Politics and results in particular challenges in its teaching.

Current and future teaching

Politics, as a subject taught within higher education is, therefore, a diverse and plural discipline. To provide students with learning experiences that will develop their understanding of this rich discipline to the full, will require a plural pedagogy that reflects this. Whether current practice reflects this is open to question. Stammers, Dittmar and Henney (1999, pp. 119–21) undertook a survey of Politics teaching in UK Politics departments in the mid-1990s and found that 'traditional lectures and small to medium seminars (between 6 and 21 students) were the most common forms of teaching', with smaller group methods declining in use, perhaps as a result of declining staff-student ratios. The QAA (2001, para. 20) *Subject Overview Report*, based on detailed reviews of every Politics course in England and Northern Ireland between 2000 and 2001 reported that 'teaching methods consist largely of lectures, seminars and tutorials'. More recent guides for students applying for or studying Politics degrees, such as Faulks, Phillips and Thompson (2003) and Leach (2008) have equally identified these as the most common forms of teaching. Survey data from the US also suggest a similar pattern of teaching (Hartlaub and Lancaster, 2008).

These are not the only types of teaching that are used in politics. As the QAA (2001, para. 20), also noted, the use of 'computer-assisted learning, internet-based discussion groups, role-play and simulation exercises, case-studies, data analysis workshops and student-led group work', were used by various institutions. In addition, the use of technology-enhanced learning has continued to evolve as new devices, applications and uses have been introduced and many universities have introduced minimum expectations for the use of their virtual learning environment in modules. Nevertheless, the predominant learning experience for most Politics students in most cases remains the lecture and the seminar, and there are different views on the efficacy of such teaching and learning practices. Dunleavy (1986, pp. 4–12) argued that the continued use of such learning methods was a result of their effectiveness in supporting students' learning. Others such as Leftwich (1987) and Cloonan (1999) have questioned the suitability of these traditional approaches which can often result in student passivity. What I would argue is that lectures and seminars will by their nature be better suited to teaching some aspects of the discipline than others. It is perhaps no coincidence that they are the teaching methods most commonly used in History and Philosophy, from which Politics has drawn so much.

What then might be the learning and teaching methods that are appropriate for other elements of our diverse discipline? A significant amount of work has been undertaken in recent years to develop teaching methods that are suited to Applied Politics. These include placements and internships which allow students to engage in experiential learning through direct engagement in political or governmental activities. Such learning opportunities can be found within almost a third of UK Politics departments and provide students with both an opportunity to gain a practical understanding of the political process and to develop the skills required for further engagement in the sector (Curtis et al., 2009). Simulations and problem-based learning approaches can provide further means through which the learning of Applied Politics can be undertaken (Craig and Hale, 2008; Usherwood, 2009). Wyman and Longwell (2010), for example, report on a model based upon a series of workshops through which students develop political skills such as public speaking and explore employment opportunities in the political sector. It is likely that despite such initiatives, there remain too few opportunities for students to engage in such learning opportunities on most Politics courses.

The teaching of Politics as a science is more established than that of Applied Politics. Nevertheless, it is an area in which there is ongoing reflection as to how it might be most effectively undertaken. Adeney and Carey (2009) observe that while there is evidence that Politics courses in the UK provide relatively little coverage of quantitative techniques and formal modelling, there is also reluctance in many departments to make this a core part of the learning experience. Such challenges are not unique to Politics and are shared by other Social Sciences (Gibbs, 2010). In their own practice Adeney and Carey (2009), have addressed this through contextualizing the teaching of statistics within the political environment and structuring learning through a range of formats including individual and group work. There is also potential to explore the teaching and learning practices that have developed in more numerate disciplines such as problem classes, regular formative feedback and diagnostic testing, which may be particularly well suited to such subject matter (Kyle and Kahn, 2009).

As I have argued above, contemporary Politics presents those studying it with particular challenges given its continuously evolving nature. Book and journal articles that confidently describe and analyse particular structures, processes and problems can quickly become dated as the world changes around them. Research-based teaching and learning methods that are required to address this issue are those that empower the student to access and evaluate information from a range of diverse sources and contextualize it within the frameworks and debates developed within the academic literature. Yet as Lightfoot (2010) has argued, research-based learning is generally less developed in Politics and the Social Sciences than in the natural sciences, and there is scope, therefore, to further develop this. In addition, as Thornton (2008) has argued, there is also a need to develop new approaches to enhance the information literacy of Politics students to support this.

Conclusion

Welch (2000, p. 102) argued that 'we should use our subject knowledge, teaching skills and commitment to students to encourage, in an active and positive way, the sort of learning that we value'. This chapter has argued that our understanding of teaching and learning in our subject should be rooted in our understanding of our discipline. In arguing this, I am not suggesting that

Politics should turn its back on generic pedagogic work or the teaching and learning approaches developed in other disciplines. On the contrary, different aspects of political studies are closely related to a range of other disciplinary areas and we can learn much from working with colleagues in these areas. Nevertheless, there is also scope to focus on what is peculiar to Politics as an area of study and to ensure that our teaching properly reflects these. In a nutshell, as Politics, Political Studies is a rich and diverse discipline so the types of learning experience that students will engage with on a Politics degree should also be rich and diverse. The plurality of the discipline should be reflected in the plurality of the pedagogy.

Notes

1. Before considering these issues further, it is important clarify the use of some key terms. Firstly, for some writers a discipline is to be differentiated from a subject. Kreber (2008b, p. 11) for example, distinguishes between a subject as something that is looked at and a discipline as the distinctive methodology through which it is looked at. An alternative approach is to consider it more as a community of practice. As Mackenzie (1975, p. ix) put it, 'I see "the discipline" as a group of people rather than a set of principles, as a continuing debate rather than an enquiry in the style of natural science, as an enterprise which is an integral part of real politics'. In this chapter, I use the terms 'discipline' and 'subject' interchangeably.
2. The focus here is on the UK, but the development of the disciplines has similar dynamics in other countries such as Australia (Crozier, 2001), Japan (Sagawa, 2006). For further analysis of the development of the discipline within a British context see Haywood, Barry and Brown (1999) and Grant (2010). Addock, Bevir and Stimson (2007) consider development in the UK and USA, while Easton, Gunnell and Graziano (1991) explore development of the subject across a number of countries.
3. The bad fairies are described as more cryptic than the good. In part they are the dark sides of the good fairies, with history accused of a certain snobbery. Other bad fairies were 'Development with the wand of progress in her hand' and 'that Liberal Anglican Lady who saw in history that pattern of the rise and fall of states' (Smellie, 1953, pp. 14–5). For a slightly later discussion in the US on the relationship between politics and other social sciences see Lipset (1969).
4. One is reminded here of the comment attributed to Zhou Enlai when asked sometime in the 1970s about that impact of the French revolution of 1789 on the world. 'It is too early to tell' was the reported response.

References

Addock, R., Bevir, M. and Stimson, S. C. (eds) (2007), *Modern Political Science: Anglo-American Exchanges Since 1880* (Princeton: Princeton University Press).
Adeney, K. and Carey, S. (2009), 'Contextualising the Teaching of Statistics in Political Science, *Politics*, 29 (3), 193–200.
Almond, G.A. (1988), 'Separate Tables: Schools and Sects in Political Science', *PS: Political Science and Politics*, 21 (4), 828–42.

APSA (American Political Science Association) (2010), 'Bachelor's Degrees Awarded in Political Science, by Sex, 1988–2006' http://www.apsanet.org/imgtest/Demographics%20Data%20BA%20degrees%2088%2006.pdf (accessed 27 November 2010).

Becher, T. (1994), 'The Significance of Disciplinary Differences', *Studies in Higher Education*, 19 (2), 151–61.

Berthiaume, D. (2009), 'Teaching in the Disciplines', in H. Fry, S. Ketteridge and S. Marshall (eds), *A Handbook for Teaching and Learning in Higher Education: Enhancing Academic Practice*, 3rd edn (New York and London: Routledge), pp. 215–26.

Biggs, J. and Tang, C. (2007), *Teaching for Quality Learning at University* (Maidenhead: Open University Press and the Society for Research in Higher Education).

Biglen, A. (1973), 'The Characteristics of Subject Matter in Different Academic Areas', *Journal of Applied Psychology*, 57 (3), 195–203.

Blondel, J. (1981), *The Discipline of Politics* (London: Butterworths).

Boyer, E. L. (1990), *Scholarship Reconsidered: the Priorities of the Professoriate* (San Francisco: The Carnegie Foundation for the Advancement of Teaching).

Chandler, J. A. (2002), 'Deregulation and the Decline of Public Administration Teaching in the UK', *Public Administration*, 80 (2), 375–90.

Chester, N. (1975), 'Political Studies in Britain: Recollections and Comments', *Political Studies*, 23, 151–64.

Cloonan, M. (1999), 'Innovation in Teaching Politics in H E: Some Observations', *Journal of Further and Higher Education*, 23 (2), 173–84.

Cole, G. D. H. (1953), 'The Status of Political Theory', *Universities Quarterly*, 8 (1), 22–33.

Craig, J. (2010), 'Practitioner-Focused Degrees in Politics', *Journal of Political Science Education*, 6 (4), 391–404.

Craig, J. and Hale, S. (2008), 'Implementing Problem-Based Learning in Politics', *European Political Science*, 7 (2), 165–74.

Crozier, M. (2001), 'A Problematic Discipline: The Identity of Australian Political Studies', *Australian Journal of Political Science*, 36 (1), 7–26.

Curtis, S., Blair, A., Axeford, B., Gibson, C., Huggins, R. and Sherrington, P. (2009), 'Rethinking Placement Learning for Politics and International Relations' in S. Curtis and A. Blair (ed.), *The Scholarship of Engagement for Politics: Placement Learning, Citizenship and Employability* (Birmingham: C-SAP), 31–59.

Donovan, C. and Larkin, P. (2006), 'The Problem of Political Science and Practical Politics', *Politics*, 26 (1), 11–17.

Dunleavy, P. (1986), *Studying for a Degree in Humanities and Social Sciences* (Basingstoke: Palgrave Macmillan).

Easton, D., Gunnell, J. G. and Graziano, L. (eds) (1991), *The Development of Political Science: A Comparative Survey* (New York and London: Routledge).

Fallows, S. and Stevens, C. (2000), 'The Skills Agenda', in S. Fallows and C. Stevens (eds), *Integrating Key Skills in Higher Education: Employability, Transferable Skills and Learning for Life* (London: Kogan Page), pp. 17–33.

Faulks, K., Phillips, K. and Thomson, A. (2003), *Get Set for Politics* (Edinburgh: Edinburgh University Press).

Finer, S. (1953), 'On the Teaching of Politics', *Universities Quarterly* 8 (1), 44–54.

Fry, H., Ketteridge, S. and Marshall, S. (2009), *A Handbook for Teaching and Learning in Higher Education*, 3rd edn (New York and London: Routledge).

Gibbs, G. R. (2010), 'Mathematics and Statistics Skills in the Social Sciences', in C. M. Marr, and M. J. Grove (eds), *Responding to the Mathematics Problem: The Implementation of Institutional Support Mechanisms* (St. Andrews: The Maths, Stats and OR Network), 44–50.

Grant, W. (2010), *The Development of a Discipline: the History of the Political Studies Association* (Chichester: Wiley-Blackwell).

Hanson, A. H. (1953), 'Politics as a University Discipline', *Universities Quarterly*, 8 (1), 34–44.

Hartlaub, S. G. and Lancaster, F. A. (2008), 'Teacher Characteristics and Pedagogy in Political Science', *Journal of Political Science Education*, 4 (4), 377–93.

Haywood, J., Barry, B. and Brown, A. (eds) (1999), *The British Study of Politics in the Twentieth Century* (Oxford: British Academy and Oxford University Press).

Haywood, J. (1991), 'Political Science in Britain', *European Journal of Political Research*, 20, 301–22.

HESA (Higher Education Statistical Agency) (2009) 'Table 2e – All HE Students by Level of Study, Mode of Study, Subject of Study (#1), Domicile and Gender 2008/09', http://www.hesa.ac.uk/index.php/component/option,com_pubs/Itemid,286/task,show_year/publd,1/versionId,4/yearId,184/, (accessed 27 November 2010).

Johnson, N. (1989), *The Limits of Political Science* (Clarendon Press: Oxford).

Johnston, C., McDonald, I. and Williams, R. (2001), 'The Scholarship of Teaching Economics', *Journal of Economic Education*, 32 (3), 195–201.

Lebow, R. N. (2010), *Forbidden Fruit: Counterfactuals and International Relations* (Princeton: Princeton University Press).

Light, G. and Cox, R. (2001), *Learning and Teaching in Higher Education: The Reflective Practitioner* (London: Paul Chapman Publishing).

Lightfoot, S., in this volume.

Kavanagh, D. (2003), 'British Political Science in The Inter-War Years: The Emergence of The Founding Fathers', *British Journal of Politics and International Relations*, 5, 594–613.

Kenny, M. (2004), 'The Case of Disciplinary History: Political Studies in the 1950s and 1960s', *British Journal of Politics and International Relations*, 6, 565–83.

King, R. F. and Marian, C. G. (2008), 'Defining Political Science: A Cross National Survey', *European Political Science*, 7 (2), 207–19.

Kreber, C. (2008a), 'The Modern Research University and its Disciplines: The Interplay Between Contextual and Context-Transcendent Influences on Teaching', in C. Kreber (ed.), *The University and its Disciplines: Teaching and Learning Within and Beyond Disciplinary Boundaries* (London and New York: Routledge), 17–31.

Kreber, C. (2008b), 'Supporting Student Learning in The Context of Diversity, Complexity and Uncertainty', in C. Kreber (ed.), *The University and its Disciplines: Teaching and Learning Within and Beyond Disciplinary Boundaries* (London and New York: Routledge), 3–18.

Kuran, T. (1991), 'Now Out of Never: The Element of Surprise in the East European Revolutions of 1989', *World Politics*, 44 (1), 7–48.

Kyle, J. and Kahn, P. (2009), 'Key Aspects of Learning in Mathematics and Statistics', in H. Fry, S. Ketteridge and S. Marshall (eds), *A Handbook For Teaching and Learning in Higher Education: Enhancing Academic Practice*, 3rd edn (New York and London: Routledge), 246–63.

Nelson, T. F. Laird, Shoup, R., Kuh, G. D. and Schwarz, M. J. (2008), 'The Effects of Disciplines on Deep Approaches to Student Learning and College Outcomes', *Research in Higher Education*, 49, 469–94.

Leach, R. (2008), *The Politics Companion* (Basingstoke: Palgrave Macmillan).

Leftwich, A. (1987), 'Room for Manoeuvre: A Report on Experiments in Alternative Teaching and Learning Methods in Politics', *Studies in Higher Education*, 12, 311–23.

Lipset, M. S. (ed.) (1969), *Politics and the Social Sciences* (New York: Oxford University Press).

Mackenzie, W. J. M. (1975), *Explorations in Government: Collected Papers 1951–1968* (Basingstoke: Macmillan).

Murray, R. (ed.) (2008), *The Scholarship of Teaching and Learning Higher Education* (Maidenhead: Society for Research into Higher Education and Open University Press).

Neumann, R., Parry, S. and Becher, T. (2002), 'Teaching and Learning in Their Disciplinary Contexts: A Conceptual Analysis', *Studies in Higher Education*, 27 (4), 405–17.

Preece, R. J. C. (1969), 'Teaching and Examining in Politics', *Universities Quarterly*, 23, 472–6.

Ramsden, P. (2003), *Learning to Teach in Higher Education*, 2nd edn (London and New York: Routledge Falmer).

Sagawa, Y. (2006), 'Political Science in Japan', *European Political Science*, 5, 304–14.

Smellie, K. B. (1953), 'The Approach to Political Studies', *Universities Quarterly*, 8 (1) 14–21.

Smith, G., Ottewill, R., Jubb, E., Sperling, E. and Wyman, M. (2008), 'Teaching Citizenship in Higher Education', *European Political Science*, 7, 135–43.

Snyder, R. C. (2001), 'Should Political Science Have a Civic Mission? An Overview of the Historical Evidence', *PS: Political Science and Politics*, 34, 301–5.

Stammers, N., Dittmar, H. and Henney, J. (1999), 'Teaching and Learning in Politics: A Survey of Practices and Change in UK Universities', *Political Studies*, 47, 114–26.

Stoker, G. and Marsh, D. (2010), 'Introduction', in D. Marsh and G. Stoker (eds), *Theory and Methods in Political Science*, 3rd edn (Basingstoke: Palgrave Macmillan), 1–12.

Thornton, S. (2008), 'Pedagogy, Politics and Information Literacy', *Politics*, 28 (1), 50–6.

Trowler, P. (2008), 'Beyond Epistemological Essentialism: Academic Tribes in the Twenty-First Century', in C. Kreber (ed.), *The University and its Disciplines: Teaching and Learning Within and Beyond Disciplinary Boundaries* (London and New York: Routledge), 181–95.

Usherwood, S. (2009), 'Grounding Simulations in Reality: A Case Study from an Undergraduate Politics Degree', *On the Horizon*, 17 (4), 296–302.

QAA (Quality Assurance Agency for Higher Education) (2001), *Subject Overview Report: Politics 2000 to 2001* Report Q07/2001.

QAA (Quality Assurance Agency for Higher Education) (2007) *Subject Benchmark: Politics and International Relations*. http://www.qaa.ac.uk/academicinfrastructure/benchmark/honours/politics.pdf (accessed 27 November 2010).

Welch, P. (2000), 'Thinking about Teaching Politics', *Politics*, 20 (2), 99–104.

Wyman, M. and Longwell, S. (2009), 'Teaching the Practice of Politics', in S. Curtis. and A. Blair (eds), *The Scholarship of Engagement for Politics: Placement Learning, Citizenship and Employability* (Birmingham: C-SAP), 123–51.

3
Can Politics Be Benchmarked?

Lisa Harrison

So far this volume has examined the teaching of Politics in relation to content and student needs. We now move on to consider the issue of status – is there consensus regarding Politics degrees in relation to what graduates know and can do? What indicators do we engage with in order to compare the quality of Politics degrees – and are there inherent problems with attempting to do so? This involves us engaging with ontological debates – what does the qualification 'a Politics degree' mean? Specifically, what are our expectations in terms of content, skills training and graduate futures?

The common distinction made in contemporary higher education is between vocational and non-vocational subjects. For some students their degree is a necessary mechanism towards a specific career path – such as nursing or architecture. The degree becomes the mechanism for ascertaining specific knowledge and skills which are deemed essential for practitioners. In this approach we might classify academic subjects on a sliding scale – at one end are those with highly stringent professional sector requirements (such as primary and secondary education and medicine). Somewhere in the middle we have subjects which *may* have professional sector requirements, but whose graduates often follow very different career paths – in the section on measuring standards we will contrast the discipline of Politics to some such examples, notably Law and Psychology. The other end of the scale is where subjects such as Politics sit; there are no professional sector hurdles to negotiate. However, it would be wrong to equate non-vocational with 'anything goes' – Politics graduates follow a multitude of careers, though there are some trends, and employers need to appreciate what our students are likely to know and be able to do. This is fundamental given the changing climate of higher education which we now face. This chapter will first reflect on the mechanisms which had been developed to benchmark the academic discipline, before moving on to consider in more detail how such benchmarks might influence the curriculum.

'Measuring' standards

While there is no overt 'national curriculum' for Politics degrees because we do not have professional sector requirements, there is nevertheless evidence of a covert curriculum, which has become formally recognized via benchmarking and audits. Inevitably, such processes lead to accusations of top-down influence which stand in the face of the concepts which lie at the heart of political analysis – freedom, organic engagement and opposition to inappropriate control. Here, we need to question what the measurement of standards is intending to achieve and what it tells us about graduates. Do benchmarks encourage an unhealthy conservatism in curriculum development?

Every student of Politics has almost certainly faced the type of questions I did as a student (and which continue well into an academic career) – 'so what do you actually study then?' and 'so what are you going to do with that – become a politician?' In most cases the short answer to the latter question is 'no', though the more explanatory response to both questions is multifaceted. Rather than viewing audits as invasive bureaucratic red tape, it is possible to see them as (1) a vehicle with which we can compare and contrast expectations regarding *essential* knowledge and skills, and (2) a regular review by which we can explore what is fit for purpose in addressing student expectations and needs. The latter is vital when we are preparing students for an unrestricted future in relation to possible careers.

This 'fuzzy' link between a Politics degree and preferred career has become a central focus for curriculum development in many universities in recent years. Students opt for our subject because they have an 'interest' in the subject matter, and enjoy the opportunity to develop skills such as critical analysis and problem solving. While these have always been central skills in what we teach, we have perhaps not been explicit enough in demonstrating that this is the case. A student of Politics needs, like many other students, to be able to articulate their achievements in a highly competitive graduate market. Employment opportunities and knowledge economies change. Well-worn pathways disappear and new ones emerge – how do we ensure that 'an introduction to Political Theory' or 'Comparative Politics 1' adapt and develop in a relevant and applicable way? To understand this further, I explore in more detail two benchmarks – those set by government and those which are derived from student opinion and experience.

Curriculum audit

The Quality Assurance Agency for Higher Education (QAA) was established by government in 1997 as an independent body with primary responsibility for evaluating academic standards and quality in UK higher education. As stated in the introduction to this chapter, some subjects are studied because they may be the route to a particular profession. The Assurance Agency benchmark statement for Psychology (2002) included in its membership group a representative of the British Psychological Society (BPS), but the report itself notes that less than a fifth of psychology graduates become professional psychologists. While BPS accreditation is highly prescriptive, the QAA benchmark is less so, though it does state that graduates should be computer literate – especially in relation to databases and statistical software packages. The QAA benchmark statement for Law (2000) is a much weightier document. In setting the benchmarks, it makes explicit distinction between 'areas of performance' – that is vocational studies, law studied as a single subject and law as an element or subsidiary of a degree. This suggests a gradation of 'lawyerliness' for which there is a consensus on knowledge and skills.

As was the case with Law, the benchmark membership group established for Politics and International Relations was wholly academic. Reporting in 2000 (and reviewed in 2007), and lacking a specific vocational driving force, it focused on *diversity* (for example, graduates are employed in a range of professions encompassing; business and research, public administration, financial services and retail) and *opportunity* – listing six major aspects expected from a degree. Notable in this list are breadth and diversity of defining principles, nature and extent of subject and skills acquisition – the implicit message is that a degree in Politics is not for the narrow minded or overly focused! As there are no formal professional requirements which bear upon curriculum content for Politics as they do for Law and Psychology, the Benchmark report recognizes three broad approaches but is not prescriptive beyond this (see Box 3.1). These approaches are normative political theory, positive/explanatory political theory and political science/analysis. Furthermore, the report acknowledges that Politics and International Relations engage with a range of research strategies and methods.

Box 3.1   Examples of thresholds of achievement as set out in the QAA Benchmark Statement (2000)

Knowledge and Understanding – Graduates in Politics will be able to

- understand the nature and significance of Politics as a human activity;
- apply concepts, theories and methods used in the study of Politics to the analysis of political ideas, institutions and practices;
- demonstrate knowledge and understanding of different political systems, the nature and distribution of power in them; the social, economic, historical and cultural contexts within which they operate, and the relationships between them; and
- evaluate different interpretations of political issues and events.

Source: Quality Assurance Agency for Higher Education (2000) *Politics and International Relations Subject Benchmark.*

The document sets out typical and threshold (minimal) levels of achievement which graduates will have developed: (1) subject knowledge and understanding, (2) generic intellectual skills and (3) personal transferable skills.

Why did a review of the Benchmark Report take place just seven years after the original statement as published?[1] The QAA had committed itself to a benchmark statements review process, and Politics and International Relations was one of the 22 subject statements that came up for review in 2007. The outcome was that very little changed, particularly in light of recommendations that may have emerged from the anticipated *Economic and Social Research Council's* international benchmarking exercise.[2] This said, there was a more explicit reference for students to recognize the ethical requirements of study, and for awards to facilitate widening participation wherever possible.

If there is such a thing, therefore, as a covert national curriculum for Politics degrees, it is at the level of broad approach – placing emphasis on the combination of theory and evidence, and upon the necessary skills of rigorous explanation, rather than indicative content. The precise nature of what is studied is not prescribed (for example: specific countries, behaviours or systems), but the expectation is they will be studied to a lesser or greater degree. We see no privileging, for example, of British or American Politics, of classical Political Theory or Public Administration. Potentially, (and putting to one side other constraints for a moment) this places the student as a powerful purchaser in a vibrant market place – enabling them to pursue a degree which they can personally construct to meet their own interests. However, such 'freedom' also brings with it risks – that it renders too implicit those aspects of knowledge and skills which our graduates will be able to market themselves by once their studies are over. We shall return to this issue when exploring the curriculum in more detail.

Student experience audit

An alternative method of measuring standards across Politics degrees is the more recently established National Student Survey (NSS). The NSS is organized by the Higher Education Funding Council for England (HEFCE) and is undertaken annually on their behalf by polling company Ipsos MORI. First taking place in 2005, the NSS asks final year students to rate their degrees, asking 22 questions which focus on six broad themes: teaching; assessment and feedback; academic support, organization and management; learning resources; and personal development. Inevitably, question 22 ('Overall, I am satisfied with the quality of the course') has become the focus of league tables, and the measure by which departments advertise themselves on websites and at open days. In addition, institutions may opt into 'optional' question banks, and students have an opportunity to present qualitative comments.

Since its introduction, the NSS has become an important yardstick for many institutions – particularly those beyond the Russell Group of higher education institutions.[3] For those departments who perform well, the reasons are clear – the NSS provides an independently organized survey which effectively asks final year students, 'would you recommend this course and institution to others?'[4] Academics are interested in two outcomes – good response rates (data is only released once a predetermined response rate is reached) and good scores. The latter is not unproblematic, with whistleblower reports of 'gentle persuasion' by university staff to encourage overgenerous positivity by participants. In contrast to the QAA Benchmark, the NSS has the advantage of currency – this is not to suggest that standards agreed upon in 2000 are no longer relevant; we would not expect a revolutionary overhaul in which decades of teaching content is rejected in favour of today's news headlines – but changes to, and innovations in, the delivery of a Politics curriculum can be recognized by the NSS (in both a positive and negative way).

The development of the NSS raises important questions regarding student ownership of the Politics curriculum. In what ways, traditionally, have students played a role in influencing what they learn about, and indeed how they learn? Universities employ their own quality management and enhancement (QME) procedures, and the most frequently employed mechanisms for capturing the student experience are via staff-student committee and course/module evaluation forms. This can be managed in two ways – for those of a highly structured course where there is little flexibility in terms of modules studied, these students can be asked to evaluate their course (think, for example, of a student who studies for a BA in Politics as opposed to one combining Politics with another subject such as History). But we have already intimated that the curriculum is not externally proscribed – options are built into programmes (as we will examine in more detail later) and as such student evaluation may be more informative if we ask students for a module-by-module evaluation, rather than at award level. While both approaches have advantages, we must recognize their limitations – evaluation of the holistic versus evaluation of the constituent parts of the whole.

The focus of the NSS is quite clearly the holistic (indeed a disadvantage is that students cannot differentiate between the experience in different subjects – a positive experience of studying Politics may be undermined by the learning experience in another subject, and vice versa). Furthermore, the NSS offers a different form of evaluation from that which focuses very heavily on module content and delivery – on heavily modular degrees we frequently ask students to rate their individual courses in terms of teaching quality and learning resources, but perhaps pay less attention to issues surrounding personal development and broader aspects of academic support (offered by services such as libraries, careers advisers and student advisers, for example).

What is less clear, however, is how departments engage with the outcomes of the NSS. To what extent is the content and delivery of a Politics degree altered by NSS results? Indeed, to what extent do academics take ownership of 'weak points'? For example, it is easy enough to say 'students complain about learning resources, give us more money to spend on the library', or 'students complain about their assessment feedback, but look how many uncollected essays are still in my office in July'. The NSS may not be the most important league table measure for some departments of Politics, but the results are available to the public at large and basking in the glory of good results is far more comfortable than wriggling through explanations of poor ratings.

Setting the curriculum

While debate in recent years has focused on the skills-versus-knowledge aspects of curriculum content and the mode of delivery, relatively little has been written about the way specific knowledge segments of the curriculum have been constructed. For example, in the first 'special edition' of the journal *Politics*[5] titled 'The State of the Art', Taggart and Lees (2006) identified four challenges that face the contemporary study of politics. These were identified as (1) introspection and independence among the sub-fields, (2) the standing of political scholarship in practical politics, (3) the relationship between the researcher and the subject matter of focus and (4) the Research Assessment Exercise – now the Research Excellence Framework.[6] It is lamentable that this reflection did not explicitly reflect on the state of the art and the curriculum. In contrast, a relatively rare example of curriculum critique has focused upon the delivery of comparative Politics in British universities. Van Biezen and Caramani (2006) suggest that for teaching purposes comparative Politics privileges a country-by-country approach (via a focus on political history and institutional framework) while overlooking important aspects such as the methods of comparison and conceptual frameworks and theories.

The reason for variation in curricula, apart from the aforementioned lack of professional body requirement is threefold. The first reason lies in the relationship between teaching and research expertise (see Lightfoot's chapter in this volume). Frequently what is offered to students as 'options' has indicative content entwined in the research interests of a single member of staff. To this end, one department's curriculum can change substantially from one academic year to the next depending upon sabbaticals and the continuity of staffing. The second reason relates to a trend in modularization – a system enabling students to select elements of their curriculum based upon interest, assessment method or timetabling convenience. Third, we must not overlook the fact that there is no overarching singular view of the nature of politics (Cloonan and Davies, 1998) – inevitably curricula will vary. A brief trawl of departmental websites and outlines of award programmes will show considerable variability in (1) the amount of compulsion in degrees and across years of study, and (2) those themes which are deemed core to a degree – such as political theory, comparative politics, political analysis and so on.

Content versus process

So far we have focused on external instruments for judging quality, and made reference to the QAA's light touch in relation to curriculum content, instead placing emphasis on knowledge, understanding and skills (see Box 3.2). A key question we may ask of Politics degrees is 'do we study the same things?' To what extent would a new undergraduate be studying what I did some 20 years ago? The QAA Politics and International Relations Benchmark document recognizes that the boundaries of what we study are 'often being contested or in movement':

> 3.1 (1) Perhaps in no other academic discipline are the subject matter and approaches so much in contention and flux. The present state of the discipline is the result of curiosity, free inquiry and debate and its future will be driven by the same forces. It is therefore not the intention of this section to lay out a 'national curriculum' for Politics and International Relations.
>
> (QAA, 2000)

This implies a great deal of curriculum ownership within the academic community – rather than slavish adherence to professional sector require-ments we are free to prioritize debates and ideas, and can swiftly respond to events such as international terrorism, democratization processes in previously authoritarian states and ideological shifts in governance. But with power comes responsibility – how exactly do we judge what is important, relevant, but equally likely to capture enthusiasm and inspire?

No one teaching Politics in higher education today can be unaware of the 'knowledge versus skills' debate. This perhaps is somewhat unfortunate as a dichotomy – seeming to assume that they are distinct qualities and that there is a preference for one over the other. The inappropriateness of this dichotomy is recognized in research based upon interviews with graduate teaching assistants in the Department of Politics at Sheffield University:

> When I first started teaching I think I approached it very much from the perspective of getting the knowledge across – that is, the content of the course. Over time I have changed it so that now I see it much more about *skills* ... If they get the skills the knowledge will follow I think ... It is also the skills which are more important: employers want *skilled* graduates.
>
> (Hayton, 2008, p. 209)

Box 3.2   Examples of thresholds of skills as set out in the QAA Benchmark statement (2000)

Generic Intellectual Skills – Graduates in Politics will be able to

- gather, organize and deploy evidence, data and information from a variety of secondary and some primary sources;
- identify, investigate, analyse, formulate and advocate solutions to problems;
- construct reasoned argument, synthesize relevant information and exercise critical judgement;
- reflect on their own learning and seek and make use of constructive feedback;
- manage their own learning self-critically.

Personal transferable skills – Graduates in Politics will be able to

- communicate effectively and fluently in speech and writing;
- use communication and information technology for the retrieval and presentation of information, including, where appropriate, statistical or numerical information;
- work independently, demonstrating initiative, self-organization and time-management;
- collaborate with others to achieve common goals.

Source: Quality Assurance Agency for Higher Education (2000) *Politics and International Relations Subject Benchmark.*

In their survey of Politics in UK universities in the 1990s, Stammers, Dittmar and Henney (1999) asked lecturers to rate the importance of student skills and qualities. Intellectual and communication skills were rated highest (these included using evidence, analytical thinking, working under constraints, writing skills, effective learning, oral skills and creative thinking). In contrast the skills least valued were group activities, empathy, computer literacy, working cooperatively and problem solving. The implicit suggestion here is that those who teach value those skills which are indicative of independence – undoubtedly the very same skills which drew them towards an academic career in the first place. Yet I am probably not alone in suggesting that academics are almost certainly not the best career advisors. In setting the curriculum we should be more willing to consult key employers – public administrators, professional communicators and business managers to ensure what we deliver is fit for purpose in relation to both academic content and skills.

A Politics graduate will be well aware of the fact that a future employer will rarely require specific subject knowledge – unlike the aforementioned requirements for professional psychologists and lawyers. In reality, employers are looking for skills – literacy, verbal communication, problem solving, planning – which Politics graduates develop and hone during their studies. Indeed, the only example I can think of where a graduate will need to explicitly evidence knowledge of political theory would be in teaching the subject! So what would a checklist of 'successfully qualified politics graduate' look like? While Part II of this text explores in greater detail particular aspects of curriculum delivery, there are two I wish to draw on here – writing a little over a decade ago Stammers, Dittmar and Henney (1999), omit two skills which have since become central to 'fit for purpose' debates. I wish to argue that any attempt to develop a Politics curriculum must embrace two challenges – information literacy (also explicit in the QAA Benchmark) and experiential learning.

Earlier in this chapter I made reference to the often-asked question – why study Politics? Indeed as a younger, less-wearied academic I always looked forward to induction – meeting and greeting new students as they embarked on their degree, though I quickly learnt that asking 'why have you chosen to study Politics?' did not always generate the type of response I had expected. I remember one student who came to see me to switch degree course; his reason for dissatisfaction with Politics was 'there's too much reading' – a requirement which most of us would see as blindingly obvious. However, how we access and consume the necessary resources upon which a Politics curriculum is built has changed dramatically in recent years, and the increased availability of more and different types of information does not necessarily imply a better or more effective learning experience.

Thornton, in Chapter 7, draws attention to challenges and opportunities offered to information literacy by new technologies. While recognizing that information literacy is itself a contested concept, by drawing on the American Library Association's 1989 definition (Thornton, 2008) we can agree that information literacy refers to the ability to locate, evaluate and use effectively required information. Indeed, the QAA Benchmarking statement identifies 'critical reading of a wide range of texts including documents, monographs, scholarly articles, statistics, newspapers, textbooks and sources on the internet' as an expected learning method. While the learning aid of a 'Reading List' may not exactly be outdated, the QAA Benchmark list of texts is rather conservative in breadth. It does not include broadcasts or e-communications. Yet 'what is out there' is one issue worthy of recognition in curriculum development, a far more complicated one is, as Thornton highlights, the challenge of how best to achieve information literacy. New technologies can influence not just what we can use to teach but also how we teach, and how we do so being mindful of challenges such as plagiarism.

A more recent development which prompts a rethinking of the Politics curriculum is the recognition of the benefits of explicitly linking learning and practice (as expanded in Chapter 6 by Curtis). The 2000 Benchmark statement made an explicit case for experiential learning – placements, internships, action research and contact with political actors. A concern I raised earlier was that 'freedom' in curriculum setting may render too implicit those aspects of knowledge and skills which our graduates take to the market place. The opportunity to engage with experiential learning can fill an important vacuum here –students are required to *apply* political theory, empirical methods and analytical frameworks in a variety of settings. The relevance of what we ask them to do in the classroom and via assessments becomes more explicit, enabling students to more effectively articulate the value of an 'academic, non-vocational' degree in a competitive market.

I refer back to the point I made earlier – how do we deliver what is important and relevant in an environment that can enthuse and inspire? How far has the Politics curriculum moved beyond the traditional lecture and seminar method of delivery? Do further changes need to be made? Part II of this text will examine the various issues and priorities in more detail and more effectively – but what is notable is the number of pilot studies and class-based experiments which 'do things differently' and receive very positive student feedback – such as Thornton's (2008) venture into information literacy via workshops.

Designing a politics module

Given the lack of professional sector requirements it would be easy to mistakenly think that 'anything goes'. It is not surprising to know that academics frequently want to teach what they research – not only because it is what they enthuse about but because they want to try out ideas and arguments on those keen to learn. It is not unusual to see reference to student cohorts in the acknowledgement section of textbooks – what better laboratory can a political researcher ask for? Yet perhaps we need to take a step back and ask whether cutting-edge research does, or indeed should, form the basis of high-quality Politics teaching? At the risk of alienating the reader at this point, I will argue why module design requires important consideration in order to best serve the needs of students – bearing in mind the diversity of the student body (see Box 3.3).

First, it is important that we can distinguish between a Politics degree in a holistic sense, as opposed to the component elements of a degree. In the latter case, we ask students to take and pass a number of modules – some will be compulsory (that is, many undergraduate degrees will require a familiarization with political theory and empirical political analysis) while others will be more specialized and be delivered by experienced researchers in that area. In contrast, those who enthuse about the teaching of Politics will argue that

Box 3.3   Developing a new politics module

- Each University operates its own Academic Governance procedures which set out the process for developing new, and reviewing the quality of, existing academic programmes. Included within this will usually be a timetable for subject reviews – often carried out at three- or five-yearly intervals.
- The prompt for the introduction of new modules can be broadly defined in two categories (1) resource driven – a programme is expanding and more needs to be offered to students, or recruitment has increased and there are more students to teach, or new members of staff are able to offer new specialism, and (2) interest/currency driven – particular subfields of the discipline move into vogue due to specific events. There is a demand from students.
- A new module proposal will go through one or more committees to ensure it attains minimum quality standards. This will focus on three aspects (1) a brief outline of content; (2) an indicative 'reading list' and (3) an outline of the assessment diet.
- The nature of committee membership is a crucial determinant in terms of the extent to which a new module has taken on board a range of needs and interests. For example, it will inevitably involve departmental members and those who provide learning resource support.
- To what extent should the curriculum development process involve groups such as current students, recent graduates, external academics familiar with similar programmes, relevant employers?

a degree is more than a sum of these constituent modules – it is about the opportunities students have to test out their skills and knowledge – be it via debating societies, field trips and visiting speakers to name just some examples. What we experience from time to time is a shift in expectations – we find that what started as 'whistles and bells' innovations in what we deliver and how we facilitate learning become 'belt and braces' requirements of a good degree. Think back to the discussion of information literacy – I rarely see a module 'reading list' that consists purely of academic texts and journal articles – there will be reference to online materials, mass media and other sources of information.

In putting together a new degree for validation we will inevitably think about the 'whole package' – what should be included as core and optional? How should assessment vary? What is the market and what are the core qualities of those we recognize as graduates? Now consider the extent to which we place priority on those same questions when it comes to designing individual modules? I would suggest that more resource-led questions lie at the heart of module design: Who can teach this? Do the existing learning resources adequately support the curriculum content? Is there overlap with existing modules? I suggest there are additional, and possibly more important, questions we should ask: Is to what extent is the assessment diet benefitting the students? To what extent does the subject content *compliment* the knowledge that students will already be expected to have acquired? To what extent can students *apply* what they have learnt to their preferred future – bearing in mind this includes almost limitless options. In designing modules we should not restrict our discussions to colleagues and librarians. Involve careers advisers and existing students – students will perform best when they appreciate *why* they are studying a particular theory or region, and understand *what* the assessment is trying to demonstrate – subject knowledge may be our primary concern but it is the skills and qualities which graduates will need to articulate once they leave our care.

Conclusion – the future of politics in the post-Browne era?

It is notable that Stammers, Dittmar and Henney (1999) reflecting on their survey of practices of teaching and learning of politics in UK universities lamented on the challenges that academics faced at that time – increasing student numbers, limited resources but a necessity to maintain traditional approaches to teaching and learning. More than a decade later the mantra has changed little – government repeatedly asks us to 'do more for less', but with a more diverse student body who have different needs and expectations and in an environment where access to information has never been so quick and far reaching. Given the impending changes to university funding, will future students want to study Politics? Of course they will, but they will probably ask different questions about courses than would have been the case 20 years ago.

Politics degrees will survive because of those qualities recognized by the QAA Benchmark Report (2000) – contentious and fluctuating subject matter exposed to rigorous enquiry and debate – hence the recent spurt in growth of International Relations, and in the study of topics such as sustainability, citizenship and engagement. It is reasonably easy to identify which aspects of theory and empirical content will be of most appeal but much more challenging to deliver in an effective way. Innovation can raise expectations, but can also ensure that Politics graduates are needed beyond the walls of a lecture theatre. With this in mind it is important that we can continue to benchmark the discipline, and ensure we do so in a constructive and effective way.

Notes

1. I am grateful to the Chair of the 2007 review group (Dr. Jacqui Briggs, University of Lincoln) for providing information on the rationale for the review. Any inaccuracies remain solely the responsibility of the author.

2. This benchmark was primarily concerned with the quality and impact of research in the UK against international standards, rather than curriculum issues *per se*.
3. The Russell Group represents 20 leading UK universities which are committed to maintaining the very best research and an outstanding teaching and learning experience. They recruit approximately a quarter of the international undergraduate students who come to the UK. Eighteen of its 20 members are in the top 20 in terms of research funding. [http://www.russellgroup.ac.uk/home/]
4. In 2009 the highest rated Politics awards were provided by; Leicester, Loughborough, Cambridge, Exeter, Birmingham, Dundee, Sheffield, De Montfort, Aberystwyth and Essex. A year later this list included Leicester, Sheffield, Strathclyde, Bradford, Cambridge, Essex, Exeter, East Anglia, Plymouth and St Andrews – only two of which are Russell Group universities.
5. One of the listed aims and scope of *Politics* is to serve as the 'bulletin board' for the discipline, providing information on conducting research and teaching politics.
6. The Research Assessment Exercise (RAE) was first conducted in 1992, undertaken by the four UK higher education funding bodies. The Research Excellence Framework (REF) is the new system for assessing the quality of research in UK higher education institutions and the next exercise is due to take place in 2014.

References

Cloonan, M. and Davies, I. (1998), 'Improving the Possibility of Better Teaching by Investigating the Nature of Student Learning: with Reference to Procedural Understanding in Politics in Higher Education', *Teaching in Higher Education*, 3 (2), 173–83.

Hayton, R. (2008), 'Teaching Politics: Graduate Students as Tutors', *Politics*, 28 (3), 50–6.

Quality Assurance Agency for Higher Education (2000), *Law Subject Benchmark* (QAA: Gloucester).

Quality Assurance Agency for Higher Education (2000), *Politics and International Relations Subject Benchmark* (QAA: Gloucester).

Quality Assurance Agency for Higher Education (2002), *Psychology Subject Benchmark* (QAA: Gloucester).

Quality Assurance Agency for Higher Education (2007), *Politics and International Relations Subject Benchmark* (QAA: Gloucester).

Stammers, N., Dittmar, H. and Henney, J. (1999), 'Teaching and Learning Politics: a Survey of Practices and Change in UK Universities', *Political Studies*, 47 (1), 114–26.

Taggart, P. and Lees, C. (2006), 'Politics – The State of the Art', *Politics*, 26 (1), 1–2.

Thornton, S. (2008), 'Pedagogy, Politics and Information Literacy', *Politics*, 28 (1), 207–14.

Van Biezen, I. and Caramani, D. (2006), '(Non) Comparative Politics in Britain, *Politics*, 26 (1), 29–37.

4
Enhancing Politics Teaching through Active Learning

Cristina Leston-Bandeira

Our student population has changed considerably over the last two decades. An increasingly popular field, Politics courses have expanded all across the country and our classes are now larger and include a wider range of ability and experience. And yet the style of teaching in Politics has not necessarily followed this path of change. Many other disciplines have adopted innovative and varied ways to respond to the characteristics of our new student population, but until the 2000s there was little evidence of Politics doing the same (Stammers, Dittmar and Henney, 1999; Welch, 2000). Since then the pedagogy of Politics has steadily developed and today many courses have moved on beyond the traditional approaches to teaching. This chapter reviews why some traditional approaches may not be suitable to teaching Politics today and how approaches embedding active learning principles may encourage better student engagement and develop more robust politics skills.

Politics as a discipline

Unlike in many other disciplines, there are seldom right or wrong answers in Politics. We research and teach a discipline in constant flux, where everyday events add to our knowledge and understanding of politics, in many cases questioning well-established assumptions about the political world. What is more, part of the discipline's nature is exactly about addressing a wide range of perspectives and opinions on a single political issue. As the Quality Assurance Agency (QAA) Politics and International Relations benchmark states: 'Perhaps in no other academic discipline are the subject matter and approaches so much in contention and in flux. The present state of the discipline is the result of curiosity, free inquiry and debate and its future will be driven by the same forces' (QAA, 2000). The elements of free enquiry and debate are crucial for an adequate understanding of the nature of Politics and International Relations studies. Although there is an established set of principles, concepts and facts that make up our knowledge of politics, which we need to convey to our students, we also need to promote strong skills of debate and independent enquiry. Besides this, the pace of change in politics can be extremely fast, requiring a constant awareness of contemporary developments.

Besides knowledge and understanding of specific principles and facts, our teaching should therefore encourage enquiry and debating skills, the identification of different perspectives, the ability to keep up-to-date with fast changing phenomena and the ability to apply complex concepts to everyday political realities in a variety of contexts. In many ways the traditional format of holding a seminar teaching session around the presentation of a paper followed by discussion recognizes the nature of our discipline, through which we start with a set of assumptions and then explore its different interpretations and possible consequences. However, this is only one way of exploring the nature of politics and one that is often not applied successfully for a full benefit of this teaching style. The other common approach, the traditional one-way delivery of a lecture, only addresses some dimensions of our discipline, namely the presentation of a set of principles and facts. It does little to promote enquiry skills, for instance. This becomes particularly important in the context of contemporary higher education which looks very different to an early twentieth century type, which inspired the teaching methods employed in many Politics classes. As Stammers, Dittmar and Henney showed in the mid 1990s, Politics teaching in the UK was still very traditional in its approach despite significant new challenges such as increased student numbers (Stammers, Dittmar and Henney, 1999, p. 124). Employed to develop deep learning and critical analysis skills, the traditional Politics approach to teaching may, in the new millennium, actually be insufficient to promote that deeper level of thinking.

Today's generation of students

The expansion of access to university education over the last decade, combined with the widening participation agenda, has resulted in increased student numbers and a much wider range of abilities and styles of learning. The resulting poorer staff-student ratios hinder individual support to students and generate considerably larger class sizes. The wide range of abilities and learning styles has therefore become very visible in Politics classes, made all the more difficult to deal with in a context of large class sizes in both lectures and seminars.

Besides this, the generation of students we currently teach are also representative of a very different generation to ours, they embody the so-called Google generation. Today's standard students are used to consuming information in smaller and more frequent portions and rely much more on information and communication technology. Most students have also had very different school experiences to the ones of most current lecturers. Many will have experienced various forms of active learning in school, with more hands-on and interactive approaches to teaching. What is more, this standard type of student often sits in the same class as mature students who embody a very different profile, a reflection of the wide range of styles that characterise the student body. Today's politics students embody, therefore, a huge variety of styles and challenges, having specific expectations towards teaching which may not always relate to their university experience.

The traditional politics approach to teaching

The combination of a lecture with seminars constitutes one of the most common approaches to teaching Politics in the UK. Through the lecture the main ideas and facts relating to a topic can be delivered to a very high number of students within a limited amount of time, and then topics can be discussed in depth in seminars. The seminars are often organized around the presentation of a paper followed by a general discussion led by the tutor. This format has traditionally served politics well, as it allows the efficient delivery of main contents whilst allowing for a forum for discussion. The combination of both should promote deep learning and critical thinking skills. However, not only does the reality often suggest a poor teaching experience, but also this format may not promote key politics skills, particularly in a context of larger classes. Before we consider how to enhance politics teaching, let us review the key aims and characteristics of lectures and seminars.

Lectures are a cost-effective method of teaching in that large amounts of content can be delivered to a high number of students within a short period of time, typically 50 minutes. It is also an efficient method to teach content that includes considerable detail or technical information. The main focus is on the lecturer who delivers the content, usually expecting little, if any, active involvement from the students. It is a one-way delivery, whereby students listen as passive learners. When taking notes, students may be less passive as they apprehend the contents being delivered, selecting and registering the information they regard as most useful. But mostly lectures tend to promote a passive style of learning. This could be effective if students were able to retain attention for the whole of the 50 minutes of a lecture. But research shows that levels of attention drop considerably after 15 to 20 minutes (Exley and Dennig, 2004, p.52; Horgan, 2003, p. 78). As Politics lecturers, we often participate in conferences or public speaking events. It may not be that difficult then to relate to the student experience and consider the last time we listened to a talk as long as 50 minutes.

Still, lectures can be an extraordinary tool for engaging students into Politics and indeed to convey a considerable volume of information; they should by no means be disregarded and are undoubtedly here to stay as they are a very cost-effective teaching method. There are many ways through which we can transform our lectures into effective and rich learning experiences, in particular if we integrate active learning techniques.

Seminars can be a very satisfying learning experience. They tend to take place in small class sizes and are geared towards participation from students. They promote a more active style of learning and individualized support from lecturers. Small class teaching suits very well the promotion of discussion whilst also encouraging more in-depth learning thanks to the active participation from students. By making an effort to participate, students have to be aware of the issues at stake, reflect on these, form an opinion and argue; a perfect outcome for a Politics seminar. However, the practical experience of many Politics lecturers falls well short of this. In reality, seminar class sizes are now much larger, it is often difficult to generate discussion and more often than not students have not read what was expected of them. What should be a very satisfying learning experience can easily become a particularly difficult one to endure, for both tutors and students.

Yet seminars should help us to promote key politics skills such as debating, free enquiry and critical analysis. Seminars constitute an essential teaching method for Politics. A number of interventions can be employed to ensure the traditional format works (Wood and Moran, 1994), but essentially seminars should follow diverse formats and styles. They provide excellent opportunities to develop a much diversified approach to teaching Politics offering substantial flexibility to employ different techniques to engage students, even in large classes. Again active learning can provide many ideas to enhance seminar teaching, in particular in a context of large classes.

Why active learning suits politics

The pedagogic value of active learning principles has been extensively recognized in a very wide range of disciplines, including Politics. Considering its wide remit and application, it is difficult to identify a universally accepted definition, but, put very simply, active learning is learning by doing; it is not simply about just doing an activity though, it requires a process of thought in the way that activity is conducted and applied by the learner. It can refer to a range of teaching techniques from problem-based learning to mock debates.

Active learning puts the student at the centre of the learning process. Instead of passive learners, students become active in the process of understanding and building knowledge. As a result, the role of the lecturer becomes one of guiding that process rather than delivering content. As a student-centred approach, active learning encourages students to build their own interpretation of knowledge which leads to better engagement and a sense of ownership of the learning process. As McManus and Taylor summarize 'the core elements of active learning are student activity, student engagement, student reflection and the use of higher-order academic skills such as analysis, synthesis and evaluation' (McManus and

Taylor, 2009, p. 10). Because active learning requires an effort and investment from students, they naturally become engaged in the process of thinking about the issues at stake in the learning process. It is therefore an excellent process to cement key higher-order politics skills such as critical thinking; whilst at the same time generating a learning process that engages students more readily.

What is more, active learning facilitates the ability to apply complex concepts to specific political phenomena, potentially sustaining better student understanding of these concepts. It also provides a vehicle for lecturers to embed the contemporary character of the discipline into its teaching; through active learning students can engage with ongoing political phenomena and keep abreast of fast changing political developments. The diverse range of teaching techniques that fall within active learning is also more likely to suit the varied learning styles of our diverse student population.

Enhancing politics teaching

Whilst active learning provides sound principles to better engage students in the learning process, it is by no means the magic wand which will transform our teaching. It is merely a starting point. Many other factors can have a huge impact on the quality of teaching, such as tutor enthusiasm. Whatever the teaching method, students' feedback often shows that what really matters for their learning experience is the tutor's enthusiasm. But then again, often problems emerge not in the final year option modules, where tutor enthusiasm is likely to be higher, but in the compulsory large first and second year modules. Below, we consider ways to enhance Politics teaching, particularly in a context of larger classes.

The importance of introductions

The introduction to a set of classes should never be underestimated. It helps students understand better how the module is organized and structured, and how it fits with the rest of their programme. It ensures a platform of minimal understanding about what to expect from the classes of that module. Timetable constraints often do not give us the luxury of having an introductory lecture, but even in those cases the first lecture should include some time to introduce the module and lecturing style; as should the first seminar. An adequate introduction should include aims of the module, methods of teaching and assessment, main reading sources, tutors' contact details and programme of classes. Setting this clear starting point is particularly important in larger classes, where communication with students is often hindered.

Structure and breaks

As seen above, it is unlikely that students' attention and ability to retain knowledge in a lecture will stay high past 15 minutes. There is a simple way of addressing this: by introducing breaks throughout the delivery of the lecture and ensuring it has a clear structure. Setting the lecture's structure at the beginning of its delivery helps students to understand and apprehend its contents better, as they know what is coming next and how themes connect. Likewise, a conclusion helps cement the understanding of the whole lecture. This also applies to seminars: establishing its aims at the start and providing a conclusion at the end enhances student understanding considerably.

The introduction of small breaks throughout a lecture ensures students' attention is maintained. Small breaks can take many forms, from a more formal and longer break to a simple diversion within the lecture of a mere few seconds. Breaks in lectures can include

- questions put to students;
- viewing of a short video;
- use of a small quiz;
- introduction of a joke;
- use of practical examples;
- referral to specific students to illustrate points;
- small activity carried out by students;
- use of different means of communication within same lecture.

Some of these ideas are developed and illustrated further below, but regardless of the type of break, these work best if casually introduced into the lecture delivery. Some of these activities are so casual and brief that they are not necessarily perceived by students as breaks as such. When the breaks are more formal and there is an expectation of (re)action from students, it is important this is made clear, as the common perception in a lecture situation is that students should sit quietly and simply listen.

Variety of means of delivery in lectures

In line with the above, the use of a variety of means of delivery also helps to keep student attention and foster understanding. It introduces a move away from the monotony of a 50-minute talk. Lectures that rely solely, for example, on a PowerPoint presentation are unlikely to do a very good job in actually conveying their key ideas. Politics offers such a wealth of means of communication and sources of information that there is plenty of choice for all subfields of politics. A PowerPoint presentation can be complemented, for example, by the simple use of a book: pausing for a couple of minutes to read from a key book is a very simple activity that has many benefits. It brings a break to the lecture, it reaffirms the importance of key readings and it can more effectively convey the enthusiasm and/or clarity of an author than a quote in a slide could ever do.

Examples of different means of delivery include

- reading a quote from a book – preferably one of particular importance;
- use of videos or audio recordings;
- inclusion of photos into slides (with copyright acknowledged);
- inclusion of non-text evidence such as graphs and figures;
- use of a significant website to illustrate points;
- use of a news item (newspaper, website, video, audio);
- bringing non-academic material to show during lecture (for example: Hansard report, UN resolution).

The application of any of the above helps not only to retain attention but, more importantly, to considerably foster understanding by providing illustrations which are invaluable for students.

Interaction in lectures

Promoting interaction in a lecture helps enhance student engagement. It is not always an easy method to apply, depending on the physical layout of a lecture room, the class size and the lecturer's level of confidence. But it should be considered nevertheless even in large classes, as it can provide for breaks, better engagement and even enjoyment of the lecture experience. Interaction can take the simple form of questions to students – as long as it is clear these are not rhetorical questions, students will answer clear questions. Asking questions can also help the lecturer to gauge the students' level of understanding. Other forms of interactive activities include

- doing a small quiz (see Box 4.1);
- use of a crosswords puzzle (tools freely available online can be used to build puzzles relevant to any topic);
- doing a small activity in the lecture, individually or in groups, and then asking for some of the conclusions deriving from the activity;
- use of buzz groups, followed-up by questions from the lecturer to identify specific ideas;
- asking students to identify a specific quote or photo displayed on a Power-Point slide;
- re-enacting a political situation where each student represents a specific element, asking them to do something very simple such as standing up to indicate a particular position. For example, parliamentary voting where students represent MPs; or a diplomatic situation where students represent different countries; or still a world economic crisis where students represent specific stakeholders. For some topics this works particularly well in large classes, being a very effective means to prove a point.

Box 4.1   Interactive activity for lectures: quiz *The Odd-One Out*

This activity is inspired by the BBC programme *Have I got News for You*. It lasts about five minutes and works best about half-way through a lecture.

The lecturer presents students with four photos, each representing a different person or idea. Three of the photos have something in common, whereas the fourth represents something contrary to the other three. Students are asked to identify which is the odd one out photo. The choice of photos should reflect the ideas being conveyed in the lecture, as should the identification of the right answer. When the right answer is identified, this should be accompanied with a clear explanation of its reasons. The following example illustrates this activity: photos of François Mitterrand, Lionel Jospin, Jean-Marie LePen and Jacques Chirac; the answer being Lionel Jospin, as he never managed to get to the second round of a French presidential election.

The quiz provides a break, some interaction and variety of delivery. In short, it engages students into the lecture being delivered, while still considering its contents. It can be used, adapted or extended in many different ways. The photos can easily be included into a PowerPoint slide or in a handout distributed to students.

Using e-learning to enhance lectures

Lectures are often seen as discrete units within a module, with start, middle and finish within a 50-minute slot. However, they can be considerably enhanced when adequately integrated with the rest of the module. This can be done through the delivery itself when links to other lectures – past and future – are made, but e-learning can also provide effective tools for this purpose. This can be used in a number of ways from storing relevant material, to developing discussions online in preparation for a lecture or as a follow-up, or still by using an announcement system providing for a regular follow-up to each lecture summarizing the main issues at stake, providing perhaps an indication of what will follow in subsequent classes. In short, e-learning can provide powerful tools to ensure clarity and communication, both are instrumental in managing large classes.

E-learning can also be used to communicate to students something to prepare for the lecture. This could include reading, a small task or simply a list of the main ideas being addressed in the lecture. Harnessing the lecture with some prior preparation helps to foster better understanding of what is being taught. It can also then be referred to during the lecture when perhaps a small activity may follow it up. For example, students could be asked to bring a specific type

Box 4.2 Integrating lectures with e-learning

This is a lecture about research design. Through information posted in the virtual learning environment, students know that prior to the lecture they have to read about research questions, their features and purpose. On the basis of this, they then write their first draft of a research question, which they bring to the lecture. Half way through the lecture students share in pairs their research questions and aim to improve their partner's question.

This helps a potentially very dry lecture to become interesting because it is made more directly relevant to each student. The activity also helps students to understand better the concept by putting it into practice.

of information to the lecture which is then used for a small buzz group activity within the lecture (see Box 4.2), or for providing answers to questions being asked during the lecture. The preparation and activity act as a simple hook to engage the students with the lecture delivery while also reinforcing the matter being taught.

Buzz groups and group work

Buzz groups are very small groups of people put together to work on a specific idea. This can be equally applied in lectures and seminars, being particularly useful to deal with large classes. Often the group has to discuss an idea and agree on a number of points (for example three main arguments used in Marx's Communist Manifesto). The value of buzz groups is that they are a very flexible method to apply. They can be used at any stage of a class and are often employed when a group is particularly quiet in a seminar; putting students into smaller groups will generate ideas more readily, and the individual groups can then report back to the larger group. Even when not planned for, the buzz group method can very easily be introduced as a way to generate ideas for discussion. It is particularly useful for large seminar classes where discussion within the whole group can sometimes be more difficult to maintain; or in lectures that address complex concepts. This method can be developed in different ways, for example in terms of the focus given for the discussion in the buzz group or by giving students specific material to record their ideas, such as flipchart paper.

Group work is often used for more complex activities, which may take longer and have a wider remit. It is very useful for seminars that deal with complex concepts or with a considerable amount of data and information (see Box 4.3). Again particularly in larger seminar classes, group work can help the weaker students understand issues better, at the same time as it provides a better framework for all students to develop analytical skills than a class wide discussion would.

Box 4.3   Group work in a seminar

The seminar is dedicated to Lijphart's typology of consensual and majoritarian democracies. Students were previously asked to bring to the seminar relevant information about a number of political systems. The aim of each group is to devise a diagrammatic representation of the typology and to then plot their political systems onto the diagram. The diagram could be a chart, a table or any other type of diagrammatic representation.

Students first have to discuss between themselves the main criteria that determine the two types of democracies, to then decide which criteria they will focus on and then consider how to represent this figuratively. They then have to explain where their own political systems would fit within the diagram. In doing so, all students have to reflect not only on what exactly the typology means, but also to review and consider differences between various political systems. Once this activity is finished, each group presents their diagram and explains their decisions.

This example illustrates an activity whereby students employ higher-level analytical skills, while also developing important transferable skills such as team work.

Role play and simulations

Role play and simulations have become extremely popular in politics especially in international relations. In fact this constitutes the one area of Politics pedagogy where there is abundant literature (for example: Shaw, 2004; Shelmann and Turan, 2006), with considerable amounts of money and time often spent to devise simulations. Simulations usually reproduce an international politics situation, often a crisis to be solved, where students take a full part in driving the development and outcome of that particular situation. Each student is given a specific role within the simulation, which will undoubtedly involve communicating, negotiating and deciding issues with other students. Simulations are usually run across several weeks and go well beyond the class room, with considerable material being specifically produced such as news briefings, maps, defence reports and so on. They can be implemented in lectures, seminars or a combination of both, working particularly well for large classes. Simulations can lead to very engaging and fun learning, with effective results in terms of learning outcomes. However, simulations are also highly time consuming to organize and support, and have little flexibility. Still they suit some classes very well.

Role plays are a mini version of simulations: also based on a political scenario and students take on specific roles. They can be as long and complex as the lecturer would like to make them, and as short and simple as needed. They are therefore a more flexible option, which again can be applied in both lectures and seminars. Good role plays require very clear instructions about the students' roles, the political scenario and the aims of the activity. As with any other method, role plays do not suit all students and so should not be overused, even if they can work very well and many students fully engage with the process. Although role plays are mainly popular within International Relations, they can be applied to any subfield of Politics; they stretch as far as each lecturer's imagination.

Problem-based learning (PBL)

PBL is a very popular method in disciplines such as Chemistry. But it can be equally useful for Politics, being similar to role plays. PBL activities also develop around specific scenarios and the attribution of roles to students. The main difference being that the scenarios include specific problems to resolve. PBL activities tend, therefore, to be more focused in their remit. There is considerable literature showing the potential of PBL indicating its many advantages in engaging students, enabling understanding of complex concepts, strengthening the ability to apply concepts to reality and developing problem-solving skills. PBL activities can be simpler than role play and merely require, for example, a sheet of paper describing a scenario, a buzz group to discuss and address the problem and then report back. This can be as easily applied in a seminar as in a lecture.

Mock debates and line-ups

Mock debates are an extremely useful method for Politics seminars, which can also be applied in lectures when they are well integrated with the rest of the module. They are an excellent means to practise and consolidate debating skills, a key element of Politics, as well as to develop an appreciation of different points of view. Mock debates are best applicable in classes that deal with a deeply dividing issue, where opinion and difference of perspectives matter. In a standard mock debate, the class is divided into two groups; each group prepares their key arguments and debating strategy; the debate then starts with an opening statement from either group developing thereafter into an open debate. As with any other method, this can be considerably adapted and extended, with varying degrees of complexity. Depending on the topic, a mock debate can be quickly organized in a seminar, requiring little preparation; in other cases, students may be put into their groups prior to the class and engage in some form of preparation for the debate. In the case of lectures, it is recommended to opt for a formal type of debate, with prior preparation, as it eases considerably the organization of the actual class. Politics students usually adhere very readily to this method and fully engage in the process; but for some students this is an intimidating method, so again it should be used where it makes most sense.

Line-ups are an alternative to mock debates. A line-up consists of the following: the tutor asks students to stand up and to place themselves along an imaginary line across the class room where the two poles represent opposing ideas. For example, the issue might be direct democracy versus representative democracy; at one end would stand students who believe that representative democracy is superior to other forms; at the other end would be those who wish to give democratic authority to the people. As students find their place along that line, they need to talk to the other students nearby to ascertain whether they are to their left- or right-hand side; by doing so, they have to review the main arguments for and against and where their view stands. If applied in a lecture, a line-up makes for a very effective break.

Line-ups can also be easily combined with other methods; for instance, to create the two groups for a mock debate, ensuring more effective opposing views to argue. Or to create groups for a role-play situation, with two groups with opposing views and a middle group acting as their mediators (see Box 4.4).

Diversity in approaches

Some teaching methods may suit some classes and topics better, but diversity of approaches is paramount to effective teaching. Thus, no single approach should be used for a set of classes; instead different techniques should be combined according to the teaching context of each class. It not only helps to keep students engaged,

Box 4.4   Line-up leading to role play in a seminar

The seminar investigates the pros and cons of new media to strengthen public engagement with politics. Students are asked to do a line-up according to the extent to which they believe new media could provide solutions for public engagement. Three groups are then formed from the line-up: one that prefers traditional forms of public engagement, one that believes new media are the solution and another, drawn from the middle of the line-up, that is undecided.

The three groups are then put into a scenario: a select committee is considering parliamentary reform to improve public engagement. The undecided group form the committee leading enquiries on the matter, and the other two groups represent organizations defending different methods to strengthen public engagement. Each group is given time to prepare their case or questions to enquire the value of each approach. This is then followed by a public hearing where each organization puts their case. At the end of the hearing, the committee decides which group presented the strongest case and which recommendations will be adopted, with a full explanation of their decision.

but it also meets the needs of our very diverse student population. A diversity of approaches will help meet varied levels of ability and different learning styles.

Preparation for classes

Prior student preparation is often a key condition for a large class to run smoothly, especially those requiring active participation from students such as seminars. However, lecturers often complain that students do not prepare. There are many ways to address this problem but the following two are paramount: (1) reasonable and clear preparation required and (2) clearly identified expectations of what is required for classes to run.

(1) Simply setting a seminar question with a long reading list may do little to encourage actual preparation, especially in first-year classes where students encounter academic articles for the first time. Faced with a task they do not know how to handle or which, if applied effectively, would take considerable effort, students often simply give up and do not even try. What is expected from students should be reasonable and adequate for the type of class they are taking. The reading list could be more focused; key issues could be suggested to guide the students' reading. In some cases this reading preparation can be accompanied by specific tasks. Students may be asked to bring news items, research data from websites, research a document of particular significance, establish a number of pro and con arguments for a specific issue and so on. The list is endless. Adding a practical side to the academic reading is more likely to engage a wider range of students. It gives a focus for the preparation and makes it doable. It also becomes more visible if the student has done no preparation, acting as a good disincentive for lax attitudes. Besides this, using non-academic material has advantages such as keeping abreast with fast-changing political phenomena and obtaining a more up-to-date perspective than academic articles would give. It also introduces students to the real stuff of politics.

(2) What is expected from students should be clearly set out, as should the consequences of not meeting that expectation. If preparation has not been done, students should understand that the class cannot run. When preparation has been poor, this should be clearly stated to students with a reminder of why preparation needs to be done for everyone's benefit. If need be, a class should simply not run; students quickly understand the rules of the game needed to be followed, if everyone is to benefit from the learning experience.

Conclusion

Politics teaching clearly faces new challenges as a result of the very different student population that has expanded since the 1990s. While many of its traditional methods of teaching have merits, they are insufficient to deal with the challenges in teaching large classes with such a diverse student population. However, active learning principles provide us with many ideas to enhance our Politics classes. This chapter reviews some of those possibilities and why they work. Though, ultimately, the key for good teaching in Politics is enthusiasm, utilizing the stuff of politics and diversity in approaches.

Further reading

Exley, K. and Dennig, R. (2004), *Giving a Lecture* (Abingdon: RoutledgeFalmer).
Hale, S. (2008), 'Innovations in Learning and Teaching Politics', *European Political Science*, 7 (2), 133–4.
Fry, H., Ketteridge, S. and Marshall, S. (eds) (2003), *A Handbook for Teaching & Learning in Higher Education* (London: Kogan Page).
Powner, L. and Allendoerfer, M. (2008), 'Evaluating Hypotheses About Active Learning', *International Studies Perspectives*, 9 (1), 75–89.
Welch, P. (2000), 'Thinking about Teaching Politics', *Politics*, 20(2), 99–104.

References

Exley, K. and Dennig, R. (2004), *Giving a Lecture* (Abingdon: RoutledgeFalmer).
Horgan, J. (2003), 'Lecturing for Learning', in H. Fry, S. Ketteridge and S. Marshall (eds) *A Handbook for Teaching & Learning in Higher Education* (London: Kogan Page), 75–90.
Lijphart, A. (1989), 'Democratic Political Systems Types, Cases, Causes, and Consequences', *Journal of Theoretical Politics*, 1 (1), 33–48.
McManus, M. and Taylor, G. (eds) (2009), *Active Learning and Active Citizenship: Theoretical Contexts*, C-SAP Monograph No.10 (Birmingham: C-SAP, the Higher Education Academy network).
Quality Assurance Agency (QAA) (2000), *Politics and International Relations subject benchmark statement* (Gloucester: QAA).
Shaw, C. (2004), 'Using Role-Play Scenarios in the IR Classroom: An Examination of Exercises on Peacekeeping Operations and Foreign Policy Decision Making', *International Studies Perspectives*, 5, 1–22.
Shelmann, S. and Turan, K. (2006), 'Do Simulations Enhance Student Learning? An Empirical Evaluation of an IR Simulation', *Journal of Political Science Education*, 2(1), 19–32.
Stammers, N., Dittmar, H. and Henney, J. (1999), 'Teaching and Learning Politics: a Survey of Practices and Change in UK Universities', *Political Studies*, XLVII, 114–26.
Welch, P. (2000), 'Thinking about Teaching Politics', *Politics*, 20(2), 99–104.
Wood, B. and Moran, M. (1994), 'The Engine Room of Instruction: Small Group Teaching', *Politics*, 14(2), 83–90.

5
Teaching Politics to Small Groups

Jacqueline Briggs

The pedagogical topic of teaching Politics to small groups may perhaps be regarded as a non-issue given the increase in applications to study Politics at university. According to Professor Wyn Grant, 2741 students took up a Politics and International Studies place in 2000 and by 2005, this had increased to 4366. Grant highlights that in '2007 there were 23,000 Politics undergraduates and 9625 postgraduates, many of them from outside the UK' (Grant, 2010, p. 164). Figures from UCAS, cited by Professor John Benyon, highlight that acceptances to study Politics were up by 90 per cent in 2009 (from 2000) (Benyon, 2010, p. 18). Having said this, even though applications and actual places are up, for a variety of reasons – some say it is the Obama Effect, coalition politics and/or the conflicts in Iraq and Afghanistan (Davies, 2009, p. 6), others cite an increasing politicization facilitated by a focus upon issues such as the increase in tuition fees – and Politics tutors are faced with increasing numbers of students, for the majority of Political Scientists/Politics tutors there will remain an optimum class size. As Bogaard et al. (2005, p. 16) state, 'Teaching in small groups is a common and highly valued practice in the Social Sciences and Humanities'. They proceed to highlight the general 'conviction that small group teaching is a particularly useful device to encourage critical learning and understanding of complex issues' (Bogaard et al., 2005, p. 16).

This chapter concentrates upon teaching Politics to small groups, as opposed to focusing, for example, upon the traditional lecture scenario. The lecture usually involves a tutor imparting information to a much larger group – some universities may have, for example, Politics lectures involving a hundred plus students. Generally, the skills that the student needs to acquire are active listening skills and note-taking. The lecture is very much a tutor-led experience, often with relatively little student participation. A much smaller learning environment, the seminar places much greater emphasis upon student participation and involvement. Seminar size varies from institution to institution and from course to course. It is probably a fair assessment, however, to say

65

that average seminar size ranges from between 15 and 30 people. Quite often, within this environment, the tutor assumes the role of facilitator or guide, the trajectory of the seminar will often be led by the students themselves with the Politics lecturer taking more of a backseat/observing role. This is, nonetheless, still a pivotal role within the classroom/learning environment.

The aim of this chapter is, therefore, to consider strategies and approaches that the Politics lecturer may employ to facilitate teaching and learning within small groups. It is hoped that the chapter offers ideas and suggestions that may be of use within the classroom situation. First of all, it is necessary to devote some discussion to this question of size. What constitutes a small group? How small is small? Is there, in fact, an optimum size for the teaching and learning of Politics? What kinds of skills will students acquire through these small groups? In addition, to enhancing their political knowledge, for example, it may be that students are acquiring various transferable skills such as team-building skills, problem-solving techniques and presentational skills. All valuable skills for the Politics graduate to possess and that should enable them to enhance their employability – especially in this new age of austerity, where anything the student can do to give them added leverage in the jobs market is to be applauded. Goldsmith and Goldsmith highlight the many challenges facing Politics tutors today, including

> maintaining the quality of provision in the face of growing student numbers; the demand on universities to address not only the academic needs of students, but also to prepare them for the labour market; and, finally, the necessity to adapt pedagogy to new developments in information and communication technology.
>
> (2010, p. 63)

In addition, one of the main points to consider is what is the purpose of a seminar? Is it to reinforce and expand upon ideas and opinions which were introduced in preceding lectures? Or, do they provide opportunities to discuss related topics which may or may not have been covered in the lectures? So, you need to think about the purpose of a particular seminar, what is it designed to achieve?

Size matters ...

The old cliché and double *entendré* comment, that tired and ubiquitous innuendo of size matters is actually rather apposite as we consider the teaching and learning of Politics. Student feedback indicates that students enjoy being taught in smaller groups and often feel that they benefit and learn to a much greater extent than if they were part of a huge lecture audience. The lecture has its place in the higher education environment; lectures can be a place to learn the key aspects of a particular topic especially when given by a tutor who is passionate about their discipline. Lectures can constitute a performance and be inspirational, instilling a desire in the recipient to go off and engage with the subject matter in greater depth. Some question the relevance of the lecture in twenty-first-century higher education; the former head of the National Union of Students, Wes Streeting (2009, p. 17), is quoted as saying that, come the revolution, in his opinion, the '... lecture would be first up against the wall'. He continues by asking why is it '... in the age of mass higher education, that we keep packing lecture theatres with hundreds of students for a format designed for teaching no more than 20 in an elite system?' (Streeting, 2009, p. 17). Some commentators question the value of lectures, in terms of average attention-span, for example and whether students do learn if they are simply being 'talked at' for 50 minutes. For many, however, the real learning takes place within the seminar/classroom environment. It is necessary, therefore, to focus upon the teaching of Politics to small groups.

Ten tips for teaching small groups: some suggestions

> 1. **Breakout sessions** – three to four in a group and relay responses to whole group. Provide three or four questions in advance of the session with short indicative reading lists. For example, political theory, questions relating to whether or not there is a right to disobey the law in a democracy.

According to recent research, size does matter as far as academic achievement is concerned (Attwood, 2010). The results of a five-year survey, conducted by the London School of Economics and University College London reveal 'robust evidence of a negative class-size effect – on average, larger classes reduce students' academic achievement' (Attwood, 2010, p. 11). If this advice is heeded, there could be a movement towards smaller class sizes as a way of improving student performance. With the increase in student numbers, size matters. Seminar size can be an issue. Some groups might be as large as 30. Breaking a large group into smaller groups to discuss a particular topic or issue and then asking them to report back is a technique which may help here. It may also encourage some of the more diffident members of the group to contribute. They may feel more confident in a smaller group.

As stated, small-group teaching does militate against the trend of increasing class sizes. We still need, however, to have an armoury of coping strategies to enable us to deal with smaller groups. There are many different strategies that the tutor of Politics may wish to employ when they are faced with a small group. Many of these techniques, strategies and approaches are considered in this chapter. One of the easiest approaches to take is to break the group up into smaller groups. Three to four students per group is often regarded as optimum. The groups are then given a task – for example discussion of three or four questions. The groups are asked to (s)elect a *rapporteur* to report the findings of the group back to the group as a whole. Alternatively, the tutor may choose the spokesperson for each group. Small group discussions ensue and then the *rapporteur*/spokesperson has to relay the findings of their small group back to the whole seminar. This strategy is useful for enabling the more reticent members of the group to relay their thoughts, knowledge and beliefs. They may feel more confident about expressing their viewpoints knowing that this will be relayed by a third party. It is also a useful device for facilitating group cohesion and for enabling students who may be meeting for the first time to get to know one another. This method works best with preparation. Tutors may wish to prepare a set of questions and an indicative reading list so that students prepare their response or at least have the opportunity to ponder the problems prior to the actual seminar.

---

2. **Debates** – for and against the motion, possibly being coerced into arguing contrary to one's own beliefs. For example, 'This House believes that prisoners should have the right to vote'. 'This House believes that feminism is *passée* as a political theory'.

Another concomitant advantage of breakout groups is that they can serve to foster a team spirit. Concepts such as leadership, problem-solving techniques and consensus building all come into focus here. The real world often involves working as part of a team and so this approach again helps to nurture those transferable skills that are important in the workplace environment. Students have to learn to listen to the views of their peers but also to know when it is appropriate and necessary to take the initiative themselves. These small groups are an ideal conduit for the acquisition of these vital team-building skills.

Student-centred

The small-group seminar should emphasize student participation and they should be very much student-centred with the tutor acting more in the capacity of a facilitator or guide. This is particularly apposite as far as students of Politics are concerned because it is fair to say that Politics students, on the whole, are not passive learners. The nature of the discipline lends itself to conflict, debate and argument. Politics students like to debate and to argue. In part, this is probably why they chose to read Politics at university. The ability to differentiate between fact and mere opinion is a key skill and debate in these small groups will probably encourage students to hone their talents in this area. Given that Politics lends itself to a multitude of opinions and differing perspectives, small groupwork is usual in this respect in that it enables differing opinions and viewpoints to come to the fore.

Involve your students as much as possible, especially given that student-centred learning is said to be more effective. The old Chinese proverb, 'I hear and I forget, I see and I remember, I do and I understand' is relevant here. This is the very essence of student-centred learning. For those wanting to see some of the best examples of student-centred learning, observe teaching practise in a primary school. This is where some of the most innovative teaching methods are taking place with respect to pupil-centred learning. A day spent observing in a local primary school will no doubt reveal pupils actively engaged in a whole host of different tasks and projects. Higher education can learn from these approaches employed at the lower echelons of education.

---

3. **Student presentations** on a particular topic – ten minutes to present, ten minutes for discussion. Students need to be well briefed and need to have plenty of preparation time. For example, a presentation on women in politics, looking at why there are relatively few women in politics and what can be done to rectify this.

Most tutors would agree that the best seminars are student-centred but, in order for them to be successful, the students need to be well-briefed. They need to have researched the topic or area under discussion beforehand. There is nothing more frustrating than when students turn up for seminars and they are obviously unprepared. But tutors need to provide adequate guidance as to the most obvious sources of reference beforehand. Extensive reading lists or even indicative reading lists ought to be provided for some, if not all, of the seminars. It can be seen then that student-centred learning is not an easy option.

'Let's have a heated debate...'

Debates are a useful device in the small-group scenario. The tutor needs to decide what role they should adopt too. They could, for example, play Devil's Advocate. In an early text about the teaching of Politics, Roberts alludes to this, 'He [in the 1960s, the assumption is that the Politics tutor is male] must therefore be skilled at guiding discussion and eliciting the views of the less voluble, as well as being competent to put an opposition case where an entire class takes one side of a controversial political question' (Roberts, 1969, p. 122). Students could choose their own stance or they may be forced to adopt a particular line of argument.

This tactic means that rather than giving the group *carte blanche* to pursue whatever perspective appeals, the tutor prescribes the approach to be taken. This means that they may have to pursue a line of argument that is countervailing to their own particular perspective or opinion. This results in a situation where they have to really think about the counter-arguments. This can work particularly well if the seminar takes the form of a debate. Students need to be given time to prepare their case so they can clearly research and rehearse the arguments to be pursued. It is fair to say that students can sometimes be reluctant to argue counter to their own thoughts and beliefs so tutors may encounter opposition initially, but it is an effective way of getting someone to at least recognize an alternative viewpoint even if they do not espouse the counter-arguments. Political theory classes often work very well in this respect. Debates centring on topics such as the arguments for and against abortion, the existence of capital punishment and whether there is a right to disobey the law in a democracy have ensured that students of political theory engage with the subject matter. The debate needs to be properly organized with plenty of preparation time and opportunity for the students to research their perspective beforehand. Each side needs to be allocated a set amount of time for them to present their case to the group and then time needs to be allowed for the whole group to discuss and debate the merits and demerits of each particular perspective.

Problem solving

The essence of small-group teaching is to encourage students to become critical thinkers. It is not, therefore, just about imparting knowledge and factual information to our tutees, it is about encouraging them to think for themselves. The acquisition of problem-solving techniques is invaluable for students both in the classroom and in the work-place environment. One way to facilitate the development of these skills is to use a case-based approach. Such case studies might be centred upon real events or fictional scenarios. The University of York and also the University of Huddersfield have both been involved in projects to devise case studies intended to help the teaching and learning of Politics. Topics are wide-ranging but include, among other aspects, cases to encourage understanding of theoretical concepts such as democracy or toleration and also contain investigations into contemporary issues such as press freedom. Students are provided with suggestions for background reading and it is certainly the case that the more the students put into their research the more they will get out of these case studies.

> 4. Create a 'Democracy Wall' – give small groups different coloured Post-it™ pads and they have to put their comments, sometimes one-word responses on the wall. For example, highlighting the basic tenets of Conservatism: Highlighting legislative changes that have impacted positively upon gay rights.

New(ish) technology

Obviously, a great deal of lecturer/student interaction takes place in seminars. New technology can be used to enhance that interaction. At the University of Lincoln (my own institution), for example, we are currently being shown the merits/possibilities offered by a system such as Optivote™ whereby an audience response system *à la Who Wants to be Millionaire?* can be used to ascertain student opinion/understanding (Gormley-Heenan and McCartan (2009) have undertaken research in this area). This enables tutors to take a quick straw poll. It can also be used to ascertain whether opinion has changed throughout the course of a class. For example, on a topic such as whether voting should be made compulsory or whether the voting age should be lowered to 16, it has been used to gauge opinion on these matters. It can also be used to ascertain the level of knowledge on any given topic. Its value should not be overestimated but it does have its uses and can, for example, enhance a debate by providing a snapshot of opinion. The system is probably more beneficial when applied to a large lecture situation but it can equally be used in seminars.

---

5. **Speed discussions** (*à la* Speed Dating) – two lines each moving in opposite directions after five minutes, have the chance to share ideas and discover alternative viewpoints. For example, students are asked to research the life and work (theoretical perspectives) of one specific political philosopher each, to ascertain the key details as they pass along the line – just a 'warm up' exercise but it does get students thinking critically.

One way of enhancing the small-group situation is by making use of the wide-range of audio-visual resources which are available. Those new to Politics teaching have an expansive variety of resources at their disposal. Older colleagues will remember using VHS clips to supplement their teaching. It is much easier to access relevant information nowadays. The Internet is an invaluable source of material – although obviously some websites are more reliable/rigorous than others. Political parties, Parliament, learned societies (such as the Political Studies Association, and the British International Studies Association), organizations such as C-SAP (the Higher Education Academy's Subject Network for the teaching and learning of Sociology, Anthropology and Politics), the University of Southampton's Citizenship project (POLIS) are all invaluable sources of information. A short visual or audio clip can enhance a small group situation by illustrating or clarifying.

The microblogging site Twitter™ has potential for use in the teaching and learning of Politics. Essentially, a tweet consists of a maximum of 140 characters. These might be in the form of a question to elicit a response or simply a point to be made. As well as being used within the classroom environment, this can also mean that discussion, on any given topic, may carry on beyond the confines of the seminar room. Some critics may argue that tweets constitute dumbing down or they may question how much one can actually say with such a limitation. It does, however, concentrate the mind and can serve to initiate a debate on any given topic area. There is talk of a digital divide between tutors who are familiar with web 2.0 technology and those who are less so. *The Times Higher Education* (Whittock, 2009, p. 20) recognizes that 'Twitter divides opinion but some scholars view it as a tool that could benefit their work'. In addition, many students are helping their tutors to understand and get to grips with the opportunities offered by this new technology.

---

6. **Runaround** – number one to five on the floor, numbers equate with 'agree strongly' through to 'disagree strongly' continuum. On any given question, students will be asked to move around the room and standby the number equating to their viewpoint or their perception of others' views. For example, 'AIDS tests should be compulsory', 'The Monarchy should be abolished' and other such controversial assertions. Students have to literally vote with their bodies/stand up and be counted.

Acting it out

Tutors may wish to use innovative techniques such as simulations and role-play. For example, cabinet committee simulations whereby students are given a particular departmental portfolio and have to argue the case for their particular department. Again students need to be well-prepared beforehand. Students seem to really enjoy doing this. Another role-play exercise is where students are asked to negotiate a constitution at the start of setting up a new state. Professor Richard Rose (2009) of Aberdeen University has a useful suggestion for a seminar. Rose himself was invited to put forward suggestions to George W Bush about ideas for policy. He was given time to prepare beforehand but was told he would only have three and a half minutes to do so (Rose, 2008). Rose sees this as a good seminar exercise, to get students to do a role-play exercise where they have three and a half minutes to present their policy ideas to, say, an incoming prime minister. He said it is also interesting to get students to prepare a policy brief when they hold opposing political opinions to the person they are told to brief!

7. **Twitter™** – microblogging sites such as Twitter can be used to expand the discussion. For example, it can be used to carry on the debate beyond the classroom scenario or it can be used actually within the seminar room itself. Students can send their questions or points to be raised in the form of tweets. This often suits the more diffident members of the group or it enables points to be raised without disrupting the flow of the session. For example, to enable students to ask questions, for points of clarification, and to air their views. The 140 character tweets mean that they have to be concise and succinct in their approach.

Keeping it real

Politics is a living subject. It is necessary to ensure that the tutor keeps abreast of contemporary affairs otherwise one's perception and awareness quickly become out of date and lacking in the basic knowledge. Keep up-to-date and well-informed. Make sure that handouts are revised on a regular basis. Anecdotal evidence recalls one university lecturer using handouts dated 1969 and this was the early 1980s! On the issue of handouts, it is a good idea to produce handouts either before the seminar for research purposes or after so that students have something to take away with them for future reference. Continuing this theme of updating, when one institution was assessed by the Quality Assurance Agency, the observer's fair comment was that the example of the poll tax protest was quite an old one to use and should be supplemented with more contemporary examples. Sad to learn that while the poll tax debacle was still fresh in the tutor's mind, it was ancient history as far as the students of the new millennium were concerned. Thompson refers to this aspect in Heater's aforementioned text, *The Teaching of Politics*, 'The whole study should involve the use of contemporary examples where appropriate, and these should be provided by the pupil as well as the teacher' (Thompson, 1969, p. 67). Illustrations should not be fossilized, as they can easily become, but draw on contemporary situations' (Thompson, 1969, p. 67). As Harold Wilson said, *circa* 1964, 'a week is a long time in politics'. That still holds true today. This is, for many, part of the appeal of Politics. The pace of change can sometimes be quite breathtaking. For many, that makes it exciting. Of course, giving a lecture, on say electoral systems, does not necessarily involve a great deal of change but, without updating (knowledge of the May 2011 referendum on the question of electoral reform, for example), you will soon find yourself behind the times.

Preparation

One of the first points to note as a tutor of small groups is to be prepared. Robert Louis Stevenson wrote, 'Politics is perhaps the only profession for which no preparation is thought necessary'. In terms of teaching Politics, however, it is paramount that you are prepared, like the good Girl Guide – even to the event of having a 'Plan B' should a seminar not go as you would have wished. Obviously, you need to ensure that you know your subject matter – content is important – although it is not everything, you may be an expert in your field but unable to convey that expertise across. Enthusiasm for the subject, displaying your love of politics, is important. Be passionate about politics – it is contagious. It is necessary to ensure that seminars have a clear set of aims and objectives. Academics are readily familiar with the notion of specific learning outcomes. These help with the planning of seminars. Tutors should ensure that seminars are well structured, that they have a clear beginning, middle and end. This will enable students can follow the 'flow' of thought and argument.

---

8. **News review** – a five minute or so review of contemporary events at the beginning of each session can be useful for getting students to engage with the discipline. The tutor needs to know when to rein in the debate and also to focus upon the more relevant aspects of the news. This ensures students get into the habit of keeping abreast of contemporary affairs.

Variety

There is a case to be made for using a variety of teaching methods and styles. Variety is the spice of life. However, do not change just for the sake of change but likewise do not stick rigidly to one method. If every week, a tutor uses the 'breakout into small groups' approach, this may become a little tedious for the students. Likewise, using Twitter every week or showing an audio or video clip, may lead to typecasting!

---

9. **Role-play and simulation exercises** – with the possibility of filming these. For example, cabinet committee simulations, model UN sessions, local council meetings (setting the budget). Student need to prepare their policy positions beforehand and to be able to debate these and to defend their positions.

Maturity

Make use of the experience of any mature students in the group. They often provide a valuable source of information (albeit somewhat anecdotal in a subject like Politics). Mature students initially may feel intimidated when faced with a class of undergraduates who have come straight from school or college, especially if they themselves are returning to study after years in a non-academic job or rearing a family. Confidence-building is crucial here and valuing their experiences in the real world. Once anxieties on both sides have been allayed, the combination of mature and mainstream undergraduates can lead to highly rewarding seminars for both parties in the equation.

---

10. **Mini-tests** – on any given topic, to ascertain the level of knowledge or to discover differences of opinion. New technology, such as audience response systems, could be used to enhance this process. For example, these can range from the more mundane/basic (such as: How many members of the UK Parliament are there? In what year did Margaret Thatcher become Leader of the Conservative Party?) through to more complicated questions requiring a more in-depth response (such as: Define the following terms: mandate, citizenship, socialism, democracy).

Bias

What about the issue of bias too? Should you adopt a particular political standpoint? Given that this is Politics, bias cannot be ignored. The tutor needs to decide whether to approach any given topic by highlighting the range of views in existence (often preferring to say 'Some people believe X, some people believe Y, etc' and not coming down in support of any given stance) or whether to adopt a particular standpoint – whether or not that accords with the tutor's own personal point of view.

Presentations

Student presentations are a useful device for the teaching and learning of Politics and also useful as an assessment method. They can be either individual or group presentations. It's a good idea for students to be able to practise their presentational skills and it is useful practice for many job interviews. The 'I'm happy to be here. I'm happy you're here' approach usually makes them laugh! This is where students are encouraged to make eye contact with their audience and to produce such an enthralling presentation that their audience would not rather be anywhere else at that particular moment in time – no mean feat. It might, at first, appear difficult to assess a presentation given the apparent subjectivity involved – just think of one's favourite actor and differences of opinion come to the fore. Having said this, a checklist of criteria can be devised to ensure that students can be taught the mechanics of what constitutes a good presentation. Content, delivery – including confidence, eye contact, volume of voice, engaging one's audience, appropriate speed of delivery, usage of audio-visual resources, time-management are all factors that come into play here.

Conclusion

Every tutor of Politics will need, at some stage, to teach small groups. As Goldsmith and Goldsmith point out, 'The goal is to produce students who are 'independent, enterprising problem solvers' rather than passive consumers of knowledge' (2010, p. 65). It is, in part, helpful that as well as using tried-and-tested methods, tutors look for new and exciting ways of teaching and learning politics. The Goldsmiths (2010, p. 65) are correct to say that 'there is a continuing need for innovation in teaching methods and for the cross-national dissemination of good teaching practice' (p. 66). The old methods are invaluable but, at the same time, there is a desire of not wanting to limit tomorrow's academics with a model of the past. It is also worth highlighting that techniques and strategies may work with one cohort of students and then, for no apparent reason, fail to work quite so effectively with another group. There may be a reason behind this, such as timing – what works effectively at 2 pm on a Thursday afternoon in April might fail to deliver the same enthusiastic response at 9 am on a Monday morning in January. In this sense, always have a Plan B at your disposal. The reality here is that we are dealing with real people with all their moods, foibles and beliefs. We are dealing with people not machines. This is, in part, what makes the teaching of Politics to small groups such a challenging and rewarding endeavour to pursue. Hopefully, this Chapter has provided some models and approaches for consideration.

References

Attwood, R. (2010), 'Size Matters to Students' Grades', *Times Higher Education*, 16 December, p. 11.

Benyon, J. (2010), 'Looking Forward to a Bright Future', *PSA News*, June, 21 (2), 18–20.

Bogaard, A., Carey, S. C., Dodd, G., Redpath, I. D. and Whitaker, R. (2005), 'Small Group Teaching: Perceptions and Problems', *Politics*, 25 (2), 116–25.

Davies, C. (2009), 'Obama Weaves his Magic Spell', *The Independent*, Education Section, 9 April, p. 6.

Goldsmith, M. and Goldsmith, C. (2010), 'Teaching Political Science in Europe', *European Political Science*, 9, S61–S71.

Gormley-Heenan, C. and McCartan, K. (2009), 'Making it Matter: Teaching and Learning in Political Science Using an Audience Response System', *European Political Science*, 8 (3), 379–91.

Grant, W. (2010), *The Development of a Discipline: the History of the Political Studies Association* (Oxford: Wiley-Blackwell).

Jaques, D. (1991), *Learning in Groups* (London: Kogan Paul).

Roberts, J. (1969), 'The Teaching of Politics in Practice' in D. B. Heater (ed.), *The Teaching of Politics* (London: Methuen), pp. 116–25.

Rose, R. (2008), 'What Would You Tell The President in Three Minutes About Iraq?', *European Political Science*, 7, 78–83.

Rose, R. (2009), Email correspondence with author 25 November.

Salmon, G. and Edirisingha, P. (2008), *Podcasting for Learning in Universities* (Maidenhead: Open University Press).

Streeting, W. (2009), 'Lectures: First Target of The Teaching Revolution', *Policy Review*, June, 17.

Thompson, D. (1969), 'The Teaching of Civics and British Constitution', in D. B. Heater (ed.), *The Teaching of Politics* (London: Methuen), pp. 50–70.

Whittock, J. (2009), 'Twitterati in the Academy', *Times Higher Education*, 30 April.

Wood, B. and Moran, M. (1994), 'The Engine Room of Instruction: Small Group Teaching', *Politics*, 14 (2), 83–90.

Useful sites re-Twitter: http://chronicle.com/wiredcampus/index.php?id=3705&utm_source=wc&utm_m http://elearningstuff.wordpress.com/2009/04/08/using-twitter/ http://www.blogscholar.com

6
How Relevant are Other Ways to Learn?

Steven Curtis

The teaching of Politics and International Relations has traditionally taken place through lectures and seminars. However, in recent years we have seen the emergence and rising prominence of other ways to learn about politics. The UK Quality Assurance Agency for Higher Education's 'benchmark statement' for Politics and International Relations includes a place for class-based debates, role-play and simulations, which can be conducted within regular teaching arrangements; but, in addition, mentions 'contact with political actors through visits, speakers, websites and, in some cases, experiential learning such as internships, placements or action research in the UK or abroad' (QAA, 2007, p. 9). This chapter argues that such activities form an important addition to the armoury of the Politics lecturer. Along with improving students' knowledge and understanding of Politics and International Relations, they can help to develop personal transferable skills, such as working independently and with others, self-organization and time-management, as well as facilitating deep learning, with students taking responsibility for their own learning; these are also benchmark goals (QAA, 2007, p. 8).

This chapter provides an overview of these alternative approaches to learning and teaching in political studies, with particular emphasis on experiential learning through placements and the use of simulations, and also explores the question of how such non-traditional forms of learning can be effectively and meaningfully assessed. Of course, any such survey will inevitably be partial, so some important developments, such as the use of case- or problem-based learning (Hale, 2006) or publicly accessible student blogs which can attract practitioners' comments (Curtis, 2010, pp. 94–5), will not be covered here. Despite the variety of non-traditional approaches to learning, the chapter argues that there are a number of common themes and benefits from adopting such methods and techniques, including deepening and enriching students' understanding of the political world as well as enhancing their personal development and employment prospects.

The advantages of learning through engaging

Forms of learning which actively engage students in their studies, by contrast to the traditional arrangement of lectures and seminars in which students play a more passive role, are often deemed to yield significant educational benefits. One frequently meets some variation of the claim, hailing from the work of Edgar Dale, that 'students retain 10% of what they read, 20 per cent of what they hear, 30 per cent of what they see, per cent of what they see and hear, 70 per cent of what they say, and 90 per cent of what they say as they do something' (quoted in Ishiyama, 2010, p. 4). While this claim is deeply problematic and unscientific, not least due to the round percentages and the fact that stimulating texts and the performances of impassioned lecturers will stay with students longer than a poorly devised simulation, there is some truth in the claim that engaging students in their studies through such techniques will improve their depth of understanding.

These advantages stem in large measure from the fact that such forms of learning are less mediated by the interventions of tutors, thus forcing students to play a greater role in interpreting and learning from such experiences (Moon, 2004). In addition, such approaches demand and encourage that students take on more responsibility for their own learning and provide an opportunity to embed a research-based approached to learning in the undergraduate politics curriculum (see Lightfoot's Chapter in this volume), as students develop higher-order academic and practical skills. They also offer students with different learning styles opportunities to excel, encouraging students who perform less well in standard assignments to engage with their studies.

But in addition to being more effective modes of learning, claims are also frequently made for the benefits of placements and simulations in terms of students' personal development and preparation for lives of active citizenship (Annette, 2005; Bernstein, 2010; Rimmerman, 2007). This touches on the contentious issue of the politicization of students and there is much debate surrounding the question of what should be the academic's proper role in all of this. Opinions vary considerably and the differences are neatly captured in the titles of recent influential books, from *Educating Citizens* (Colby et al., 2003) and *Educating for Democracy* (Colby et al., 2007), on the one hand, to the declaration that as an academic you should *Save the World on Your Own Time* (Fish, 2008), on the other. But even if we bracket the issue of educating citizens for one moment, we can see that there are related additional benefits from such approaches to learning.

Studies have demonstrated that both simulations and placements have the capacity to enhance students' sense of personal efficacy (Bernstein, 2010, p. 20; Curtis and Blair, 2010b), that is, their sense that their thoughts and opinions matter and that they have the ability to affect change in the world.

They are also very popular with students, who often say that such activities are the best thing they have done at university, which is of no small importance given the rising significance of the National Student Survey and university league tables.

Finally, deploying other approaches to learning enables the disciplines of Politics and International Relations to more successfully address the issue of employability. The UK Minister for Universities and Science requires that information about every degree programme include an 'employability statement', clearly indicating how the course will prepare graduates for work (Willetts, 2010). However, this is merely the culmination of a trend, with employers, governments and students alike demanding that degree subjects bear more relevance to future careers (Tomlinson, 2008), with similar concerns also recently emerging in the United States (for example, Colby et al., 2007, pp. 234–5; Peters and Beeson, 2010).

Politics has traditionally been seen as a largely non-vocation subject, which has led to the framing of employability of politics graduates primarily in terms of both subject knowledge and the study skills that one would expect of social sciences graduates (Higher Education Academy, 2006). Embracing approaches to learning which involve the active participation of students in one form or another means that students can become more aware of the range of careers that are available to politics graduates as well as developing a broader range of skills that will be attractive to employers. Even Oxford University exposes its undergraduates to an element of experiential learning through extra-curricular activities, to provide students with more business awareness (Black, 2010). But as we will see in this chapter, Oxford is missing a trick here, as there are many ways of integrating and embedding such experiential learning into the Politics curriculum and providing students with academic credit for such work.

Placements and other forms of community engagement

In recent decades there has been a growth of learning opportunities which provide students with some direct experience of the political world. These can take a variety of forms, including internships with political actors, work placements, service-learning, volunteering, action research projects in collaboration with community actors, and contact with practitioners facilitated through educational visits and outside speakers entering the classroom (see Box 6.1). Many of these activities take place on a co-curricular or extra-curricular basis, as activities which students can engage in alongside and in addition to their studies, with the main aim the development of their CVs. However, there are a variety of means through which learning from these experiences can be linked to and captured through a unit or module of study and thus more fully integrated into the Politics curriculum. Such activities have been demonstrated to

Box 6.1   Getting started with placement learning: some tips

Identifying placements: While high profile national actors such as MPs can offer prestigious internships, local organizations often provide more meaningful opportunities to learn about politics. Smaller NGOs are usually more flexible in dealing with interns and allow them to experience a wider range of activities than larger organizations which tend to have rigid ideas of what an internship should require.

Making the student useful: Placement providers will incur costs by taking on a student, if only in terms of staff time answering questions and guiding the student's activities. Find out if the student can undertake a small piece of research in return. Most political actors will have a number of research projects they have wanted to undertake but haven't had time.

Documentation: Learning agreements or memoranda of understanding between university, student and placement provider are important means of setting out the responsibilities and expectations of each partner, especially in terms of ensuring the student learns while on placement.

Health and safety: Make sure you comply with your institution's health and safety regulations and that your health and safety officer know what you are up to. It may be necessary for your institution to take out additional insurance for students on certain placements.

provide opportunities for an enriched understanding of politics, so embedding experiential learning in the curriculum will benefit students' learning, as well as addressing the citizenship, employability and personal development agendas (for example, Markus, Howard and King, 1993).

But before we attempt to embed such forms of learning in the curriculum, it is important to be clear about what the main intended learning outcomes of the placement should be. Do we want students to gain work experience or do we want them to learn about how politics works in practice? While many forms of placement activities will achieve both outcomes to one degree or another, how we set up, embed and assess such activities will have an impact on what students get out of them. In this regard, there appears to be a continuum of learning outcomes, with work experience and the acquisition of work-related skills and competences at one end and the enhancement of students' disciplinary knowledge and understanding at the other. If we wish to develop the former, then lengthy exposure to the world of work would be appropriate, to give students the opportunity to develop generic work-related skills such as teamwork, time management and so on. If that is the sole aim, it matters little whether the experience takes place in the world of politics or not. Hence, sandwich degree programmes in the UK, in which students experience a year of work between the second and final year of their four-year degree programmes, generally allow students to explore any area of employment that they can demonstrate an interest in, regardless of whether the work is relevant to their degree.

However, if we intend that students should use the experience to improve and develop their understanding of politics, then we will want their experiences to be more closely related to – and ideally integrated into – the Politics curriculum. In such cases, there is less concern with students demonstrating work-related skills and more of a focus on learning about politics, so that activities such as shadowing an official may be more productive than students actually engaging in workplace activities themselves. Of course, this notional continuum simplifies matters somewhat, and the art is in devising placement opportunities that bend the continuum in order to develop students' learning and work-related skills simultaneously.

There are a number of ways of integrating experiential learning into Politics degree programmes, from a full-time semester or year-long placement with a political actor to shorter periods of activity during vacations or in term time. While there tends to be an emphasis on lengthy placements, short placements have been demonstrated to yield tangible benefits in terms of students' learning about politics, their sense of personal efficacy and their employability (Curtis et al., 2009a; Curtis and Blair, 2010b). Such experiences can be integrated into the curriculum, through a year or semester-long placement as a formal requirement of a programme. This is often the case with degrees in Public Administration, Public Policy and Legislative Studies, which are more vocationally-directed programmes and which are concerned with developing students' workplace competencies in a relevant environment. This is where we come closest to work-based learning in politics, where the work itself forms part of the curriculum. But for most Politics programmes, there will be a greater concern with learning about the subject of politics, in which case the curriculum will remain entirely with the university and the exposure to the real world of politics should provide students with concrete experiences to illustrate and compare against their campus-based studies.

Experiential learning can also be embedded in Politics programmes at the level of the unit or module of study. This can be achieved though a designated placement module, which involves a certain minimum amount of activity combined with a pattern of assessment. Alternatively, experiential learning opportunities can be linked to and assessed through a content module, in which a direct connection between a specific area of the Politics curriculum and a related realm of the political world is established so that each reinforces the other: students can put their specialist knowledge into practice while simultaneously enriching their understanding of that area of study through exposure to concrete examples. For example, a student taking a module on the European Union who is placed with a Member of the European Parliament can put her knowledge of the EU's institutions to work on the placement while gaining new insights into the workings of the EU at the same time. This is the approach which most successfully integrates experiential learning into the curriculum. By comparison, other approaches often appear as 'bolt-ons', relatively free-floating affairs in which it is more incumbent on the student to make the connection between their experiences and their degree programmes. Tying experiential learning to units of study more closely relates such experiences to intended learning outcomes.

There are a number of challenges posed by these forms of activity. For lecturers there is the time commitment that setting up and monitoring these opportunities for learning requires. Even if the responsibility for finding and negotiating the content of placements is devolved to university careers service staff or to the students themselves, which is the most popular approach in the UK, academic staff will still need to ensure that the experiences are meaningful in academic terms and that various procedural issues have been satisfied, such as health and safety clearance and confirmation from placement providers that the students actually undertook activities of the nature and duration they claim to have done in their assessed work. And devolving the responsibility for setting up placements to other parties increases the risk that the experiences will not be closely related to the intended learning outcomes of the unit of study to which they are linked.

There is also the issue of what counts as a placement relevant to Politics degree programmes. In the United States service-learning, an approach which attempts to combine service to the community through volunteering with the enrichment of students' learning, has become very popular, especially as it is seen as a way of developing students as active citizens (Astin, 2002; Barber and Battistoni, 1993). However, there is a concern that most service activities are not in any way political and do not enhance students' learning about the discipline (Colby et al., 2007, 5), although other commentators prefer to see service to the community as an expression of a new politics, free from the cynicism that is often attached to party politics and other more traditional forms of political activity (Rimmerman, 2007).

There is also the challenge posed by the changing demographics of the student body. With increasing numbers of so-called 'non-traditional' students (that is, mature students with families and work commitments and those from less well-off backgrounds), coupled with the increasing financial pressure on students to work while studying, many students will not be able to participate in such activities (Butin, 2010, pp. 145–6; Curtis and Blair, 2010b, pp. 374–6). This renders it difficult to extend this sort of learning opportunity across politics programmes generally, and makes other activities more attractive. For example, short educational visits to political actors, organizations and exhibitions and outside speakers coming onto campus, can both enrich students' understanding of the discipline and enhance their personal development and employability by putting them into contact with practitioners and broadening their career horizons. All students on a unit should be able to participate in such activities, which both widens participation and undermines the 'individualist bias' in most experiential learning opportunities (Moon, 2004, p. 118). Students can learn from each other's insights when they learn together.

Nonetheless, experiential learning opportunities can yield significant results in terms of enriching student learning and enhancing their personal development and employment prospects. Lecturers will also find that many community and political actors have their own 'community engagement' boxes to tick, and that frequently government departments, local government offices and non-governmental organizations will be looking to forge such partnerships.

Simulations

Simulations, role-play activities and games have become very popular in the disciplines of politics and international relations and there is a growing body of literature on the subject. The entire range of real-world political activity can be simulated on campus, from local assemblies to national legislatures to meetings of the United Nations Security Council and international conferences. It is also possible to explore the nature of violent conflict and peacebuilding in the safety of the university environment, when to seek to do so through more direct experiential learning would raise a host of health and safety issues. Finally, it is possible to blend simulations with other forms of active learning, such as service-learning (Jenkins, 2010) or with films (Simpson and Kaussler, 2009), so that these novel methods of learning reinforce each other, as well as providing opportunities for drawing professional bodies and other organisations into the university to assist in the running and/or assessment of such activities. For example, peacebuilding NGOs can provide skills training and run simulations based on their experiences of conflict and the training which peace workers require to survive and succeed in warzones (Curtis, 2010, p. 94; Curtis and Blair, 2010a, chapters 6–8).

As simulations can be run during normal class hours, they provide a means of learning which can engage the whole module cohort simultaneously, thereby overcoming some of the limitations of placement learning noted above (although if extended simulations which run over a number of days are used, many of the problems of inclusion may reappear in class-based activities).

When devising simulations, just as when embedding placements into the curriculum, it is important to determine what the main purpose of the activity is. Like placements, simulations can be used for a variety of purposes, and how the activity is set up will determine what students learn from it. Simulations also range across a continuum, from the recreation of actual historical events, in which students are assigned and re-enact the roles of real figures, at one extreme, to hypothetical situations in which the outcomes are not predetermined and through which students can develop their negotiating skills and their ability to frame and articulate arguments clearly and authoritatively. Of course, most simulations will involve both aspects to varying degrees, but considering the intended learning outcomes of the unit on which the simulation is to be employed should determine which end of the continuum the activity should address.

If the intention is that students should understand the origins of the First World War, for example, then the simulation will tend towards the re-enactment end of the continuum, as students assume the positions of the various statesmen and go through the motions of August 1914. The main value of this activity is in enriching students' understanding of the alliance politics of the period and giving them refined insights into what the policy makers were thinking and the constraints they operated within. It works to improve their understanding of events, similar to Hans Morgenthau's famous claim that we can understand the reasoning of a statesman by rationally reconstructing his thoughts and actions, as we 'look over his shoulder' (Morgenthau, 1985, p. 5), with the added advantage that the students are exploring such actions through embodying the statesmen.

By contrast, at the hypothetical end of the continuum, simulations deploying contrived settings can be used to introduce students to the nature of debate, negotiation and organization by having them work through a situation the outcome of which is not determined in advance (Bernstein, 2010, p. 20). If the intention is to develop students' skills of negotiation rather than providing insights into real-world events, a hypothetical situation will be more appropriate. Without a predetermined outcome, students have the freedom to develop their negotiating and teamwork skills to the full. Tutors will often still want students to glean some insights into how such activities work in practice, and therefore the hypothetical situation will usually bear some resemblance to actual events, regions or conflicts; but here the emphasis lies on nurturing a skills set that cannot be developed through the usual learning and teaching configuration of lectures and seminars.

In the middle of the continuum lie simulations which introduce students to actual situations but which encourage them to think about how to move things forward, for example through how to go about resolving the conflict between the Israelis and the Palestinians. This approach will offer up both insights into the causes and constraints of the current situation along with creative but realistic thinking and activity directed towards improving the situation – it will both enrich students' understanding of the present historical juncture and enable them to develop their negotiating skills.

Many lecturers are often put off of the idea of embedding simulations in their classes as they view it as a very time-consuming undertaking. Frequently simulations do require tutors to produce a pack of materials, sometimes for each actor, setting out the background to the situation to be simulated as well as the positions, values and interests of each actor. This is especially the case towards the re-enactment end of the continuum, where tutors expect students to emerge with an improvement understanding of an event or situation.

However, there are two possible ways forward for tutors who are put off at the thought of producing such information packs: to procure a simulation package, many of which are freely available online; or to set up the unit in which the simulation is to be embedded in a way that requires students to research and produce their own position papers ahead of the simulation. Of course, the former approach depends on the prior existence of suitable off-the-shelf simulations that are ready to go (see Box 6.2). A simulation that is shoehorned into a unit with which it bears little resemblance will be less effective as a learning opportunity. The second approach therefore has the benefit of more precisely tailoring the preparatory materials and the simulation itself to the content and nature of the unit of study. In addition, it nods in the direction of a research-based approach to learning, as requiring students to research and produce their actors' position papers demands independent research and a more practical form of academic work than the standard essay (Usherwood, 2009, p. 299).

Whichever form of simulation is decided upon, space needs to be set aside at the end for reflection so that learning from the exercise can be accumulated

Box 6.2   Getting started with simulations: online resources

To save you the time of devising your own simulations, there are a number of online repositories of simulations, role-play exercises and games. You can tailor many of them to meet the requirements of your module. The following is just a selection:

Archive of Simulations and Games (University of Westminster and University of Surrey): http://en.wikiversity.org/wiki/Portal:Simulation_and_Gaming_Archive

Simulations for Teaching Political Science (American Political Science Association): www.apsanet.org/content_15404.cfm

The Program on Negotiation (Harvard Law School): www.pon.org/catalog/index.php

United Nations Security Council Role-Play Exercise (University of Western Australia): www.learningdesigns.uow.edu.au/exemplars/info/LD25/index.html

Conflict Simulations (Professor Philip Sabin, King's College London): www.kcl.ac.uk/sspp/departments/warstudies/people/professors/sabin/consim.aspx

and consolidated. This can take the form of individual or group debriefing sessions, which can involve students writing about their experiences. This leads us to matters of assessment.

Assessing other ways to learn

Due to the unconventional nature of these forms of learning opportunities, a variety of novel assessment techniques have been developed to capture and facilitate student learning. To maximize the impact on learning, assessment practices should be constructed with care and attention. For example, students engaged in such activities are frequently required to maintain learning journals of one form or another, to record and reflect upon their experiences. However, depending on the lecturing outcomes that tutors are aiming for, reflective journals may not always be the best form of assessment, at least not as the final piece of work that is submitted at the end of the experience. It may be better to view journals as 'an aid to learning', which can then form a source of information for an essay or report, rather than a form of assessed work in their own right (Moon, 2004, p. 156).

Thinking about assessment and its purpose returns us once again to the issue of where we wish to situate the aims of learning on the continuum between engendering certain competencies in practice, on the one hand, and enriching students' knowledge and understanding of an area of activity, on the other. If we are attempting to achieve the former, then it may be appropriate to develop ways of assessing each student's performance *in situ*. In this case, we are assessing the student's ability to perform certain tasks. In work-based learning, the employer will then play a role in commenting on and possibly even grading a student's performance against the regular expected standards of performance in the workplace. In the context of simulations, a student's performance during the simulation itself can be assessed against a predefined range of criteria. Professional organizations, such as the peacebuilding NGO referred to above, which specialize in providing training, may be able to observe the simulation and then to grade the performance of students in groups or individually. Nonetheless, this approach to assessment is fraught with a number of problems. In particular, involving employers in the assessment of work-based learning frequently leads to inconsistency in the grades awarded (assuming that all students have not been placed with the same employer). In addition, the grades awarded by employers and other bodies will rarely neatly correspond to university marking schemes. For these reasons in particular, academics often prefer to retain the prerogative of awarding marks, even if that means translating the comments and grades of employers into marks that universities understand.

If the purpose of unconventional learning activities is to enhance students' understanding of a dimension of the political world rather than to develop certain professional competencies, then other forms of assessment, which bear a greater resemblance to more traditional forms of assessment, will be appropriate. The most popular forms of assessing such activities include learning journals, diaries and portfolios, essays and reports, and oral presentations (Curtis et al., 2009b; Donahue and Ishiyama, 2009; Fanthome, 2004, pp. 114–25). What they have in common is an emphasis on reflection. As Jenny Moon points out, due to its relatively unmediated nature, experiential learning is almost always associated with reflection (Moon, 2004), although how we assess such activities will exert a profound shaping effect on the experience itself (Curtis et al., 2009a, pp. 67–8; Moon, 2004, pp. 150–5). It is therefore a mistake to think of such forms of learning as entirely unmediated and pure experiences. Embedding them in the curriculum and assessing them will shape how students approach and learn from them.

Conclusion

Besides being very popular with students in their own right, in part due to the breaking of the traditional routines of learning and teaching in higher education, the approaches to learning outlined in this Chapter hold out the possibility of enriching students' understanding of the world of politics and complementing their regular class-based study of the subject by providing concrete experiences with which to illustrate and in some cases challenge formal conceptual approaches to the study of politics. In addition, there are also profound benefits in terms of enhancing students' personal development and employment prospects, which is of increasing importance in a world where students are expected to invest more and more in their futures through higher tuition fees.

Guide to further reading

There is an established and growing body of articles on the benefits of experiential learning for students of Politics, such as Markus, Howard and King (1993) and Dicklitch (2003). Service-learning and placement learning in Political Studies have received book-length treatments in Battistoni and Hudson (1997) and Curtis and Blair (2010a) respectively, with the latter also including chapters on simulations and other forms of active learning. Contrasting approaches to the role of politics placements can be found in Norton (2008) and Curtis et al. (2009a). Fathome (2004) contains some good general advice about setting up and getting the most from placements from a student's perspective, while Moon (2004) provides consistently thought-provoking guidance on the purposes and assessment of experiential learning. A fine collection of essays on active learning techniques can be found in Shaw (2010), and there are many excellent articles on the uses of simulations in the learning and teaching of Politics and International Relations, which can be found in journals including *PS: Political Science and Politics*, *Journal of Political Science Education* and *International Studies Perspectives*, such as Sasley (2010). Finally, two seminal texts from an American perspective, which explore and evaluate the educational and other benefits of a wide variety of approaches to learning, are Colby et al. (2003) and Colby et al. (2007).

References

Annette, J. (2005), 'Character, Civic Renewal and Service Learning for Democratic Citizenship in Higher Education', *British Journal of Educational Studies* 53(3), 326–40.

Astin, A. W. (2002), 'Higher Education and the Cultivation of Citizenship' in D. Allman and M. Beaty (eds), *Cultivating Citizens: Soulcraft and Citizenship in Contemporary America* (Lanham, MD: Lexington Books), pp. 91–120.

Barber, B. R. and Battistoni, R. (1993), 'A Season of Service', *PS: Political Science and Politics* 26(2), 235–40.

Battistoni, R. M. and Hudson, W. E. (eds) (1997), *Experiencing Citizenship: Concepts and Models for Service-Learning in Political Science* (Washington, DC: American Association for Higher Education).

Bernstein, J. L. (2010), 'Citizenship-Oriented Approaches to the American Government Course' in M. B. Smith, R. S. Nowacek and J. L. Bernstein (eds), *Citizenship Across the Curriculum* (Bloomington: Indiana University Press), pp. 13–35.

Black, J. (2010), 'The Issue is not Numbers of Graduates, but Their Skills' in *The Guardian*, Education Section, 13 July, available at www.guardian.co.uk/education/2010/jul/13/graduate-jobs-skills (accessed 20 July 2010).

Butin, D. (2010), *Service-Learning in Theory and Practice: The Future of Community Engagement in Higher Education* (New York: Palgrave Macmillan).

Colby, A., Beaumont, E., Ehrlich, T., and Corngold, J. (2007), *Educating for Democracy: Preparing Undergraduates for Responsible Political Engagement* (San Francisco: Jossey-Bass).

Colby, A., Ehrlich, T., Beaumont, E. and Stephens, J. (2003), *Educating Citizens: Preparing America's Undergraduates for Lives of Moral and Civic Responsibility* (San Francisco: Jossey-Bass).

Curtis, S. (2010), 'Learning in Public: Connecting Politics Students with Practitioners in "the Edgeless University"', *Political Insight* 1 (3), 93–5.

Curtis, S., Axford, B., Blair, A., Gibson, C., Huggins, R. and Sherrington, P. (2009a), 'Making Short Politics Placements Work', *Politics* 29 (1), 62–70.

Curtis, S., Axford, B., Blair, A., Gibson, C., Huggins, R. and Sherrington, P. (2009b), 'Placement Blogging: The Benefits and Limitations of Online Journaling', *ELiSS: Enhancing Learning in the Social Sciences* 1 (3), available at www.eliss.org.uk/.

Curtis, S., and Blair, A. (eds) (2010a), *The Scholarship of Engagement for Politics: Placement Learning, Citizenship and Employability*, Birmingham: C-SAP Monographs, available at www.lulu.com/product/file-download/the-scholarship-of-engagement-for-politics/6427740 (accessed 1 December 2010).

Curtis, S. and Blair, A. (2010b), 'Experiencing Politics in Action: Widening Participation in Placement Learning and Politics as a Vocation', *Journal of Political Science Education* 6 (4), 369–90.

Dicklitch, S. (2003), 'Real Service=Real Learning: Making Political Science Relevant Through Service-Learning', *PS: Political Science and Politics* 36(4), 773–6.

Donahue, V. and Ishiyama, J. (2009) 'The Critical Portfolio: Facilitating the Reflective Political Science Student in the Experiential Environment', in M. D. Deardorff, K. Hamann and J. Ishiyama (eds), *Assessment in Political Science* (Washington DC: American Political Science Association).

Fanthome, C. (2004), *Work Placements – A Survival Guide for Students* (Basingstoke: Palgrave Macmillan).

Fish, S. (2008), *Save the World on Your Own Time* (Oxford: Oxford University Press).

Hale, S. (2006), 'Politics and the Real World: A Case-Study in Developing Case-Based Learning', *European Political Science* 5 (1), 84–96.

Higher Education Academy (2006), 'Student Employability Profiles: Politics and International Relations', available at www.heacademy.ac.uk/assets/York/documents/ourwork/tla/employability/student_employability_profiles_politics.pdf (accessed 21 March 2009).

Ishiyama, J. (2010), 'What is the Impact of In-Class Active Learning Techniques? A Meta Analysis of the Existing Literature', paper at the American Political Studies Association 2010 Annual Meeting, 2–5 September, Washington D.C., available at SSRN: http://ssrn.com/abstract=1644146 (accessed 15 November 2010).

Jenkins, S. (2010), 'Service Learning and Simulations', *PS: Political Science and Politics* 43 (3), 541–5.

Markus, G. B., Howard, J. P. F. and King, D. C. (1993), 'Integrating Community Service and Classroom Instruction Enhances Learning: Results from an Experiment', *Education Evaluation and Policy Analysis* 15(4), 410–19.

Moon, J. A. (2004), *A Handbook of Reflective and Experiential Learning: Theory and Practice* (London: Routledge Falmer).

Morgenthau, H. J. (1985), *Politics Among Nations: The Struggle for Power and Peace*, 6th edn (New York: McGraw-Hill).

Norton, P. (2008), 'Parliamentary Placements: The Benefits and Challenges', *ELiSS: Enhancing Learning in the Social Sciences* 1 (1), available at www.eliss.org.uk/ (accessed 11 May 2011).

Quality Assurance Agency for Higher Education (QAA) (2007), 'Politics and International Relations Subject Benchmark Statement', available online at www.qaa.ac.uk/academicinfrastructure/benchmark/statements/Politics.pdf (accessed 21 March 2010).

Peters, R. and Beeson, M. (2010), 'Reducing the Gap Between Skills Sought by Employers and Developed by Education', *PS: Political Science and Politics* 43 (4), 773–7.

Rimmerman, C. (2007), *The New Citizenship: Unconventional Politics, Activism and Service*, 3rd edn (Boulder, CO: Westview).

Sasley, B. E. (2010), 'Teaching Students How to Fail: Simulations as Tools of Explanation', *International Studies Perspectives* 11 (1), 61–74.

Shaw, C. (ed.) (2010), 'Active Learning in International Affairs', in R. A. Denmark (ed.), *The International Studies Encylopedia*, Blackwell Reference Online, available at www.isacompendium.com/subscriber/tocnode?id=g9781444336597_chunk_g97814443365972 (accessed 15 February 2011).

Simpson, A. W. and Kaussler, B. (2009), 'IR Teaching Reloaded: Using Films and Simulations in the Teaching of International Relations', *International Studies Perspectives* 10 (4), 413–27.

Tomlinson, M. (2008), '"The Degree is Not Enough": Students' Perceptions of the Role of Higher Education Credentials for Graduate Work and Employability', *British Journal of Sociology of Education*, 29 (1), 49–61.

Usherwood, S. (2009), 'Grounding Simulations in Reality: A Case Study from an Undergraduate Politics Degree', *On the Horizon* 17 (4), 296–302.

Willetts, D. (2010), 'University Challenge', speech at Oxford Brookes University, 10 June, available at www.berr.gov.uk/news/speeches/david-willetts-oxford-brookes-university-challenge (accessed 17 July 2010).

7
Issues and Controversies Associated with the Use of New Technologies

Stephen Thornton

Some within the discipline of Politics are keenly aware that the development of certain new technologies could help shape the future of the subject. For example, Newell and Bull warn that, for the discipline to 'survive and thrive', Political Scientists 'need to stay abreast of and exploit these [technological] changes' (Newell and Bull, 2008, p. 131). Moreover, some academics within the discipline are attempting to shape this future through innovative work utilizing these new technologies, including many contributors to this particular book. Examples include Leston-Bandeira's (2009) thoughtful utilization of e-learning to promote critical thinking in Politics; Gormley-Heenan and McCartan's (2009) innovative utilization of an audience response system; Curtis and colleagues' exciting take on blogging (2009); and Ralph, Head and Lightfoot's stimulating work developing the use of podcasting (2010). However, despite the exhortations made by Newell and Bull, and many others, and the plentiful examples of good practice, there remains a strong suggestion that the discipline in general has yet to treat new technologies seriously. As Blair, Bromage and Curtis have indicated, Politics has a habit of trudging in the footsteps of more technology-savvy disciplines, notably the physical sciences (2006, p. 119). Furthermore, it is not simply a pedagogic concern, as Margetts has illustrated, in terms of research and study, Politics again trails behind some other disciplines such as Economics and Sociology in appreciating the significance of the Internet and other related technologies (Margatts, 2010, p. 66).

The reluctance of many within the discipline to embrace some of the opportunities provided by new technologies is surprising, and – to some extent – regrettable. Margetts makes a very convincing case in support of her contention that mainstream Politics research has suffered by largely ignoring the implications of Internet-based activity (2010, pp. 64–87). Likewise, turning to the focus of this book – learning and teaching – an equally valid case can be made to claim that significant opportunities for improving student learning are being missed through disciplinary tardiness. James Sloam, for one, has argued that the teaching of Politics in the UK tends towards the conservative, with an over-dependence on the behaviouralist model of education; one which generally favours hierarchically structured systems of knowledge-transmission (Sloam, 2008, p. 513). Among many suggestions designed to take the learning of Politics forward in a more interactive, student-centred direction – one that prejudices the development of understanding more than simple knowledge acquisition – Sloam suggests that the thoughtful deployment of new technologies in the field of education, sometimes called 'e-learning', can be used for 'a multitude of purposes' (2008, p. 519). These include using e-learning facilities to provide a valuable resource for relevant information, to encourage problem-solving, to aid collaborative learning, and to encourage interaction inside and outside the classroom.

Like many others writing about teaching and learning in the university sector, Sloam is influenced by the work of influential educationalist, John Biggs. Though most celebrated for popularizing the concept of constructive alignment (Biggs, 1996) – in which learning objectives, teaching methods and assessment are consciously put together in a systematic manner to facilitate deep learning – Biggs has also explored the issue of e-learning. Though critical of some of the ways in which new technologies have been applied in the classroom, Biggs has identified four particular areas where such technologies can provide opportunities for improved learning across the university curriculum (2003, pp. 214–5; see Box 7.1):

Box 7.1 Biggs' uses of ET ('educational technology')

Use	Description	Typical technologies used
Managing learning	To assist the administration and management of learning, through providing information about programmes, modules regulations, etc., and to facilitate communication to, from and between students.	Virtual Learning Environments (VLEs), such as Moodle and Blackboard
Engaging learners in appropriate learning activity	To aid learning activities (many interactive) that are not practical under conventional teaching	Audience response systems, such as TurningPoint
Assessing learning	Providing opportunities for computer-assisted assessment, both summative and formative, that can, *inter alia*, provide immediate feedback and allow more than one attempt	Assessment management systems, such as QuestionMark, Perception

Use	Description	Typical technologies used
Distance and off-campus learning setting.	Providing opportunities for increasing the variety of creative learning experiences outside the traditional campus	Lecture capture systems – systems to record video, audio and content of lectures or presentations – such as Echo360; web conferencing systems, such as DimDim.

Details of an excellent example from within the Politics discipline that achieves many of Biggs' aspirations for what he calls '*educational* technology (ET)' – to distinguish it from '*information* technology (IT)' (Biggs, 2003, p. 213, italics in the original) – will be examined later in this Chapter. However, before lauding the pedagogic opportunities technology promises further, it is essential to highlight that, accompanying these opportunities, come many substantial challenges. Indeed, as Biggs, and others, have argued, technology is a double-edged sword, one – when used carelessly – with the potential to damage learning as likely as enhance it. Two of these challenges will be examined here: 'IT' as 'inappropriate technology' and the threat of 'information obesity'.

'IT' as 'inappropriate technology'

There is nothing intrinsically pedagogically beneficial about technological advancement. To take one popular example, despite its clear technological superiority over its late twentieth-century rival, the overhead projector (OHP), the current near-ubiquity of the presentation software Microsoft PowerPoint has not consequentially led to the delivery of better lectures. Indeed, some would argue the reverse has occurred, that PowerPoint encourages over-simplification, rewards style over substance, and, essentially, becomes a crutch for poor speakers. It was Edward Tufte, channelling the spirit of Lord Acton, who coined the memorable: 'Power corrupts. PowerPoint corrupts absolutely' (Tufte, 2003a, see also Tufte, 2003b). Thus, as Craig has argued, regarding teaching and learning in particular, one path that must be avoided is the one that leads to 'a kind of technological determinism that assumes that the newest technology must be better simply because it is new' (Craig, 2010, p. 2).

Unfortunately, as Middleton explains (2010, pp. 7–9), many of those who use and write about e-learning are prone to exactly this type of technological determinism, and, once under the thrall of some exciting new piece of hardware or software, throw their critical faculties away with the plastic wrapping. As a result, many evaluations of new products in the field of e-learning tend to focus less on assessing pedagogic efficacy and more on rating simple popularity

(Booth, 2007). Indeed, it seems that a number of those involved in promoting technology as a enhancement for teaching and learning have lost sight of the reality that most technology is not designed with pedagogy in mind. This is not a new observation: Davies was making the point that most of the technology used in the classroom was 'primarily developed for other purposes' before the arrival of the first personal computer (1972, p. 2). Davies was referring to devices such as television, overhead and slide projectors, and convenient sound recording, all which all began as products for markets other than the educational one, and had to be adapted – with varying levels of success – for the purposes of teaching and learning. In the twenty-first century, it is the electronic gaming and communications industries that are forcing the pace in terms of civilian technology, however – just as before – innovations taken up by the educational world are, in many cases, clumsy adaptations of products designed for other markets.

This issue of appropriateness of certain techniques and technologies for the educational purposes has been investigated by Ishiyama (2010). In particular, Ishiyama has investigated the popularity in many US Political Science classrooms for simulations – which regularly come supported by a variety of information and communication technologies – and he has arrived at the conclusion that proven pedagogical effectiveness is not the main factor to explain their attractiveness; a deduction that rests on the convincing grounds that little such evidence exists. Rather, Ishiyama speculates, the simple 'fun' gained through simulations, by students and teaching staff alike, is a more significant driver, as is the growing market in such products: 'Simulations have become a business, and to some extent the supply has created the demand for their use' (Ishiyama, 2010, pp. 12–13). The result, Ishiyama believes, is that political scientists – in the US at least – have become over-reliant on simulations and now overlook 'other active learning techniques that are potentially just as effective' (2010, p. 13). In the UK the situation is slightly different in that, according to Sloam (2008), many political scientists tend overlook active learning in the first place.

Returning to the main issue, it is quite evident that pedagogic concerns are not always the main drivers behind the take-up of particular technologies. Neophilia and market pressures are also major factors, as is a desire to stimulate students without necessarily considering other equally pedagogically sound, but less technologically ostentatious, options. Furthermore, this desire to stimulate the young may be the result of a possible over-reaction made by an older generation to the arrival into the higher education system of a new generation referred to – among a number of competing epithets – as the 'Net Generation', 'Digital Natives', or 'Millenials'. The presumption of theorists such as Prensky (2001) – who coined 'Digital Natives' – is that this young generation is distinctive in that has been immersed since birth in a world of new technologies, and higher education needs to adjust rapidly to match the novel set of skills and expectations shaped by such digital experiences. This assumption has led to suggestions that often focus on the much greater involvement in the education process of 'Web 2.0 technologies' - such as social networking sites like Facebook and MySpace – and has prompted the publication of many articles with urgent titles such as 'Web 2.0: A New Wave of Innovation for Teaching and Learning?' (Alexander, 2006) and 'Is Education 1.0 Ready for Web 2.0 Students?' (Thompson, 2007).

With the publication of such pieces, and the evident massive popularity explosion of social networking sites, it is understandable that many academics have reacted by embracing technology wholeheartedly, and sometimes successfully. However, it ought to be highlighted that some argue that Prensky's assumption is flawed; not least the expectation that an entire generation of students is technologically savvy. For example, Kennedy and his colleagues in Australia have convincingly demonstrated that there is a much greater diversity in the frequency of use in the study and general lives of students than many would expect and, moreover, that 'the use of collaborative and self-publishing "Web 2.0" technologies that have often been associated with this generation is quite low' (Kennedy et al., 2007, p. 517). Herring makes a different point, noting that it is not members of the younger generation who have dubbed themselves this exotic 'Net Generation' moniker; rather this, and similar tags, are the construction of 'experts' from older generations. Herring adds that the 'hyperbolic idealizations [of these older observers] reflect the digital optimism of educated, presumably early adopter adults who tend to be pro-technology and committed to integrating technology into their educational vision for youth' (Herring, 2008, p. 76). Thus, though not to dismiss the significance of Web 2.0 technologies, as they clearly do have a significant role to play in higher education, it pays not to get carried away by the hype.

Other than neophilia, market pressures, and the urge to get 'down with the kids', there are yet more forces at play encouraging an uncritical embrace of e-learning. As Middleton has noted, 'universities are more concerned than ever to cut their costs. E-learning is seen as an important way to deliver mass education economically': indeed it is plausible to suggest that 'the "e" in e-learning can be said to stand for economic rather than electronic' (Middleton, 2010: 6). This observation is particularly insightful an era where any developments in e-learning which permit a university to expand its intake at little cost, not least through the possibilities of remote learning, are going to be jumped on like a starving dog at a juicy bone. However, the economic possibilities of new technology in the education system have long since excited interest among certain managerial types. As Davies remarked back in 1972, 'the process of teaching has been mechanized through the production of teaching aids. These transmit, amplify, distribute, record and reproduce stimuli materials with a consequent increase in teacher impact; at the same time, the teacher can deal with larger and larger groups of students' with consequent potential reductions in cost (Davies, 1972, p. 2). Clearly, economic issues have long since been important factors in the story of using new technologies in educational settings, and remain so more than ever; despite, as Middleton points out, the many instances in which the promise of 'efficiencies' through e-learning have proven to be sadly illusory (Middleton, 2010, p. 11).

To conclude this section on 'inappropriate technology', it is evident that many factors are at play when new technologies are brought into the classroom, and enhancement of learning is not always prominent among them. However, from this it should not be concluded that e-learning has earned banishment from the teaching of Politics; that really would be throwing the technological baby out with the defunct OHP machines and daisy-wheel printers. Rather, the challenge for teachers of Politics is to choose the most appropriate technology when only a modest proportion of the information provided to encourage that choice is based on notions of pedagogic efficacy.

Information obesity

The theme of being wary about all the promises made by hard-core enthusiasts for new technologies continues into this section. Biggs, for one, is fully aware of the siren song that trills, 'use IT, and teaching problems will disappear as we join the globalized, online, knowledge economy' (2003, p. 213); but he is not impressed. In particular, Biggs is unconvinced about some of the claims made about the supposed educational value of the Internet, not least the promises that widespread access to Internet will necessarily herald the arrival of a more intelligent, well-informed, and democratic society (Biggs, 2003, p. 214). Biggs is not suggesting that the Internet is malign, indeed he declares its ability to store and access information as 'impressive', however he does insist we need be aware that some misguidedly 'see the "educational" value of electronic information beginning and ending with its ability to access information from the World Wide Web' (2003, p. 217). Using sarcasm as a weapon, Biggs continues:

> If teaching is about the transfer of knowledge from teacher to student, then the World Wide Web, with virtually unlimited information a mouse-click away, has to be a top quality teaching device. This view is also implied in the phrase 'surfing the Net': surface indeed, with cut-and-paste here, cut-and-paste there, link up with a few connecting sentences in your own very personalized style, and bingo ... an assignment that looks terrific but contains no original or deep thinking.
>
> (Biggs, 2003, p. 214)

Focusing on the use of the Internet in Politics, Burnham et al. make a similar point about the virtues and vices of the Internet. On the positive side,

> government documents that might formerly only have been available by visiting a foreign country, xeroxing them and mailing them home can now in principle be accessed and downloaded within a matter of minutes.
>
> (Burnham et al, 2008, p. 214).

The interactive potential of the Internet is also highly commended; however, midst the excitement, 'a note of caution is necessary' (2008, p. 214). Many students, they suggest, are resorting to resources such as online encyclopaedia Wikipedia which, as the authors acknowledge, has its merits, but also bitterly exposes the user to important questions of academic reliability and validity that they may be unable to respond to effectively (2008, p. 213). In their influential guide to Politics on the Internet, Buckler and Dolowitz concur, suggesting that

> The relatively easy and unregulated way in which information is published online, whilst in some ways a cause for celebration, might also prompt some caution when it comes to the use of such material in academic contexts. Discernment with respect to the origin and quality of the information you find on the Internet is certainly called for.
>
> (Buckler and Dolowitz, 2005, p. 7)

Going beyond the Politics classroom, this issue of discernment of information is tackled particularly strikingly by Andrew Whitworth, an information specialist with a background in critical theory. 'We are suffering from a condition called "information obesity"', Whitworth argues, rather alarmingly, in the first sentence of his monograph on the subject (Whitworth, 2009, p. xi). He argues that technology has rapidly transformed the relationship between society and information in often damaging ways, and that the process of education has been slow to catch up. In particular, Whitworth likens the large quantities of often unreliable information available through the Internet to the concept of 'fast food': both are extremely convenient, cleverly marketed and deeply unhealthy when consumed to excess. As too many hamburgers, with too little exercise, can lead to physical obesity, so the consumption of too many gobbets of information gleaned indiscriminately from search engines, without the mental exercise of critical analysis, can lead to information obesity (Whitworth, 2009, pp. xi–xii). Whitworth is calling for the education system to become more focused on developing critical capabilities.

Concern that uncritical use of the Internet is dulling the critical faculties of current and future university students is not just the subject of academic debate; it is also becoming an increasingly prominent feature in discussions about the future of higher education in the UK. For example, *Higher Education in a Web 2.0 World* (2009), an influential report written by the Committee of Inquiry into the Changing Learner Experience (CLEX) chaired by Sir David Melville, considered this matter as among the most critical facing the UK university education system (CLEX 2009, p. 7). Among the welter of evidence the committee considered, the report highlighted the response of one student involved in the learner experience project who remarked: 'The internet is a world of information. You don't have to go anywhere, it's all on one database' (CLEX, 2009, p. 19).

Though not the focus of this chapter, it is worth highlighting that suggestions for remedies exist, most of which involve the inculcation of 'information literacy'. For the authors of the CLEX report, this concept means 'activities such as search, retrieval and critical evaluation from a range of sources, and also its responsible use from the point of view of attribution' (2009, p. 34), and they recommend wide-ranging changes to the university curriculum to accommodate these activities. More tailored suggestions for improving information literacy within the Politics classroom have also been made (Stevens and Campbell, 2007; Thornton, 2008; 2010). These include encouraging closer collaboration between academic and information professionals, and providing students with discipline-related research assignments that encourage the collection, analysis, and synthesis of multiple viewpoints from a variety of sources.

To summarize this section, many have argued that the information technology revolution, for all its manifold virtues, has not always proven to be an altogether glorious one. Victims include all those who have developed an 'uncritical trust in branded search engines' (CLEX, 2009, p. 34), and – to use Whitworth's terminology – have thus become 'information obese'. There are remedies, but the key point, again, is that the Internet – like other forms of technology – clearly has a place in the teaching and learning of Politics, but it must be used with a clear-sighted awareness of the problems it brings along to the party.

A case study

As suggested throughout this Chapter, despite the various challenges, new technologies are useful tools in the armoury of the Politics lecturer, when used appropriately. One example of the thoughtful application of technology to assist the learning in politics is PARLE, the Politics Active Research Learning Environment, as described by Middleton and Bridge (2008). It is a particularly useful example as it demonstrates the considerable potential of technology as a vehicle to support the tackling of a specific pedagogical issue. Vague claims about 'enriching the curriculum' are carefully avoided. Furthermore – and again in contrast to some pieces extolling the virtues of e-learning – Middleton and Bridge deliberately expose serious problems and pitfalls encountered along the way.

PARLE was designed as an interactive multi-media package containing audio, visual and textual components designed to enhance the learning experience of Politics postgraduate students participating on research methods courses. This area was not chosen because it was particularly applicable for technological solutions, but, rather, to address a specific pedagogical issue that had recently been highlighted: namely a deficiency noted by the Economic and Social Research Council (ESRC) in the way in which research skills were taught in many of the UK's Social Science disciplines, including Politics (Middleton and Bridge, 2008, p. 145). The failure of most orthodox methods courses to encourage more than a surface learning approach was regarded as one factor explaining this shortcoming; that these courses tended to be taught by generalists rather than those with a particular interest in a specific discipline was another. Thus the aim was to close this deficit, at least among Politics postgraduates, by creating materials that encouraged a more active learning response and were subject specific. With this pedagogical goal in mind, the decision was then made 'to exploit the new technologies available to us' (Middleton and Bridge, 2008, p. 145). To that end, the PARLE project created an interactive tool – 'Doing Political Research' – based around a series of tutorials which encouraged students to tackle a series of increasingly challenging tasks which utilized a wide range of research methods. These tasks were supported by a number of authentic materials, such as articles from *Prospect* magazine, and involved elements of 'virtual role-play': students were to take the guise of a political researcher for an MP.

Though technology played second fiddle to pedagogic priorities in the initial stages of the PARLE project, Middleton and Bridge make it clear that the possibilities and limitations of technology did play an important part in the subsequent shaping of it. For example, though the intention was to migrate the PARLE interface directly onto university VLE systems, the large amount of video material that needed to be streamed from a central server necessitated the application initially being available in the form of a DVD (Middleton and Bridge, 2008, p. 144). Nevertheless, throughout the development, in most cases it appears that pedagogical concerns rather than technological ones took precedence – indeed, in the light of student feedback, one of the most innovative technological aspects, 'virtual role play', was partially removed: Middleton and Bridge wisely commenting that it often best 'to avoid being too clever just because you can' (2008, p.150). In addition, the technological aspect had cost implications. 'Doing Political Research' was only produced because of the substantial assistance of a £250,000 grant from the Higher Education Funding Council for England (HEFCE). Furthermore, it was very labour intensive, involving an array of contributors from a variety of institutions including the Open University, York

University and the University of Birmingham, many of whom initially struggled in adapting their style of writing for multi-media applications (2008, p. 149).

Yet, for all these problems, the PARLE project remains an admirable example of what Biggs' calls 'educational technology'. Indeed, to some extent, PARLE fulfils each of Biggs' four categories in which technology can play a particularly worthwhile role in the curriculum. In terms of the simple management of information, PARLE became the repository of a large array of relevant texts, video and audio clips, even cartoons – as Middleton and Bridge state, a decision was made early on in the process 'to create a course that could also act as a resource' (2008, p. 145). More significantly, PARLE was expressly designed to engage students in appropriate learning activities, of both an interactive and non-interactive variety. Indeed, the PARLE project was heavily informed by Laurillard's concept of blended learning in which traditional face-to-face provision is combined with other forms of media to form an enhanced learning environment (1993), furthermore 'Doing Political Research' was designed in such a way that tutors could use as much, or as little, of the course as was deemed appropriate. The e-learning element was not designed to monopolize more traditional learning activities, such as face-to-face tutorials. Feedback reported from approximately 300 students suggested that the package was regarded as a positive learning experience (Middleton and Bridge, 2008, p. 150). In terms of Biggs' third category, 'Doing Political Research' was designed to provide many opportunities for formative assessment, including multiple-choice quizzes and drag-and-drop exercises, and – if completed – summative assessment was possible as part of the whole learning package. Finally, as befits a learning tool with strong links to the Open University, 'Doing Political Research' was expressly designed to be a portable device creating many opportunities for students to learn away from the campus setting, though as noted earlier, there was no intention from PARLE's creators completely 'to replace campus-based learning with e-learning' (2008, p. 147).

Middleton and Bridge concluded their description of the creation of 'Doing Political Research' with some helpful hints for others who may be keen to emulate their achievement; advice which deserves a wide audience (2008, p.151; see Box 7.2):

Box 7.2   Advice from Middleton and Bridge for those attempting a major technology-informed project in teaching and learning

Hints	Commentary
Be prepared to spend a lot of time, effort and money in developing the product	The nature of such projects – which involve combining the efforts of many individuals from many different fields – will almost always put a strain on budgets, time-scales and patience.

Hints	Commentary
Be aware of the limitations of the medium	Awareness of the medium is the central point of Middleton and Bridge's account. It is easy to get carried away by the technological possibilities – or, contrarily, become quickly disillusioned – but, by keeping pedagogical priorities uppermost, positive results should occur.
Be aware also of the potential of the medium	
Do not allow the medium to detract from the learning objectives	
Make sure that collaborators are well briefed	As with many similar projects, most of those involved in PARLE were operating well outside traditional working environments, and this led to serious problems and delays.
Bring people together to be productive as early and as often as feasible	Collaborative one-day workshops were found to be more productive than individuals working in relative isolation.
Involve the user groups as early as possible.	What might seem good ideas – such as, in the PARLE project, the 'virtual role play' – can prove unpopular or ineffective. This is inevitable.
Be prepared to rip things up and go back to the drawing board when they don't work.	Early utilization of user groups should at least minimize the disruption

One final tip worth making is that, if you can get discipline-related scholars engaged in pedagogical-informed e-learning innovation to do much of the work for you – people such as Middleton, Bridge, and the rest of the PARLE team – then free-riding off their hard work seems a very sensible option.

Conclusion

It might appear that much of this Chapter has concentrated less on providing traditional suggestions of 'what to do', instead focusing more on warnings of 'what not to do' (see Box 7.3). Though an accurate impression, this Chapter should not be interpreted as contributing to a neo-Luddite argument in favour of not bringing technology into the Politics classroom. E-learning does have an important role to play, not least in pepping up the slightly moribund pedagogic orthodoxy that Sloam argues surrounds much Politics education in UK universities. However, the trick, of course, is to use the technology shrewdly, and not

Box 7.3   Now warned of the dangers, here are a few technologies you could try for teaching and learning purposes

Type	Good example, with website
Audience response systems	TurningPoint (http://www.turningtechnologies.co.uk)
Blogs, wikis and discussion boards	these tend to be well supported by individual institutions' VLEs
E-assessment	Questionmark Perception (http://www.questionmark.co.uk)
Lecture capture	Echo360 (http://echo360.com)
Presentation program	Prezi (http://prezi.com) (a good alternative to PowerPoint)
Texting	Txttools (https://www.txttools.co.uk)
Web conferencing	DimDim (http://www.dimdim.com)

be swayed by the siren songs that suggest that the latest bit of kit will prove some sort of pedagogic panacea. As Lee writes, when considering the use of e-learning in the Politics classroom, it should be remembered that 'the medium is not the message', and that teaching and learning methods should be 'supported by the new technologies, not dictated by them' (Lee, 2003, p. 67).

Perhaps the final word should be made by much-missed writer and IT enthusiast Douglas Adams. A man of immense wit and intelligence, he wrote some of the most insightful comments about the technological revolution, including the famous – if not completely accurate – set of rules that describe our reactions to technologies (Adams, 2002, p. 95):

1. Anything that is in the world when you're born is normal and ordinary and is just a natural part of the way the world works.
2. Anything that's invented between when you're fifteen and thirty-five is new and exciting and revolutionary and you can probably get a career in it.
3. Anything invented after you're thirty-five is against the natural order of things.

On the matter of use of technology in everyday life, including the Politics classroom, Adams foresightedly summarized this chapter in three short sentences:

We are stuck with technology when what we really want is just stuff that works. How do you recognize something that is still technology? A good clue is if it comes with a manual.

(2002, p. 115).

References

All websites cited here were accessed on 26 January 2011.

Adams, D. (2002), *The Salmon of Doubt: Hitchhiking the Galaxy One Last Time* (Basingstoke: Macmillan).

Alexander, B. (2006), 'Web 2.0: A New Wave of Innovation for Teaching and Learning?' *Educause Review*, 41 (2), 32–44. Available at: http://net.educause.edu/ir/library/pdf/ERM0621.pdf.

Biggs, J. (1996), 'Enhancing Teaching Through Constructive Alignment', *Higher Education*, 32 (3), 1–18.

Biggs, J. (2003), *Teaching for Quality Learning at University*, 2nd edn (Maidenhead: The Society for Research into Higher Education and Open University Press).

Blair, A., Bromage, A. and Curtis, S. (2006), 'Teaching Politics in UK Universities: A Survey of the Profession', *LATISS: Learning and Teaching in the Social Sciences*, 3 (2), 119–32.

Booth, A. (2007), 'Blogs, Wikis and Podcasts: The Evaluation Bypass', *Health Information and Libraries Journal*, 24 (4), 298–302.

Buckler, S. and Dolowitz, D. (2005), *Politics on the Internet* (Abingdon: Routledge).

Burnham, P., Gilland, K., Grant, W., Layton-Henry, Z. (2008). *Research Methods in Politics*, 2nd edn (Basingstoke: Palgrave Macmillan).

Committee of Inquiry into the Changing Learner Experience (CLEX), 2009a *Higher Education in a Web 2.0 World*. Available at: http://www.jisc.ac.uk/media/documents/publications/heweb20rptv1.pdf

Craig, J. (2010), 'Introduction: E-learning in Politics', *European Political Science*, 9 (1), 1–4.

Curtis, S. et al. (2009), 'Placement Blogging: The Benefits and Limitations of Online Journaling', *EliSS: Enhancing Learning in the Social Sciences*, 1 (3). Available at: http://www.heacademy.ac.uk/resources/detail/subjects/csap/eliss/1-3-Curtis.

Davies, I. (1972), 'The Nature of Educational Technology', in I. Davies and J. Hartley (eds) *Contributions to an Educational Technology* (London: Butterworths), pp. 1–14.

Gormley-Heenan, C. and McCartan, K. (2009), 'Making it Matter: Teaching and Learning in Political Science Using an Audience Response System', *European Political Science*, 8 (3), 379–91.

Herring, S. (2008), 'Questioning the Generational Divide: Technological Exoticism and Adult Constructions of Online Youth Identity' in D. Buckingham (ed.) *Youth, Identity, and Digital Media* (Cambridge MA: MIT Press), pp. 71–92.

Ishiyama, J. (2010), 'What is the Impact of In-Class Active Learning Techniques? A Meta Analysis of the Existing Literature' APSA 2010 Annual Meeting Paper. Available at: http://ssrn.com/abstract=1644146

Kennedy, G., Dalgarno, B., Gray, K., Judd, T., Waycott. J., Bennett, S., Maton, K. Krause, K.-L., Bishop, A., Chang, R. and Churchward, A. (2007), 'The Net Generation are Not Big Users of Web 2.0 Technologies: Preliminary Findings', in *ICT: Providing Choices for Learners and Learning. Proceedings ASCILITE Singapore*. Available at: www.ascilite.org.au/conferences/singapore07/procs/kennedy.pdf.

Laurillard, D. (1993), *Rethinking University Teaching: A Framework for the Effective Use of Educational Technology* (London: Routledge).

Lee, D. (2003), 'New Technologies in the Politics Classroom: Using Internet Classrooms to Support Learning and Teaching', *Politics*, 23 (1), 66–73.

Leston-Bandeira, C. (2009), 'Using E-learning to Promote Critical Thinking in Politics', *EliSS: Enhancing Learning in the Social Sciences*, 1 (3), 1–14.

Margatts, H. (2010), 'The Internet in Political Science' in C. Hay (ed.) *New Directions in Political Science* (Basingstoke: Palgrave Macmillan), pp. 64–87.

Middleton, D. (2010), 'Putting the Learning into E-learning', *European Political Science*, 9 (1), 5–12.

Middleton, D. and Bridge, K. (2008), 'Multimedia Learning: Lessons from the PARLE Project', *European Political Science*, 7 (2), 144–52.

Newell, J. and Bull, M. (2008), 'Political Science Innovations, Good and Bad', *European Political Science*, 7 (2), 131–2.

Prensky, M. (2001), 'Digital Natives, Digital Immigrants', *On the Horizon*, 9 (5), 1–2.

Ralph, J., Head, N. and Lightfoot, S. (2010), 'Pol-casting: The Use of Podcasting in the Teaching and Learning of Politics and International Relations', *European Political Science*, 9 (1), 13–24.

Sloam, J. (2008), 'Teaching Democracy: The Role of Political Science Education', *British Journal of Politics & International Relations*, 10 (3), 509–24.

Stevens, C. and Campbell, P. (2007), 'The Politics of Information Literacy: Integrating Information Literacy into the Political Science Curriculum' in Jacobson, T. and Mackey, T. (eds) *Information Literacy Collaborations that Work* (New York: Neal-Schuman), pp. 123–46.

Thompson, J. (2007), 'Is Education 1.0 Ready for Web 2.0 Students?', *Innovate*, 3 (4). Available at: http://innovateonline.info/pdf/vol3_issue4/Is_Education_1.0_Ready_for_Web_2.0_Students.pdf.

Thornton, S. (2008), 'Pedagogy, Politics, and Information Literacy', *Politics*, 28 (1), 50–6.

Thornton, S. (2010), 'From "Scuba Diving" to "Jet Skiing"? Information Behaviour, Political Science, and the Google Generation', *Journal of Political Science Education*, 6 (4), 353–68.

Tufte, E. (2003a), 'Power Point is Evil', *Wired*, 11(9). Available at http://www.wired.com/wired/archive/11.09/ppt2.html

Tufte, E. (2003b), *The Cognitive Style of PowerPoint* (Cheshire, CT: Graphics Press).

Whitworth, A. (2009), *Information Obesity* (Oxford: Chandos Publishing).

8
Developing Assessment Practices in Politics

Alasdair Blair and Sam McGinty

Up until the early 1990s the traditional approach to teaching and learning in Politics was to use examinations and essays as the primary method of assessing students. This was somewhat in contrast to other subject-based disciplines, such as the Sciences, where the nature of the discipline necessitated the use of a wider pattern of assessment, including class-based tests in the form of laboratory work. Other subjects, such as Business Studies, tended to make greater use of work placements and case studies. Over the last two decades there has been a steady expansion in research on teaching and learning from a Politics perspective, with a considerable focus being attached to the dissemination of different approaches to teaching and learning. This chapter draws on one aspect of this work by focussing on the importance of the assessment regime in the teaching of Politics. In doing so, it draws on the work of a National Teaching Fellowship Scheme (NTFS) project, 'It's Good to Talk: Feedback, Dialogue and Learning' that seeks to identify, evaluate, develop and promote ways to improve feedback to students within the disciplines of History and Politics/International Relations. At the centre of the project is the issue of encouraging teacher and peer dialogue around learning by drawing on feedback approaches in three universities: De Montfort University, London Metropolitan University, and the University of Warwick. The chapter proceeds as follows. First, it reviews the context of assessment within the teaching and learning of Politics. Second, it analyses the significance of assessment. Third, it investigates different types of assessment. Fourth, it examines the importance of assessment feedback for students. Finally, it presents a concluding argument that a central feature of any method of assessment should be the objective of developing student engagement in 'deep' rather than 'surface' learning.

Changing times

One of the most notable developments in the British system of higher education over the last two decades has been the altering nature of the student body. Student numbers have increased due to government policies to widen participation and the 'massification' (Schuetze and Slowey, 2000) of higher education. There has been a shift away from standard A-level applicants, with a presupposed level of knowledge and understanding, to an acceptance of applicants possessing a range of relevant experiences to gain entry to university. Just as universities have been faced with responding to an increase in student numbers, they have also faced the challenge of responding to external audit. This has principally taken the form of the work of the Quality Assurance Agency (QAA) for Higher Education. Of the Politics subject reviews that were undertaken in 65 Politics departments in 2000–1, the weakest area of departmental provision was teaching, learning and assessment. The reviews that were undertaken were numerically graded 1–4, with 4 representing the highest grade. And while the QAA's overview report for Politics notes that in the area of teaching, learning and assessment some 55 per cent of departments were judged to make a full contribution to the achievement of the aims and objectives (grade 4), with the remaining 45 per cent making a substantial contribution (grade 3), this has to be sat against a background that with the exception of one university, the lowest grade given in the review of Politics was a 3 (QAA, 2001, p. 17). Of the factors that influenced the lower scores for teaching, learning and assessment, the review reported that just over one-quarter of departments (26 per cent) failed to link teaching and assessment practices to the development of knowledge, critical, analytical and key transferable skills (QAA, 2001: 22). This is something that was not just akin to Politics, but was common with the experience of broader subject reviews, of which 'the reason is almost always something to do with inconsistent assessment practices' aRust, 2002, p. 147).

The years since the period of subject review have seen a considerable expansion in the body of literature devoted to the teaching and learning of Politics. One of the key drivers in this process was the Politics projects that were supported by the Higher Education Academy Subject Network for Sociology, Anthropology and Politics (C-SAP) from 2000 to 2011, as well as those projects that were supported by the Fund for the Development of Teaching and Learning (FDTL) between 2004 and 2007. The findings of these projects have primarily appeared in a limited number of journals such as *Politics, European Political Science* and *International Studies Perspectives*. A cursory glance at the titles of these publications highlights that there is a general absence of articles that are explicitly written about assessment from a Politics perspective. Instead, the articles report on specific innovations on teaching and learning, such as blogs, e-learning, simulations, placements and teaching particular subjects like the Middle East. As far as assessment is concerned, this has meant that there has been less attention devoted to critically analysing the appropriateness, reliability and validity of assessment practices from the perspective of the Politics discipline. This is despite the fact that a general theme of the last decade has been a need to look more closely – and in some cases re-evaluate – assessment methods for undergraduate students in particular.

Significance of assessment

It is only in recent years that there has been a significant amount of change incorporated into to the design of Politics degrees in the UK (Goldsmith and Goldsmith, 2010). This has (among other reasons) been driven by an increased realization of the necessity of ensuring that degree programmes offer a wider variety of assessment methods that now incorporates the likes of presentations, learning journals, reports and class tests, albeit with lectures and seminars still accounting for the main method of teaching content. This has resulted in a gradual shift away from end of year exams to mid-course assessment, as well as the introduction of diagnostic pieces of assessment at the start of a course. Arguments in favour of a reduction in the weighting of exams arose out of an appreciation that exams often encourage surface learning (Marton and Säljö, 1997). This approach is associated with memorization, the segmentation of learning materials, an absence of reflective practice, and learning being driven purely by the completion of assignment tasks (see Box 8.1). As a first year History student from our NTFS project commented 'I don't think exams are a good test of your skills, particularly in History where an exam is basically a memory test. I think coursework is a much better method of assessment.' And because exams often attach as much (if not more) importance to technique rather than subject knowledge, they therefore do not necessarily provide a complete indication of student performance (Race, 2001, p. 43). To this end, it is possible for students to obtain very good exam results and yet at the same time have serious misconceptions about the subject that they have studied.

The fact that the nature of assessment plays the critical role in student learning is a point that is widely acknowledged. Gibbs has commented that 'assessment systems dominate what students are orientated towards in their learning' (Gibbs, 1992, p. 10), and while it has also been noted that assessment has been identified as the single most influential factor in student learning (Snyder, 1971; Miller and Parlett in Gibbs and Simpson, 2004). Brown notes that 'assessment defines what students regard as important ... If you want to change student learning then change the methods of assessment' (Brown, 1997, p. 7). It is commonly acknowledged that assessment is the sole factor that is uppermost in students' minds when they examine a curriculum. To this end, students' assumptions as to what they will be assessed on will govern what they will learn, which is in contradistinction to the topics that they will have been exposed to in lectures and tutorials. In practical terms, this often means that the possibility for students to succeed in exams with limited reading and the selection of a narrow number of topics can result in students' knowledge and understanding of

Box 8.1 Deep and surface approaches to learning

	Deep approaches	Surface approaches
Characteristics	• Embeds a critical approach to knowledge and understanding, whereby ideas and concepts are examined in a reflective manner that promotes linkages in knowledge. • Develops critical analysis of the subject matter. • Promotes understanding of the subject. • Active learning. • Creates links between modules to promote knowledge and understanding. • Modules are structured to link with previous knowledge. • Advances reflective practice that allows new concepts and ideas to be developed.	• Entrenches an approach that seeks to develop knowledge and understanding as distinct building blocks with little or no linkages between ideas. • Prioritizes the memorization of information. • Passive learning. • Divides modules and learning materials into component chunks. • Modules are structured by the need to complete assignments. • Avoids reflective practice that seeks to get students to link concepts and ideas.
Teaching strategies	• Strong personal interest in teaching the subject. • Create an active learning environment that allows students to engage in discussion. • Balanced delivery of teaching content. • Allowing time for teaching material to be discussed.	• Little or no interest in teaching the subject. • Information is presented in a passive manner that allows little or no time for engagement and discussion. • Overloading the content and transmission of teaching material. • Rushing the delivery of teaching material.
Assessment strategies	• Broad range of assessments used that challenge students. • Assessments that link ideas and concepts together. • Assessment strategies that reward effort.	• Narrowly focussed assessment strategy. • Assessments that focus on independent facts. • Assessment strategies that penalize mistakes.

modules being patchy. Such a state of affairs can be in contrast to the very aims that have been set out in the learning outcomes of modules, including students obtaining a wide knowledge of the relevant subject matter. A key intention of revising methods of assessment is that they should embed a deep approach to learning (Marton and Säljö, p. 1997). To this end, assessment regimes should foster; a critical analysis of the subject matter, understanding, reflective practice and activities that motivate student involvement (Gibbs, 1992: 10–11). A pertinent issue is therefore that the methods of assessment should be reflective of the learning outcomes that students are expected to achieve.

Deciding on the most appropriate means of assessment

As Box 8.2 illustrates, there is a considerable variety of assessment practices and it is important that the right method of assessment is used (Race, Brown and Smith, 2005). In essence, the method of assessment is directly correlated to the reasons for the need to assess. We are, therefore, concerned with not just undertaking assessment in a broad setting, but directing assessment towards the provision of a mapping exercise which examines a whole range of skills and processes. We now discuss four of these assessment methods which may have particular relevance within the discipline of Politics in more detail.

The practice of assessment – oral presentations

In looking at particular examples of the practice of assessment, oral presentations are particularly valuable as they develop important transferable skills in students. Such presentations obviously require the important discipline of structure and clarity of argument, but they also attach emphasis to the variety of tools that can be used to deliver presentations, such as PowerPoint. This use of non-written assessment is an important method of developing student's verbal reasoning skills. For oral presentations to be effective they should be assessed by assessment criteria that differ from the requirements of written work such as essays or case study reports. This is because they are clearly testing different skills. One of the benefits of oral presentations is that they lend themselves to student peer evaluation which is a particularly valuable form of learning. Where a presentation contributes to the final degree mark, then it should always be double marked by two members of staff. The grade can otherwise be regarded as overly subjective. It is also helpful to video presentations as this can then assist with student feedback as well as forming part of the assessments that are reviewed by external examiners.

Written assessment

The use of oral presentations goes in tandem with written assessment procedures as it is important that graduates have both the ability to convey information

Box 8.2 Comparing assessment methods

Method	Description	Advantages	Disadvantages
Essays	An extended piece of writing that tackles a particular subject.	• Students and staff are most familiar with this type of assessment. • Students tend to have well-established routines for tackling essay writing. • Essays help develop writing and analytical skills. • Essays provide an ability to distinguish performance between students. • Essay writing is a way in which students can show originality and depth of knowledge on a subject.	• Essay writing is something of an art and is as much about style as content. • Essays do not lend themselves to precise marking standards. Marks are subjective and there can be considerable variation in standards. • Essays are time consuming to write and student choice of topic is influenced by module progression. • Essays can be problematic for students with learning support needs, such as dyslexia. • Can take time for students to receive feedback.
Written Reports	The presentation of information on a particular theme in a structured manner. Reports tend to use a progressive numbering system such as 1,2,3 and be divided into specific sections	• Has a real-world element to the assessment task. • Can encourage generic skills such as use of computers. • Allows a broad range of topics and areas of investigation to be tackled.	• Without proper guidance, students can find it difficult to undertake an assessment that they are not familiar with. • Marking criteria need to reflect a different form of assessment exercise, such as the effort involved in producing data tables.

Dissertations and Research projects	An extended piece of writing involving detailed research.	• Provides an opportunity for students to examine subject matter in more depth. • Promotes student creativity and reinforces independent learning. • Individual nature of the dissertation means that there is less chance of plagiarism.	• Very time consuming. • Requires considerable student support with time-management and organizational skills. • Students do not always get adequate supervision.
Unseen Exams	A written exam which the students will not have previously seen.	• Students and staff are familiar with this type of assessment. • Helps to demonstrate knowledge and understanding of the subject matter. • All students face the same challenge. • Encourages students to engage with the subject material. • Little or no chance of cheating or plagiarism.	• Exams favour some students more than others as technique of how to answer an exam is crucial. • Exams can reinforce surface rather than deep learning. • Often tests memory more than knowledge, understanding and analysis. • Exams do not always provide a complete picture of student performance. • Students rarely get feedback on exams. Therefore no sense of how they can improve.

Method	Description	Advantages	Disadvantages
Seen Exams	The contents of the exam are provided to the student at a time period before the exam is taken.	• As students are provided with questions prior to the exam, this allows them to undertake focussed research prior to the exam. • Has the advantage of providing a formative element to the assessment task. • Can be viewed as being less stressful for students.	• Encourages students to focus on particular aspects of the curriculum. • Students can spend too much time researching their questions and committing answers to memory which can encourage a surface learning approach.
Open-book Exams	Students are allowed to take certain learning aids, such as books, into the exam.	• Less stress and emphasis on students having to memorize information. • Focuses on the ability of students to find out information in a defined time period.	• Students can spend too much time trying to find information and not enough time writing. • Students need to have equal access to the books that they can bring into the exam.

Multiple-choice tests	Comprises many questions and answers, of which one answer is correct.	• Provides an opportunity to test a wide range of subject coverage. • Not dependent on such skills as handwriting speed. • Saves on staff time as they are quick and easy to grade. • Provides an opportunity for swift feedback on performance to students. • Good for gaining understanding of student progress.	• Designing multiple-choice tests can take time. • Students may 'guess' the correct answer. • Students with learning difficulties may find it difficult to answer questions which all look the same. • Multiple-choice questions do not always provide an opportunity for students to show a deep level of knowledge and understanding. • Can create undue concern by some students if they obtain a poor result.
Presentations	Where students make a presentation to a class utilizing the likes of PowerPoint and providing handouts. Can be individual or in groups.	• Provides an opportunity for individual and collaborative work. • Creates a good environment to demonstrate verbal reasoning skills through question and answer sessions. • Develops technological skills in terms of the use of PowerPoint slides. • Offers the opportunity for students to learn from their peers and reinforces reflective practice.	• It can be hard to distinguish performance on collaborative work. • Not all students are comfortable with presentations. • Presentations can lead to accusations of subject bias because they are not anonymous. To ensure this does not happen there is a need for presentations to be recorded or double marked which can be time consuming.

Method	Description	Advantages	Disadvantages
Book reviews and annotated bibliographies	Book reviews pick out the strengths and weaknesses of an individual or a collective piece of writing. Annotated bibliographies require a list of sources to be annotated with a short summary of their strengths and weaknesses.	• A very useful means of developing analytical skills. • Creates an opportunity for students to examine a wide range of reading materials. • Is a useful method of developing skills that are relevant for research projects such as a dissertation.	• It can be difficult to compare students work if the reviews are of different books. • Reviews of individual books require sufficient copies in the library. • Book reviews can be a time consuming process that does not involve collaborative effort.
Reflective journals	Reflective journals are written over a specific time period to enable a student to reflect on their own learning.	• Provides an opportunity to chart the development of student learning over a period of time. • Helps to embed a reflective approach to learning. • Relatively easy to demonstrate student ownership of the work through an oral *viva*, therefore overcoming concerns of plagiarism.	• It can be difficult to evaluate this type of work as the individual nature of the exercise can mean that is hard to establish a common assessment format. • They can be time consuming in terms of commenting on student work and marking the final product.
Blogs	Posting and responding to comments online.	• Provide an opportunity for students to work in a learning environment that many are familiar with. • Allows individual expression for students who might otherwise not talk in class.	• Requires monitoring to ensure that the discussion retains a focus on the task in hand and does not drift into other unrelated topics.

Placements	Engages students in a real life learning environment.	• Provides students with an opportunity to test their knowledge and understanding in the 'real world'. • Develops skills and experiences that future employers are interested in. • Creates a sense of student independence. • Allows students to bring lessons from the placement into their degree programme.	• Difficult to achieve a common method of assessment. One student's experience is going to be considerably different to another. • Increases the chance of things going wrong as the university does not control the learning experience. • Financial costs of travel and dress codes can impact on students. • It can be difficult to align placement learning with learning outcomes of the module and degree.
Simulations	Involves a role play enactment of an event.	• Allows student to appreciate the complexity of decision-making exercises. • Puts learning into practice.	• Involves a lot of effort to set up the simulation. • Not all students are comfortable with taking on this type of assessment.

in an oral and written form. While skills of clarity, structure, argument and analysis are important in both oral and written methods of assessment, written assessment involves a different range of skills, including spelling, punctuation, grammar and syntax. Written forms of assessment are also an important means of diagnosing if a student is dyslexic, for instance. Of the forms of written assessment that are available, the most common format is the standard essay and dissertation. Reports are another written assessment method. The relevance of this form of assessment flows from the reality that graduates will be more likely be engaged in report writing rather than essay writing and therefore it is important that they are made aware of the different skills and practices that are involved in the construction of reports.

Placements

While presentations and report writing help to assist with developing a broader set of skills, they do not provide a substitute from the real world of work. One solution is for students to engage in placement learning (Curtis et al., 2009a; Curtis and Blair, 2010a and 2010b). For disciplines such as Politics, where there has not been a formal requirement for placements, this adjustment of the curriculum can create a number of challenges for academics and students. This particularly applies to the extent to which it is possible to develop a reliable means of assessment. Such a point of view is reflective of the fact that there will inevitably be a degree of variety between the experiences of each and every work placement. An important point is therefore that the methods of assessment to be used need to be able to offer the opportunity for students to demonstrate their learning experience irrespective of the nature or the success of the placement.

Reflective journals and blogs

As students are to be exposed to the demands of the 'real-world' then the tasks to be set should be reflective of the 'real-world' placement environment (Marr and Leach, 2005). This can be achieved through the use of a learning contract that is developed by the student in collaboration with the work placement and the academic supervisor. Learning contracts are particularly useful because they are an optimum means of maximizing student engagement and motivation and ensure that students are aware of the tasks to be undertaken. This is in line with the reality that there is a clear link in improving the performance of students when they have a clearer understanding of the assessment criteria. Reflective journals and blogs are particularly helpful methods of assessing students undertaking work placements because they lend themselves to online electronic formats that provide an opportunity to develop peer supported learning by creating a community of student learners (Curtis et al., 2009b). They also enable staff to provide supportive feedback on an ongoing process as a means of aiding a deep approach to learning. In this context, Boud has commented that 'web-based activities appear to be most effective when there is direct interaction between staff and students and among students themselves' (Boud, 2001 p. 6).

Summative versus formative assessment

Whatever the method of assessment used, it is important to ensure that the approach provides sufficient opportunity for students to demonstrate their subject understanding. Here it is important to ensure that students are not over-assessed as this can result in a surface approach to learning rather than a deep approach. And while a key underlying factor in summative assessment is the need to grade student achievement and to provide a data set that indicates the level of individual and group cohort student achievement, there are, of course, many other reasons to undertake a process of assessment. This includes motivating students by concentrating their energies on a particular piece of coursework. But crucially, assessment does require a feedback element in order to provide students with information on their level of achievement and in doing so providing direction for future improvement.

It is therefore important that some method of performance indicators can be obtained at a relatively early stage of the learning process, not least to flag up any students who may require extra assistance. This can take the form of formative and summative methods of assessment. Summative assessment is 'a judgement which encapsulates all the evidence up to a given point' (Taras, 2005, p. 468), for example this may take the form of a grade or percentage mark on an assignment. Formative assessment is concerned with providing student feedback that helps to provide clarifications in the student learning process and in this sense 'can be used to shape and improve the student's competence' (Sadler, 1989, p. 120). This might include the pre-submission of coursework to ensure that it has the correct level of focus. This type of assessment tends not to be formally graded. By contrast, summative assessment is generally associated with the end point of the learning cycle, with the focus being on obtaining a grade that reflects student performance. This might include an end of module exam or written assessment.

The significance of feedback

A potential pitfall in any method of assessment is the way in which feedback is provided. This is a point that has been noted in the literature, with a common theme being that students often find feedback to be problematic. This has been further borne out by the evidence of the National Student Survey (NSS). Feedback is, however, extremely subjective and there is evidence to highlight that students' views on feedback are heavily influenced by the grade awarded. For instance, students who receive a high grade are often less likely to query feedback because they may be content with the grade awarded (Duncan, 2007). This is despite the fact that there could be room for more constructive feedback to further develop their work. One of the issues here is that students are rarely given guidance on how to best use their feedback (Burke, 2009) and this can in turn lead to frustration on the behalf of students and academic staff. There is evidence that the use of academic language is one of the reasons students do not follow-up on their feedback (Ivanic, Clark and Rimmershaw, 2000; Lea and Street, 1998, Weaver, 2006). And while this non-engagement can be frustrating for academic staff, one of the problems is that students who receive poor quality feedback on a regular basis tend then to completely disengage from the feedback process (Sadler, 2005).

Such a state of affairs is problematic because feedback is recognized to be of great value in improving student performance (Black and Wiliam, 1998). One of the challenges is therefore to develop effective feedback strategies (Blair and McGinty, 2010). This is particularly important in the case of exams taken at the end of the academic year which do not automatically lead to feedback because students tend no longer to be in formal teaching sessions (Brown, 2007). In this context a single piece of assessed coursework, such as an essay, towards the end of a module and the provision of an exam is a less than satisfactory method of assessment. This is because of four factors. First, the chosen methods will not provide sufficient feedback to students at an early enough stage so that methods of improvement can be implemented. Second, the assessment timing creates a gap between present student practice and future implementation. Third, a narrow method of assessment is more than likely to embed a surface approach to learning whereby students deliberately focus their energies on segmenting learning materials into chunks to complete the tasks in hand. Fourth, leaving assessment towards the end of a module increases the likelihood of students dropping out of their studies (Race, Brown and Smith, 2005, p. 10–11).

Of the reasons that high quality feedback is crucial, a key point to note is that it helps to develop students as independent learners though a self-regulation model (Butler and Winne, 1995). In other words, students are encouraged to establish strategies such as their management of the amount of time they have available to study, planning for the use of learning materials in the library, as well as the way that they can utilize and build on the feedback that they receive. As Sadler (1989) has noted, for such a strategy to be effective, it is clearly important that students need to be able to understand what good performance actually is, what the difference is between current performance and good performance, as well as the methods that can be employed to 'close the gap' between current and good performance. Nicol and MacFarlane-Dick (2006, p. 205) have further refined these thoughts by identifying seven principles of good feedback practice:

1. helps clarify what good performance is (goals, criteria, expected standards);
2. facilitates the development of self-assessment (reflection) in learning;
3. delivers high quality information to students about their learning;
4. encourages teacher and peer dialogue around learning;
5. encourages positive motivational beliefs and self-esteem;
6. provides opportunities to close the gap between current and desired performance;
7. provides information to teachers that can be used to help shape their teaching.

Nevertheless, several structural factors within the university system, such as the modularization of courses, assessments at the end of each semester and

Box 8.3   SMART assessment

Scaffolded	Students are given more support at the start of their studies to assist with their development and understanding of the subject matter. This could involve extra seminars and greater attention to providing feedback and advice on assessments. As student knowledge and learning increases, then the level of support can taper off.
Motivating	Learning and assessment needs to be motivational, otherwise students just go through the motions of completing tasks that reflect a surface approach.
Active	Allowing students to undertake assessments that facilitate collaborative and independent tasks which facilitate dialogue and encourages deeper thought processes that make links between different modules and areas of knowledge.
Reflective	Providing students with sufficient opportunity to reflect on their assessment so that they can set their own goals and targets, thereby promoting self-regulated and independent learning.
Timely	Assessment strategies need to be set at strategic points within the academic year to avoid bunching and to prevent a surface approach to learning as students have sufficient time to complete tasks. This also creates the space to provide feedback that can be transferred to the next assignment.

increased class sizes have influenced the quality and timing of feedback according to Hounsell (2003). The modularization of courses within the division of two semesters has meant that students need to be 'tested' for each module, often at the end of each semester. The impact on feedback is that the timing of assignments and feedback are at the end of each module. The feedback may then be given at the start of the next semester, often when the student has 'moved on'. At the same time larger classes have meant an increased marking load for staff. The result is that lecturers have less time to write detailed feedback and there is less opportunity for dialogue around feedback within tutorial sessions.

The particular significance of this is that just as it is important for academic staff to consider the relevance of their existing assessment and feedback processes, so too it is important for universities to consider the way in which they monitor quality standards with a view to their having a clearer sense of linkage between student grades and profiles and the reality of the assessment and feedback process. This means moving away from a traditional view of assessment which 'involves making judgments about students' summative achievement for purposes of selection and certification, and it also acts as a focus for institutional accountability and quality assurance' (Bloxham and Boyd, 2007, p. 15). In implementing a system of assessment it is helpful to structure the tasks that are to be undertaken by students at appropriate intervals in their overall degree programme. This notably includes the need to avoid bunching of assessment. Apart from the fact that having too many assessments in a concentrated time period is problematic in terms of student workload, it has the additional problem of putting excess stress on library resources and results in students not being able to benefit from feedback in a timely fashion that can in turn inform future assignments.

Conclusion

This Chapter has argued that both assessment and feedback benefit from a reflective approach that encourages deep rather than surface learning. Whatever the methods of assessment that are used, it is important to achieve a balance between different types of assessment. And while assessment is in itself of value in terms of recording student achievement, its broader value is that it assists with motivating students, consolidates their learning and ensures that they are able to remedy mistakes. But for this to happen, it is crucial that effective feedback is provided as means of not just reflecting on the work undertaken, but crucially as a mechanism for providing a structured pathway for student progression and achievement. We have developed the acronym SMART assessment and suggest this is a potential way forward for the discipline of Politics, as outlined in Box 8.3.

Further reading

There is a wide body of literature on assessment. A useful introductory text on assessment practice is Bloxham and Boyd (2007). Key journals for future reference include *Assessment and Evaluation in Higher Education* and *Studies in Higher Education*. Useful 'how to' guides include Race, Brown and Smith (2005). Nicol and Macfarlane–Dick (2006) provide a useful set of strategies for developing good feedback. The most up-to-date surveys on e-learning in Politics can be found in the special issue of *European Political Science*, 9 (1), 2010. Issues relating to the assessment of placements can be found in Curtis and Blair (2010a).

References

Black, P. and Wiliam, D. (1998), 'Assessment and Classroom Learning', *Assessment in Education: Principles, Policy and Practice*, 5 (1), 7–74.

Blair, A. and McGinty, S. (2010), 'It's Good to Talk? Developing Feedback Practices', *Gateway Journal*, 1, 18-26, available online at: http://moriarty.tech.dmu.ac.uk/webapps/journal/index.php/gateway/article/view/39/8 (last accessed 30 March 2010).

Bloxham, S. and Boyd, P. (2007), *Developing Effective Assessment in Higher Education: A Practical Guide* (Maidenhead: Open University).

Boud, D (2001), 'Introduction: Making the Move to Peer Learning', in D. Boud, R. Cohen and J. Sampson (eds) *Peer Learning in Higher Education: Learning From and With Each Other* (London: Kogan Page), pp. 1–19.

Brown, J. (2007), 'Feedback: The student Perspective', *Research in Post-Compulsory Education*, 12 (1), 33–51.

Brown, G. (1997), *Assessing Student Learning in Higher Education* (London: Routledge).

Burke, D. (2009), 'Strategies for Using Feedback Students Bring to Higher Education', *Assessment and Evaluation in Higher Education*, 34 (1), 41–50.

Butler, D. and Winne, P. (1995), 'Feedback and Self – Regulated Learning: A Theoretical Synthesis', *Review of Educational Research*, 65 (3), 245–81.

Curtis, S. B., Axford, A., Blair, C., Gibson, R., Huggins, R. and Sherrington, P. (2009a), 'Making Short Politics Placements Work', *Politics* 29 (1), 62–70.

Curtis, S., Axford, B., Blair, A., Gibson, C., Huggins, R. and Sherrington, P. (2009b), 'Placement Blogging: The Benefits and Limitations of Online Journaling', *ELiSS: Enhancing Learning in the Social Sciences* 1 (3), available at www.eliss.org.uk/.

Curtis, S. and Blair, A. (eds) (2010a), *The Scholarship of Engagement for Politics: Placement Learning, Citizenship and Employability*, Birmingham: C-SAP Monographs, available at www.lulu.com/product/file-download/the-scholarship-of-engagement-for-politics/6427740 (last accessed 30 March 2011).

Curtis, S. and Blair, A. (2010b), 'Experiencing Politics in Action: Widening Participation in Placement Learning and Politics as a Vocation', *Journal of Political Science Education* 6 (4), 369–90.

Duncan, N. (2007), '"Feed – Forward": Improving Students' Use of Tutor Comments', *Assessment and Evaluation in Higher Education*, 32 (3), 271–83.

Gibbs, G. (1992), *Improving the Quality of Student Learning* (Bristol: TES).

Gibbs, G. and Simpson, C. (2004), 'Conditions Under Which Assessment Supports Students' Learning, *Learning and Teaching in Higher Education*, 1, 3-31.

Goldsmith, M. and Goldsmith, C. (2010), 'Teaching Political Science in Europe', *European Political Science*, 9 (1), 61–71.

Hounsell, D. (2003), 'Student Feedback, Learning and Development' in M. Slowey and D. Watson (eds) *Higher education and the Lifecourse* (Buckingham: Society for Research into Higher Education and Open University Press), pp. 67–78.

Ivanic, R., Clark, R. and Rimmershaw, R. (2000), 'What Am I Supposed to Make of This? The Messages Conveyed to Students by Tutors' Written Comments', in M. R. Lea and B. Stierer (eds) *Student Writing in Higher Education: New Contexts* (Buckingham, Open University Press), pp. 47–65.

Lea, M. and Street, B. (1998), 'Student Writing in Higher Education: An Academic Literacies Approach', *Studies in Higher Education*, 23 (2), 157–72.

Marr, L. and Leach, B. (2005), 'What Are We Doing This For? Widening Participation, Employability and Doing Sociology', *LATISS: Learning and Teaching in the Social Sciences*, 2 (1), 25–38.

Marton, F. and Säljö, R. (1997), 'Approaches to Learning', in F. Marton, D. J. Hounsell and N. J. Entwistle (eds) *The Experience of Learning*, 2nd edn (Edinburgh: Scottish Academic Press), pp. 39–58.

Miller, C. and Parlett, M. (1974), 'Up to the Mark: A Study of the Examination Game' in G. Gibbs and C. Simpson (2004) 'Conditions Under Which Assessment Supports Students' Learning', *Learning and Teaching in Higher Education*, 1, pp. 3–31.

Nicol, D. J. and Macfarlane-Dick, D. (2006), 'Formative Assessment and Self – Regulated Learning: A Model and Seven Principles of Good Feedback Practice', *Studies in Higher Education*, 31 (2), 199–218.

Quality Assurance Agency for Higher Education (QAA) (2001), *Subject Overview Report Politics – 2000 to 2001 QO7*, available online at: http://www.qaa.ac.uk/reviews/reports/subjectlevel/qo7_01_textonly.htm (last accessed 30 March 2011).

Race, P. (2001), *The Lecturer's Toolkit: A Practical Guide to Learning, Teaching and Assessment*, 2nd edn (London: Kogan Page).

Race, S. Brown, S. and B. Smith (2005), *500 Tips on Assessment*, 2nd edn (London: Routledge).

Rust, C. (2002), 'The Impact of Assessment on Student Learning: How Can The Research Literature Practically Help to Inform The Development of Departmental Assessment Strategies and Learner-Centred Assessment Practices?', *Active Learning in Higher Education*, 3 (2) 145–58.

Sadler, D. R. (1989), 'Formative Assessment and the Design of Instructional Systems', *Instructional Science*, 18, 119–44.

Sadler, D. R. (2005), 'Interpretations of Criteria-based Assessment and Grading in Higher Education', *Assessment and Evaluation in Higher Education*, 30 (2), 175–94.

Schuetze, H. G. and Slowey, M. (2000), 'Traditions and New Directions in Higher Education', in: H. G. Schuetze and M. Slowey (eds) *Higher Education and Lifelong Learners, International Perspectives on Change* (London and New York: Routledge Falmer), pp. 127–44.

Slowey, M. and Watson, D. (eds) (2003), *Higher Education and the Lifecourse* (Buckingham: Society for Research into Higher Education and Open University Press).

Snyder, B. R. (1971), *The Hidden Curriculum* (Cambridge, MA: MIT Press) quoted in G. Gibbs and C. Simpson (2004) 'Conditions Under Which Assessment Supports Students' Learning', *Learning and Teaching in Higher Education*, 1, 3–31.

Taras, M. (2005), 'Assessment – Summative and Formative – Some Theoretical Reflections', *British Journal of Educational Studies*, 53 (4), 466–78.

Weaver, M. R. (2006), 'Do Students Value Feedback? Students' Perceptions of Tutors' Written Responses', *Assessment and Evaluation in Higher Education*, 31 (3), 379–94.

9
The Importance of Being Theoretical: Analysing Contemporary Politics

Lee Marsden and Heather Savigny

The aim of this chapter is to give an overview of the ways in which we seek to engage students in the idea of using theory in their studies and to reflect on why this matters. While we are aware that there are different ways in which students can 'do' political analysis, here our focus is upon the application of theoretical frameworks as a mechanism to understand, or attempt to explain 'real world' events or phenomena. Our argument is that through understanding the way in which theoretical frameworks may be used and applied, students are provided with the tools and skills that they need to analyse political phenomena, event(s) or action(s).

Introduction

A simple e-mail request to colleagues requesting recent examples of examination answers from first year Politics and International Relations students produced a catalogue of unorthodox statements including:

In the 1980s the Labour Party was taken over by extreme socialites

From an essay on green ideologies – 'People really should recycle more, but basically they just can't be arsed'

From an essay on Hobbes – 'Clearly war must have its ultimate roots in human beings, as it is no-one else that humans are in war with (like war with aliens and animals)'

Or our own favourite from an essay on the clash of civilizations – 'there are five main civilizations – fire, earth, water, metal and wood'

We assume, hopefully not too naively, that such bizarre statements are not limited to our own students. For us, they do, however, reflect a need for all students to learn at the earliest stage the theoretical and analytical foundations for subsequent engagement in the discipline. In this chapter we set out our approach to engaging students, and suggest that a key way to think about the way in which we carry out our analysis is through the application of theory, to a particular 'real world' event.

In this chapter we have four key assumptions: (a) that an important way to study Politics is through the application of theory; (b) that Politics is increasingly interconnected, both by 'real world' events and phenomena and by the way in which their theoretical frameworks have been applied and have developed; (c) once students understand the way in which theory works, they will have acquired the skills to analyse political phenomena or events independently; (d) that differing theoretical perspectives focus upon differing aspects of the same event or phenomena. As such, we argue that showing students the theoretical 'tricks of the trade' means that they are able to understand not only how we approach our topics, and how to do it themselves, but also, why there are competing explanations and understandings of the real worlds of politics and international relations.

Rationale

When we were reflecting upon what it was we wanted our students to know, and understand, we also were thinking about what we would like our graduates to be competent in when they leave. While league tables and NSS and government rhetoric all emphasize 'employability', the emphasis upon vocational skills, we argue, can lead to a de-emphasis upon the importance of students having a command of their subject (and while the authors have a commitment to this as an important aim in its own right, this can also be an indicator of confidence, which in turn can be seen to contribute to the category of 'confidence' for example, deemed important by the Employability Barometer). In this chapter, and in our book which informs this chapter (2011) one of our key aims is to encourage students to reflect upon what it means to be a Political Scientist, analyst or IR scholar. As Craig (2009) observes, this is one of the few, if not the only, discipline(s) where real world events can change the discipline or subject matter, or indeed the ability to answer an exam question dramatically (for example consider the largely unpredicted events of 1989 or September 2001, or in Tunisia, Jordan and Egypt in 2011). In this way, what is crucial then is to encourage students not only to be able to describe what is happening in the contemporary world, but to give them the skills to be able to analyse the contemporary world; to be able to attempt to explain or understand it.

As we are all aware, good political analysis is something that comes not from pure description, or indeed, from the abstract modelling (for example, that we might find in economics), but from an ability not only to research and to be able to process, to organize, and to analyse that research. We argue that one of the key ways in which we do this is through the application of a theoretical framework to a particular event or set of circumstances. We are also cognisant however, of the general resistance of students to the teaching of theory. Indeed, teaching theory can often be extremely challenging, be seen as 'dry' by the students, or irrelevant. We have also found that theory tends to be taught as one course, and empirics and descriptions of political systems as a different course. This is largely reflected in the textbook market, with book such as Dunleavy and O'Leary's (1987) *Theories of the State* in the former, and as Smith (1999) observes many first year undergraduate Politics textbooks fall into the latter category, and our aim is to suggest that theory and empirics can be taught interdependently.

McAnulla's (2005) excellent *British Politics: A Critical Introduction* is theoretically and empirically rich and highlights the integration between theory and practice. However, and this related to our broader theme, we suggest that the contemporary 'real world' of politics and international relations is characterized by issues which transcend disciplinary boundaries: for example, climate change; globalization and security (to name but a few), and so in order to make sense, or analyse, these issues and events, we can draw on theories from both International Relations and Political Studies/Science. When reflecting upon the character of the contemporary political environment, it is increasingly impossible (although that does assume it was once possible) to disaggregate the domestic from the international. In making this assumption we reject the realist paradigm (dominant in IR) which seeks to separate the domestic from the international. We argue that this arbitrary division serves to obscure first the complexity of 'real world politics and second the utility that alternate perspectives may bring to analysis. In this way, we suggest that Political Science and International Relations are interlinked disciplines, which can usefully inform each other.

The overlap in subject matter is one area where the two disciplines converge. The other is around methodological debates over the way in which both disciplines do and should proceed. Both Politics and IR as disciplines are dominated by a commitment to a scientific approach as being the dominant organizing principle (see for example, Almond, 1988; Schmidt, 2008) for some the existence of a fragmentation of approaches in the discipline represents a healthy pluralism (see Goodin and Klingeman, 1995) although for others this represents a form of intellectual gatekeeping (see Marsh and Savigny, 2004). Our argument adopts the position that there is more than one way to 'do' Political Science and International Relations (see Marsh and Smith, 2001). For us this entails the discussion of competing theoretical perspectives, their insights, assumptions and objectives; the way in which differing positions render visible and invisible different aspects of analysis. For us, awareness of these competing positions also encourages students to think through carefully the claims that they are making, and with what justification they are able to do so.

We also argue that theoretical positions (across the epistemological spectrum) contain normative assumptions about how domestic and international politics should operate. Some positions are less explicit about this than others; however, for us those normative claims are inherently intertwined with the analytical ones. As such, we are encouraging students to think not only about the claims to knowledge that they are making when analysing political phenomena, but also to think about the normative claims, the assumptions they make about how politics should work.

How do we teach this?

We start from the assumption that the 'real world' of Politics and IR is messy, interconnected and incredibly complex. We also assume that Politics and IR necessarily must be theoretically informed. We are of the view that each discipline can offer insights to the other, and as such we seek to integrate the two in our teaching. We do this through reflecting the underlying debates which inform both disciplines, (for example the debate around structure and agency Hay, 2002; Wendt, 1987). But we take one step back from this, and in seeking to integrate the two disciplines, and given that both disciplines are divided as to how their respective discipline should proceed we present students with theoretical positions according to their ontological and epistemological position, rather than according to their discipline (which will be illustrated below).

To do this we adopt Marsh and Furlong's (2002) typology which gives a simple overview of ontological and epistemological positions. While we are aware there are debates around the utility, or the accuracy of teaching students these defined boundaries (for example, Bates and Jenkins, 2007) our aim here is to suggest to students that this represents the start (not the end) of their thinking. We do not wish to simply (?!) illustrate issues about ontology and epistemology, but rather to highlight to students how the metatheoretical issues that inform theories that we use in our analysis, in turn influence what we look for, and therefore what we can find, describe and analyse.

Within our teaching the way in which we have approached this is through the presentation of a case study, followed by summaries of competing theoretical explanations around that topic from both Politics and IR. These theoretical frameworks have been organized not around the disciplinary split, but around their ontological and epistemological underpinnings. We take each theory and apply it to the given example, in order to illustrate to students: (a) the way in which theory can be useful in illuminating what is significant: (b) the way in which some theory can attempt to provide a causal explanation whereas others seek to provide understanding: (c) that theories are partial and that critical analysis of theories are able to show us what is missing in our evaluation of an event. An example is given below.

Example – how we might teach theory in political science to our students: the state

The state historically has been one of the central actors in the study of both Politics and IR. This dominance has been challenged in recent years and efforts have been made to refocus attention, or 'bring the state back in' to political analysis (Evans, Rueschemeyer and Skocpol, 1985; see also Hay, Lister and Marsh, 2005). We set out differing theories of the state provided by both Politics and IR, but organize them according to their ontological and epistemological positions.

We begin with an overview of foundational positivist theories: pluralism, elitism, realism/neorealism, liberal institutionalism, public choice. We then move to give an overview of foundational critical realism, as drawn out through variants of Marxism in both domestic and international theorising. We then turn to antifoundational interpretivist approaches and explore the role of poststructuralism. We acknowledge that this is not entirely a level playing field in terms of representing approaches which diverge from the mainstream; however, we do feel that this is reasonably reflective of the field. Our aim in introducing it in this way is to encourage students to understand that the mainstream is not all there is.

Prior, however, to introducing the differing theoretical positions, we begin with an overview of our case study. When referring to the state, we use the example of the recent financial crisis. We give a brief 'journalistic' overview of the crisis – the kind we might expect to find in a newspaper (rather than an academically researched piece on the topic). The reason for this is to get students to think about events that we may have experienced, or things that we may read or hear about every day (such as news items on the credit crunch) and illustrate to them through the application of the differing theories they have been introduced to, how they might 'do' political analysis/IR. This also means that in seminars, students bring in news items which can then be split into theoretical approaches to offer an account of that 'real world' event through discussion from their perspective.

We then illustrate through the case study how differing theories can be used to provide differing accounts or explanations of events. So for example, foundational positivist approaches would posit the financial crisis as something which is observable and measurable. We would need to look at the key actors involved, observe and measure their behaviour: A pluralist analysis which would highlight the role of observable decisions being taken providing a description of events; a liberal institutionalist, on the other hand, would draw attention to the interdependence and interconnectivity of state economies, and the theorizing performs a normative function in providing for the possibility of cooperative solutions. As such the credit crunch is positioned as a 'problem'. In contrast Marxism provides a mechanism to problemat*ize* and can be used to suggest that the financial crisis can be viewed as a logical consequence of the inherent contradictions of capitalism. And so we illustrate the ways in which foundational critical/scientific realist accounts might draw attention to unobservable features of 'reality' while highlighting the causal role they play in structuring and shaping outcomes. Here, then, the unobservable workings of capitalism, and inherent tensions and contradictions, serve to generate an outcome: the financial crisis.

The third perspective we introduce students to, antifoundational interpretivism, draws our attention to the contingent nature of reality; that there is not a unified truth which exists rather interpretations of reality, which are dependent upon our relation to it. Poststructural accounts in this tradition would look at the way in which dominant discourses have defined the financial crisis and the way in which this has served to benefit privileged interests. These approaches serve to deconstruct these dominant discourses, expose and challenge dominant power relationships. As such through analysis of the discourse surrounding the financial crisis we might argue that this was a useful mechanism through which the state sought to reassert its significance in the face of globalization, or, we may see that politicians (with an eye on the electoral arena) seek to distance themselves (emphasizing the lack of effective regulation) from the crisis, placing the blame on the 'greedy bankers'.

Our aim here then is to draw students' attention to the idea that different theories not only focus upon differing aspects of a problem, but the theories themselves perform different roles. Some describe, some problematize, some explain, some seek to predict, some seek to understand and challenge.

A brief summary of the various ways in which the differing theories used can be applied and their focus of attention, and the role that theory performs in analysis is given below (Table 9.1).

Using theory: why does it matter?

Educational literature highlights the need for a more reflective approach to the relationship between theory and practice (Korthagen and Kessels, 1999). Our argument is premised upon the pedagogical benefits of the use and application of theory. These, we suggest, don't only provide the opportunity for political analysts to differentiate themselves from journalists, and to produce academic writings. Rather the use of theory also provides possibilities for students' emancipation. While we are seeking to provide students with an education, not only in subject matter, but to encourage and support more broadly their capacity to become independent, autonomous thinkers. Where education helps us do this according to Biesta (2010) is through enabling students to question the site and workings of power. More critical approaches suggest that power is reflected in people's understandings of their positioning within the system (Biesta, 2010,

Table 9.1 Summary of focus in credit crunch analysis (KEY FP – Foundational Positivism; FCR – Foundational Critical realism; AFI – Anti-foundational interpretivism)

Theory	What questions do we ask?	How do we use theory?
Pluralism (FP)	Who do we observe as key players in the process? How do they achieve their goals? Where does power lie and how is it dispersed?	Theory here is used to describe the observable actions of those individuals directly involved in the credit crunch: bankers; governments and banks. Individuals operate in a minimally specified context.
Elitism (FP)	How do key political and economic elites behave? What can we find out from observing their behaviour?	Again, here theory is used to inform the description of elite level action. Focus again is upon individuals, with whom power is assumed to lie.
Public Choice (FP)	What assumptions do we make about the way in which politicians are behaving? If we think they operate to maximise their own utility what outcomes might we expect?	Uses economic assumptions to model behaviour of politicians. Once we have established assumptions and motivations we can predict outcomes.
Realism/ Neorealism (FP)	What are states doing to ensure their own survival?	The focus here is upon observable behaviour. This theory also provides explanations of conflict.
Neoliberalism (FP)	What is the role of non-state actors? And what opportunities are there for cooperation?	Again, the theory focuses upon observable behaviour, but extends the range of actors to included both state and non-state actors. The emphasis is on cooperation (in contrast to realism).
Marxism (FCR)	How have the contradictions within capitalism caused the financial crisis? Rather than end, how has capitalism continued to be reproduced?	Here the theory provides not only an explanation of why the crisis occurs (with reference to underlying unobservable structures) but also explains why capitalism is enduring and the inequalities which result from this.
Poststructuralism (AFI)	What narratives does this crisis fit into? Which discourses have been used to legitimate behaviour and actions of political and economic elites?	Here theory is used to critique the dominant orthodoxy. This approach draws attention to the ways in which power relations are constructed and negotiated

p. 40). Emancipation flows from recognition of this positioning and the task of social science is thus to make visible, to reveal, those power structures (ibid.). For us, two ways in which we view this as possible are: (a) through the use of theory and (b) through the introduction of competing approaches.

Scardamalia and Bereiter (2006) highlight the similarities between the pedagogical assumptions of the way in which learning occurs and the way in which knowledge advances within disciplines. Knowledge building, they argue, is not an isolated activity but one which is an activity undertaken within a community (2006, p. 99). To this end, we suggest that theoretical frameworks themselves provide both an accessible route in to that wider 'community', as well as being constitutive of that wider community. Access to this vocabulary and organized sets of ideas provides a mechanism through which students can begin to situate themselves and give voice and vocabulary to their own perspectives and interpretations/understandings of events or issues. For us, it is the introduction of competing approaches which facilities this emancipating potential: through recognition of the existence of differing 'world views' and subsequent accounts of an issue or event; as a means to enable students to articulate their views and analysis and situate themselves within a wider knowledge-building community.

Conclusion

Our central argument is that the analysis of Political Science and International Relations should be theoretically informed. This enables students of Politics to produce rigorous analysis of the event, political phenomenon/a, or issue which they are studying. For us, the way we seek to encourage our students to become political analysts is through the application of a series of competing theoretical perspectives to a particular area of enquiry within the disciplines. We believe that the key to understand and appreciate theory is for students to apply it, and thus to see its 'real world' relevance. We all seek to develop our students as active rather than passive learners and for us a key way to do so is through illustrating how theory may shed light on an issue, or indeed, how theory show us what is kept invisible. In this way we believe theory also has a wider emancipatory potential not only in the building of knowledge but as a basis from which existing power relations may be rendered explicit and challenged. To paraphrase Marx (1845) – the point is not (just) to interpret the world, but to change i.

Guide to further reading

The use and application of theory to 'real world' politics is developed further in our (forthcoming, 2011) textbook *Doing Political Science and International Relations* (Palgrave Macmillan).

Other useful texts that draw out the wider themes and issues raised here include the extremely useful *Political Analysis* (Hay, 2002); *Theory and Methods in Political Science* 3rd edn (Marsh and Stoker, 2010); *Ways of Knowing* (Moses and Knutsen, 2007) all from Palgrave Macmillan.

References

Almond, G. (1988), 'Separate Tables: Schools and Sects in Political Science', *PS. Political Science and Politics*, 21 (4), 828–42.

Bates, S. R. and Jenkins, L. (2007), 'Teaching and Learning Ontology and Epistemology in Political Science', *Politics*, 27 (1), 55–63.

Biesta, G. (2010), 'A New Logic of Emancipation: The Methodology of Jacques Ranciere', *Educational Theory*, 60 (1), 39–59.

Craig, J. (2009), 'What's the Difference about Teaching and Learning in Politics and IR' paper presented at 2nd PSA Learning and Teaching Conference/C-SAP Open day, University of Leeds, UK 8 and 9 September 2009.

Dunleavy, P. and O'Leary, B. (1987), *Theories of the State* (Basingstoke: Macmillan).

Evans, B., Rueschemeyer, D. and Skocpol, T. (eds) (1985), *Bringing the State Back in* (Cambridge: Cambridge University Press).

Goodin, R. and Klingemann, D. (1995), *A New Handbook of Political Science* (Oxford: Oxford University Press).

Hay, C. (2002), *Political Analysis* (Basingstoke: Palgrave Macmillan).

Hay, C., Lister, M. and Marsh, D. (eds) (2005), *The State* (Basingstoke: Palgrave Macmillan).

Korthagen, F. A. J. and Kessels, J. P. A. M. (1999), 'Linking Theory and Practice: Changing the Pedagogy of Teacher Education', *Educational Researcher*, 28 (4), 4–17

Marsh, D. and Smith, M. (2001), 'There is More than One Way to Do Political Science: on Different Ways to Study Policy Networks', *Political Studies*, 49 (3), 528–41.

Marsh, D. and Furlong, P. (2002), 'A Skin Not a Sweater: Ontology and Epistemology in Political Science' in D. Marsh and G. Stoker, *Theory and Methods in Political Science*, 2nd edn (Basingstoke: Palgrave Macmillan), pp. 17–44.

Marsh, D. and Savigny, H. (2004), 'Political Science as a Broad Church: The Search for a Pluralist Discipline', *Politics*, 24 (3), 155–68.

Marx, K. (1845), *Theses on Feuerbach*, available at http://www.marxists.org/archive/marx/works/1845/theses/theses.htm#018.

McAnulla, S. (2005), *British Politics. A Critical Introduction* (London: Macmillan).

Savigny, H. and Marsden, L. (forthcoming), *Doing Political Science and International Relations* (Basingstoke: Palgrave Macmillan).

Scardamalia, M. and Bereiter, C. (2006), 'Knowledge Building: Theory, Pedagogy, and Technology' in K. Sawyer (ed.) *Cambridge Handbook of Learning Sciences* (New York: Cambridge University Press), pp. 97–118.

Schmidt, B. C. (2008), 'On the History and Historiography of International Relations' in W. Carlsnaes, T. Risse and B. Simmons (eds) *Handbook of International Relations* (London: Sage), pp. 52–72.

Smith, M. J. (1999), 'Institutionalising the "Eternal Return": Textbooks and the Study of British Politics', *British Journal of Politics and International Relations* 1 (1), 106–18.

Wendt, A. (1987), 'The Agent-Structure Problem in International Relations Theory', *International Organization*, 41, 335–70.

10
Teaching Politics and Political Bias

Cathy Gormley-Heenan

Teaching Politics can be a dangerous business. Some individual academics have been accused of distortion and political bias by their students and have found themselves the subject of internal investigations and inquiry (Losco and De Ollos, 2007). Universities have had to defend themselves against claims of departments teaching 'propaganda' in class (Herring, 2008; Newman, 2008). This has now become something of an international phenomenon with accusations and rebuttals regarding political biases featuring regularly in the news. For example, a diplomatic cable written by a US Embassy official and later released by Wikileaks claimed that Canadian universities displayed tendencies of 'anti-American' bias (REF). US academia, *en masse*, has been accused of having overtly liberal and left wing tendencies which could create a cold house for conservative-minded faculties and students alike (Horowitz, 2007). Small scale and case study based research to test such claims have found to the contrary (La Falce and Gomez, 2007). Nonetheless, students in the US have been offered money to record their 'liberal' lecturers so that they and their alleged liberal biases can be exposed (Younge, 2006) and a similar story can be found in Australia, where the allegations of liberal biases in the universities eventually led to a full Senate Inquiry into Academic Freedom in 2008 (Gelber, 2009).

New entrants to the profession might be concerned by this recent upsurge of interest in the political biases of academics and the implications of this (if any) for the students. Understandably, many will believe that they have to approach the teaching of sensitive, contested and politically charged topics with a large degree of trepidation and will vow to be 'neutral' in the classroom. More established colleagues might argue that the academic freedoms bestowed upon them with their tenure and appointments, give them the freedom to teach how and what they want and hold the view that a professor's job is 'to profess'. The reality for both is that the lack of formal pedagogical training in most Political Science doctoral programs has resulted in the development of a body of lecturers whose teaching philosophies, styles and strategies largely reflect these academics' experiences, personalities and identities; and tend to do so implicitly rather than explicitly. A straw poll of our own colleagues will reveal a wide range of opinions on how to teach Politics and how to deal with issues of partisanship and neutrality. So, how do you teach Politics? There are, of course, two basic fundamentals. Firstly, you need to be reflective enough of your own pedagogy to be able understand and to accept why you teach in the way that you do. Secondly, you need to be able to communicate clearly to your students why you teach in the way that you do. Such reflection and communication will, no doubt, address the most important questions around teaching Politics and political bias: what are academic responsibilities of Politics teaching staff and how does this role sit alongside an academic's personal beliefs during teaching? To what extent should academics admit their own political viewpoints in the classroom, if at all? Can a lecturer ever be neutral when teaching a subject like Politics within which every concept, ideology and political belief is contestable? How does a position of 'neutrality' sit alongside the need to encourage and develop 'critical' students? These are not easy questions to answer and opinions will vary widely. That said, the purpose of this chapter is not to tell you how to teach Politics in relation to issues of political bias. Rather, its purpose is to reflect on some of our specific teaching practices, our own political biases (acknowledged or otherwise), the student perceptions of such political bias and possible implications of this.

The academic debate

It is important to begin by explaining the nature and extent of the current debate around political bias in the classroom. David Horowitz, a conservative activist and writer in the US with a particular interest in American academia, argues that the US universities are politically biased against conservatism, that they engage in the indoctrination of students and that they fail students whose world view does not sit with the views of the academe (Horowitz, 2006). He has called for the establishment of measures to redress, what he sees as, the political imbalance of the higher education system in the US. His campaign group 'Students for Academic Freedom' actively promotes its Academic Bill of Rights (ABOR), a Bill of Rights which, it claims will promote academic pluralism and protect academic freedom (see Box 10.1). Its critics argue that the Bill's effect will be the reverse; that it will rein in such freedoms (Millteman, 2007); and that the campaign group is itself a politically motivated and biased group with a distinctly conservative agenda (Giroux, 2006). Choice quotations from republican politicians seem to validate the claims. Republican, Newt Gingrich, referring to one academic who was sacked by the University of Colorado said:

> We are going to nail this guy and send the dominoes tumbling. And everybody who has an opinion out there and entire disciplines like ethnic

Box 10.1   The Academic Bill of Rights (ABOR)

1. All faculty shall be hired, fired, promoted and granted tenure on the basis of their competence and appropriate knowledge in the field of their expertise and, in the humanities, the social sciences, and the arts, with a view toward fostering a plurality of methodologies and perspectives. No faculty member shall be hired or fired or denied promotion or tenure on the basis of his or her political or religious beliefs.

2. No faculty member will be excluded from tenure, search and hiring committees on the basis of their political or religious beliefs.

3. Students will be graded solely on the basis of their reasoned answers and appropriate knowledge of the subjects and disciplines they study, not on the basis of their political or religious beliefs.

4. Curricula and reading lists in the humanities and social sciences should reflect the uncertainty and unsettled character of all human knowledge in these areas by providing students with dissenting sources and viewpoints where appropriate. While teachers are and should be free to pursue their own findings and perspectives in presenting their views, they should consider and make their students aware of other viewpoints. Academic disciplines should welcome a diversity of approaches to unsettled questions.

5. Exposing students to the spectrum of significant scholarly viewpoints on the subjects examined in their courses is a major responsibility of faculty. Faculty will not use their courses for the purpose of political, ideological, religious or anti-religious indoctrination.

6. Selection of speakers, allocation of funds for speakers' programs and other student activities will observe the principles of academic freedom and promote intellectual pluralism.

7. An environment conducive to the civil exchange of ideas being an essential component of a free university, the obstruction of invited campus speakers, destruction of campus literature or other effort to obstruct this exchange will not be tolerated.

8. Knowledge advances when individual scholars are left free to reach their own conclusions about which methods, facts, and theories have been validated by research. Academic institutions and professional societies formed to advance knowledge within an area of research, maintain the integrity of the research process, and organize the professional lives of related researchers serve as indispensable venues within which scholars circulate research findings and debate their interpretation. To perform these functions adequately, academic institutions and professional societies should maintain a posture of organizational neutrality with respect to the substantive disagreements that divide researchers on questions within, or outside, their fields of inquiry.

studies and women's studies and cultural studies and queer studies that we don't like won't be there anymore.

(Smallwood, 2005).

Such professed political interference with what can be taught in universities is alarming and runs contrary to the very essence and purpose of higher education.

This Academic Bill of Rights (ABOR) has come in for considerable criticism, not least from the American Association of University Professors (AAUP) who have noted that while they agree with the principles of freedom, equality and pluralism, they disagree with the ideological stance behind the development of the Bill and how the very freedoms that need to be protected will be undermined by such a bill. In short, they argue that this conservative ideological stance which equates a questioning and critical approach within many of the social sciences and humanities subjects as unpatriotic and anti-American as opposed to evidence of a critical pedagogy within the disciplines.

The debates around higher education and issues of political bias are, of course, not restricted to the US though the debate is certainly amplified in the US in a way that is less obvious in other countries. In the UK, it has been suggested that

Barely a week goes by when *Times Higher Education* does not carry a complaint or a warning from an academic about threats to their cherished right to speak out. And it is not just high-profile people - there is a real sense of unease among rank-and-file academics that their right to speak truth to power, to set their own research and teaching agendas and to voice their opinions about the management of their institutions is being stripped away.

(Corbyn, 2010, p. 32)

Threats to academic freedom, however, are less explicitly connected to allegations of political bias. Indeed, much of the recent UK debate has focused on whether the universities have become 'breeding grounds for Islamic radicalism' (Reisz, 2011). In one case, the University of Nottingham began to vet the reading lists of Politics lecturers after it was discovered that a student had downloaded an al-Qaeda training manual (Corbyn, 2010). One of these Politics lecturers was subsequently suspended for presenting a conference paper relating to the student who had downloaded the manual and his treatment by the university in the aftermath of his arrest and release without charge (BBC, 2011).

These stories, and others, give us cause for reflection about what we teach, how we teach and the need for academic freedom in our work and calls for illuminating the range of ways that colleagues have and do teach in universities. This shows that there are a series of ways of approaching the teaching, learning and assessment of Politics, each with their own merits and limitations.

Five approaches to teaching politics

1. Neutrality

The neutrality issue has dominated debates on the pedagogy of teaching controversial and political issues in the UK. In theory, such an approach would necessitate a detached, dispassionate and non partisan lecture, devoid of any partiality or opinion.

The reality is that this unlikely to be possible, despite even one's best intentions to try to be neutral. Given the biases, assumptions and explicit and implicit worldviews that pattern all of our social relationships, as well as the ways that we interpret the world, it seems impossible that there can ever be such a thing as neutrality. People might strive to be impartial and to report the various sides of an argument but they will still do so using narratives that have been prepared in socially constructed contexts. So even those claiming to be neutral rest their arguments on a series of pre conceived assumptions. The very title of the course or module; the core texts, recommended books and required reading; the weekly topics for discussion; the seminar questions; and the final examination questions are all conditioned by our own world view. Therefore, as teachers we should apply to ourselves what we often teach to our students – we should recognize that we are creatures of a long process of political socialization – and that consequently our own political position is not necessarily the product of cool, and detached, purely rational thinking and, by extension, is unlikely to be considered neutral. For most then, the solution would be to accurately and fairly represent the continuous development of ideas in political discourse as outlined below in a form of alternative neutrality.

Tip one:

Acknowledge that there is no such things as complete neutrality – no matter how much once might strive to attain it.

Tip two:

Become sensitive to forms of bias and help your students to become sensitive to their own forms of bias by acknowledging issues of upbringing, education, socialization, religion and other such influences that have helped shape our political understanding and the lens through which we view the world.

---

2. Engaged neutrality

Realizing the difficulties in actualizing 'neutrality' in the classroom, scholars have considered degrees and variations of such neutrality which might be more realizable. Stenhouse (1983) proposes what he called 'procedural neutrality', in which the teacher acts as a neutral chairperson during classroom debates. Kelly (1986) proposes 'committed impartiality' in which the teacher attempts to provide all sides of an argument but *does* share their own views with the class. An extension of this might be called 'engaged neutrality' which would mean explaining the various political theories, policies and/or ideologies *in* their own terms but not necessarily *on* their own terms. This involves firstly explaining something in terms which fairly represent it, which would be acceptable by its advocates, and which treats the 'subject matter' as cogent, coherent and captures any complexity. The second stage is the introduction of the critical approaches which expose the students to the internal tensions and the real world applicability of these theories, policies and ideologies. The final stage is to address these critical approaches and to evaluate the strength of the critique.

Tip three:

Be careful of overly compensating for your own acknowledged biases by swinging the proverbial pendulum too far in the other direction and/or by going overboard to try to accommodate the range of views in the class.

---

3. Constructive ambiguity

Another approach is to illustrate how all of the political ideas and beliefs contained within the curriculum can be best explained using a constructive ambiguity framework of analysis. Constructive ambiguity in Politics is the use of ambiguous language which moves an agenda forward in order that the things do not get 'stuck'. The teaching of Politics in this way involves alerting a student to how the language(s) of politics is/are deployed in the practice of politics and in the interpretation of politics and then trying to clarify at different levels (the historical and philosophical etc), the ambiguity and ambivalence which can be identified as a political craft. To formulate ideas and proposals in such a manner as to be both distinctive and ambiguous was an experience that Vargas Llosa, the Peruvian writer and Nobel prize winner, found challenging and profoundly disturbing. But it was part and parcel of the political craft. Not to acknowledge its necessity and therefore to fail to become proficient in the lexicon of ambiguity was *not* to become a serious politician. When one engages in the craft of politics, in other words, one cannot indulge the honesty of the tender conscience. Ambiguity is often necessary not only to attain self-interested ends but also to avoid destructive – or self-destructive – political dogmatism (Vargas Llosa, 1991). This, in short, is the art of 'constructive ambiguity'. A pedagogic focus on the language of politics and what it means is critical to its understanding. As Michael Oakeshott said also: 'Politics in a university is appropriately concerned with the study of a 'language' and with 'literatures' only as paradigms of this 'languages' (1991, p. 211).

Tip four:

Remember the power of your own language and your choice of specific words in the class. In Northern Ireland, for example, terms such as 'the north of Ireland; the north; the province; and Ulster are all loaded with political meaning even though they refer to the same geographic location.

Tip five:

Acknowledge that ALL of the language is up for debate in the class.

---

4. Public intellectual

Of course, the aforementioned approaches are all quite detached in terms of perspective where the emphasis is not about an academic's political disclosure, even if such disclosure does end up happening during the class. A contrasting approach is that of the public intellectual – the academic whose 'politics' are shared in the public domain as a matter of course, whether through a weekly newspaper column or regularly commentary on television and radio. There is a strong tradition of public intellectuals who are also university academics. *Prospect Magazine*'s 'Britain's Top 100 Public Intellectuals', to celebrate its 100th anniversary in 2004 revealed the following academics among others: Bernard Crick (Political writer and citizenship expert); Lawrence Freedman (Professor of War Studies); Timothy Garton Ashe (Historian and commentator); Anthony Giddens (Social and political theorist); Fred Halliday (International Relations professor); Peter Hennessy (Historian of government); Michael Ignatieff (Human Rights theorist and author); and Bhikhu Parekh (Political theorist). In each case, their political opinions are in the public domain. Giroux, (1995) believes that more academics should reclaim their roles as public intellectuals despite the constraining forces of the critics and the authorities who suggest that everything must be neutral and apolitical, particularly in the US. There is much merit in this argument when examined in the context of the developing forms of new social media through which it has become increasingly difficult to separate our private and public lives. Facebook, 24/7 e-mail, student expectations of instant replies, web profiles, blogs, encouragement that we write op-ed pieces for national newspaper to help with our 'impact' profile all help to contribute to a blurring of the public and private personas of many academics. In such a context, there is a risk that our privately held views seep more readily into the public domain through our writing and mean that the approaches to teaching as outlined above are negated, to an extent, by very public displays of our own political positions and perspectives in arenas beyond the classroom.

Tip six:

Be provocative and encourage students to disagree with you. For example, if you have written an op-ed piece for a newspaper ask your students to craft a response for discussion in class.

---

5. Advocacy/activist scholarship

Others are also equally comfortable in the public sphere. The activist scholarship approach is: 'one in which scholarship is directed towards supporting non-violent action against oppression' (Herring, 2008, p.3) and whose intent is on creating active engagement between the academy and the communities of resistance involved in feminist, antiracist, indigenous sovereignty, transgender liberation, anti globalization, antimilitary, and anti prison movements (Sudbury and Okazawa-Rey, 2009). In making the case for activist scholarship, Herring (2006) argues that British IR academics have failed to hold the British state to account for its responsibilities in foreign policy and uses his own past record of 'neglect' of these issues as an illustration of the need for scholars to engage in educational activism. It is true that activist scholarship is quite uncommon in our universities and Calhoun (2008) explains that the reasons for this primarily due to an ideal of knowledge that is based on detached and objective observation; that scholarship is more related to academic agendas and career structures; and that activism is seen as an expression of individual interests rather than a concern with broader social issues. In addition, such an approach faces criticisms of positivism, objectivity and rigour. The counterargument is that such scholarship is a necessity for helping different movements have more success in trying to change the world. Unimpressed, critics of such an activist scholarship approach to teaching such as Stanley Fish argue that 'The moment a professor does embrace and urge [a particular viewpoint] academic study has ceased and been replaced by partisan advocacy' (Fish, 2007, np). But as Herring suggests:

> The normative and political are unavoidable in deciding what to study and what not to study, how to study it and to whom the results of that study are directed. Hence scholarship is enhanced by realising that this is the case (a necessary prior stage often missed or denied by traditionalists) and accounting explicitly for those choices.
>
> (2008, pp. 197–8)

Taking an activist scholarship approach requires, then, the clearest of communication with students, beginning with an explanation of exactly how the normative and the political are unavoidable in our line of work (much like the explanations that will be offered when using the informed neutrality approach) and why you support a particular position or cause. In short, be explicit.

Tip seven:

Put your (political) cards on the table when taking an activist scholarship approach to teaching. Tell your students who you are, what you stand for and why and assure your students that this is a personal position from which they are free to disagree.

Tip eight:

Remember that you have a duty of care to your students – despite the fact that they are Politics and IR students, many may not be overtly political nor have a particular world view that they are wedded to and have come to class to learn, to be informed and to be guided. Because of this a student might not 'hear' the perspective that you offer in class and may interpret this as being the 'truth' (whatever that may be).

Creating your personal pedagogy for politics

There are, of course, limitations and drawbacks to each of the approaches outlined above and there are other approaches. Despite this, those discussed here can act as a starting point from which you can begin develop and/or revise and reframe your own pedagogical approach to teaching Politics. At one extreme, neutrality is impossible. At the other, students might just be turned off by an approach that is too didactic, ideological and moralizing. Even so, how do you propose to teach those political, ideas, opinions and ideologies that don't rest easily with your own world view? The main thing is always good pedagogy and so creating your personal pedagogy for Politics is important. Begin by asking yourself 'What is my philosophy of teaching'? In other words, what are your beliefs about teaching and learning? What do you see as your specific role as in the classroom? What might affect your ability to fulfill your defined role in the classroom? Once you have ascertained the answers to these basic questions, make them explicit. Good pedagogy begins with good communication in class and so you need to explain to your class your specific beliefs about teaching and learning and what you see as your role in the classroom. Invite comment and debate around your explanations. In particular, ask your students what they see as *your* role in the classroom. Ask them what they see

Box 10.2   Oulton, Dillon and Grace (2004) Teaching principles

1. Focus on the nature of controversy and controversial issues; that is, that people disagree; have different worldviews, value and limitations of science, political understanding, power, and so on;
2. Motivate [students] to recognize the notion that a person's stance on an issue will be affected by their worldview;
3. Emphasize the importance of teachers and learners reflecting critically on their own stance and recognize the need to avoid the prejudice that comes from a lack of critical reflection;
4. Give pupils the skills and abilities to identify bias for themselves, encouraging them to take a critical stance towards claims of neutrality, a lack of bias and claims to offer a balanced view;
5. Promote open mindedness, a thirst for more information and more sources of information and a willingness to change one's view as appropriate, and avoid strategies that encourage pupils to actually make up their minds on an issue too hastily; and
6. Motivate teachers, as much as possible, to share their views with pupils and make explicit the way in which they arrive at their own stance on an issue.

as *their* role in the classroom and ask them to think about their own pedagogy of learning. Reflecting on the similarities and differences in your beliefs about teaching and learning in Politics will help you develop your own critical pedagogy for Politics. Box 10.2 is an example of how this might look (or not as the case may be)!

Why does all of this matter?

That said, there is much within the Politics curriculum that engages with competing values and interests and sensitive subjects which can lead to strong emotional reactions from students. An academic's own politics is always going to be an area of interest for your students. Some students will choose specific universities and colleges because of their perceptions of the politics of certain professors (usually based on those that are also public intellectuals or more widely read). Some students think they need to know your politics in order to write the 'right' answer! This can lead to a situation where students 'suppress their own convictions, writing what they imagine will please their tutors rather than what they believe themselves' (Leach, 2008, p. 31). Some students even believe that they will be penalized for expressing their own views or for writing 'conservative' answers (Kelly-Woessner and Woessner, 2006) despite the research which suggests that professors' political beliefs have no measurable effect on students (Kemmelmeier, Danielson and Basten, 2005). Leach (2008) recalls:

> I once caught an able student (who might have been fairly described as 'New Right' or 'neoconservative') scribbling graffiti, "Marx means marks", suggesting that Marxist views would be well rewarded (a comment that was perhaps directed more against one or two of my colleagues than myself). After he and his fellow students had graduated I asked him whether he still thought that 'Marx meant marks' on his degree course. He grinned sheepishly and replied, 'No! Not after I've seen the results'.
>
> (2008: 31).

So, student perceptions are their reality unless proven otherwise and it is important to discuss with the students any such perceptions at the beginning of the class. The simplest way to address these perceptions, and any related concerns, is through the use of *clear* assessment criteria. Do not leave the assessment criteria hidden in a course handbook or a syllabus. Be upfront in addressing perceived fears about 'Marx means marks'. Take a steer from Michael Bérubé, who has been extensively criticized by David Horowitz (see The Academic Debate above) and says:

> All I ask is that their interpretations be plausible, and my criteria are lawyerly and austere. One, I read their essays to see how well they handle textual evidence, that is, how well they support whatever claims they make by reference to the material in front of them; and two, I want to know how well they anticipate and head off possible counterarguments. That's it. Meet those two criteria in my classroom, and the field of interpretation is open.
>
> (Bérubé, 2006, p.).

Tip nine:

Communication and clarity of message is key. Discuss with your students the anecdote of 'Marx means marks' as a starting point and use this as a launch pad into the specific assessment criteria for your class. Reinforce these criteria each week as you move through different topics. Refer specifically to the assessment criteria in your feedback to students and to the ways in which they have met the criteria as well as ways to improve further.

Conclusion

The possibility of government enquiries, internal university investigations, exposés in the newspapers and through the various forms of the new social media can certainly concentrate the mind. The chapter might not seem to be radical enough to some. It is not intended to be. Rather, its intention is to alert those teaching in Politics and International Relations to examine their personal pedagogy and to question why they teach the way that they do. If they can articulate this to their students that would be a step in the right direction towards teaching Politics and International Relations while remaining cognisant of implicit and explicit biases of both lecturer and student alike. Continued self reflection about our role in the classroom, in higher education more broadly, and in society more generally is important in rising to the challenge of teaching Politics in the twenty-first century.

Tip ten:

Remember your professional associations when reflecting on your personal pedagogy of teaching and your role in the classroom. For example, the American Political Science Association (APSA), *A Guide to Professional Ethics in Political Science* (2008) says: 'Academic political scientists must be very careful not to impose their partisan views, conventional or otherwise, upon students or colleagues'. The UK Political Studies Association (PSA) *Guidelines for Good Professional Conduct* (undated) says: 'Members have a general duty to promote the growth and spreading of knowledge of the highest academic standards, to protect academic freedom, and to promote a working environment appropriate to these aims. The content of teaching and research in Political Studies is diverse and subject to change. Members should be prepared to recognize the diversity of their subject. Members are entitled to hold political opinions and to act politically. However they have a general duty not to present their own political convictions as though they carry the authority of professional knowledge'.

Further reading

For those most interested in the practicalities of teaching Politics and political biases there are a number of quick reflective guides that are useful for consideration before the class. See, for example, Hartlaub, Stephen G. and Lancaster, Frank A. (2008) 'Teacher Characteristics and Pedagogy in Political Science', *Journal of Political Science Education*, 4 (4), 377–93 which discusses the different factors that help to shape why we might teach in the way that we do and looks at how professional training, current professional situation, and other personal characteristics (including political affiliations) affect how and what we teach. Yale's Graduate School of Arts and Sciences has produced a useful reflective guide which provides the tools and principles that a teacher should consider

before going into the classroom. See: http://www.yale.edu/graduateschool/
teaching/forms/papers/controversial_subjects_outline.pdf.

References

BBC (2011), 'Nottingham University Expert "Suspended" in Terror Row', BBC News Online, 5 May. Available at http://www.bbc.co.uk/news/uk-england-nottinghamshire-13294132 (accessed 2 February 2012).

Bérubé, M. (2006), *What's Liberal about the Liberal Arts? Classroom Politics and 'Bias' in Higher Education* (New York: W. W. Norton & Company).

Calhoun, C. (2008), 'Foreword' in C. Hale (ed.) *Engaging Contradictions: Theory, Politics, and Methods of Activist Scholarship* (California: University of California Press), p xiii.

Corbyn, Z. (2010), 'A Clear and Present Danger', *Times Higher Education Supplement*, 11 February. Available at http://www.timeshighereducation.co.uk/story.asp?sectioncode=26&storycode=410297 (accessed 12 February 2010).

Fish, S. (2007), 'Teaching and Advocacy' *New York Times* 23 March. Available at http://opinionator.blogs.nytimes.com/2007/03/23/advocacy-and-teaching/ (accessed 2 February 2012).

Frueh, J., Blaney, D. L., Dunn, K., Goff, P., Leonard, E. K., and Sharoni, S. (2008), 'Political Beliefs and the Academic Responsibilities of Undergraduate Teaching', *Journal of Political Science Education*, 4 (4), 447–62.

Gelber, K. (2009), 'Academic Freedom and the "Intellectual Diversity" Movement in Australia', *Australian Journal of Human Rights*, 14 (2), 95–114.

Giroux, H. A. (1995), 'Academics as Public Intellectuals: Rethinking Classroom Politics' in J. Williams (ed.) *PC Wars: Politics and Theory in the Academy* (New York and London: Routledge), pp. 49–64.

Giroux, H. A. (2006), 'Academic Freedom Under Fire: The Case for Critical Pedagogy', *College Literature*, 33 (4), 1–42.

Herring, E. (2008), 'Critical Terrorism Studies: An Activist Scholar Perspective', *Critical Studies on Terrorism*, 1 (2), 197–212.

Herring, E. (2006), 'Remaking the Mainstream: The Case for Activist IR Scholarship', *Millennium – Journal of International Studies*, 35 (1), 105–18 .

Horowitz, D. (2007), *Indoctrination U: The Left's War Against Academic Freedom* (New York: Encounter Books).

Horowitz, D. (2006), *The Professors: The 101 Most Dangerous Academics in America* (Washington: Regnery Press).

Kelly, T. E. (1986), 'Discussing Controversial Issues: Four Perspectives on the Teacher's Role', *Theory and Research in Social Education*, 14 (2), 113–38.

Kelly-Woessner, A. and Woessner, M. C. (2006). 'My Professor is a Partisan Hack: How Perceptions of a Professor's Political Views Affect Student Course Evaluations', *PS: Political Science & Politics*, 39, 495–501.

Kemmelmeier, M., Danielson, C. and Basten, J. (2005), 'What's in a Grade? Academic Success and Political Orientation', *Personality and Social Psychology Bulletin*, 31, 1386–99.

La Falce, D. and Gomez, S. P. (2007), 'Political Attitudes in the Classroom: Is Academia the Last Bastion of Liberalism?', *Journal of Political Science Education*, 3 (1), 1–20.

Leach, R. (2008), *The Politics Companion* (Basingstoke: Palgrave Macmillan).

Losco, J. and DeOllos, I. (2007), 'Fear and Loathing in College Classrooms: A Survey of Political Science Department Chairs Regarding Political Bias', *Journal of Political Science Education*, 3 (3), 251–64.

Millteman, J. H. (2007), 'Who Governs Academic Freedoms in International Studies', *International Studies Perspectives*, 8 (4), 358–68.

Newman, M. (2008), 'Aberystwyth Refutes Claims of "Hateful" Anti-Israel Teaching Bias', *Times Higher Education*, 26 June. Available at http://www.timeshighereducation.co.uk/story.asp?storycode=402506 (accessed 2 February 2012).

Oakeshott, M. (1991), *Rationalism in Politics and Other Essays* (Indianapolis: Liberty).

Oulton, C., Dillon, J. and Grace, M. M. (2004), 'Reconceptualizing the Teaching of Controversial Issues', *International Journal of Science Education*, 26 (4), 411–23.

Reisz, M. (2011), 'Contravene or Intervene', *Times Higher Education* Supplement, 6 January. Available at http://www.timeshighereducation.co.uk/story.asp?sectioncode=26&storycode=414746 (accessed 2 February 2012).

Smallwood, S. (2005), Newt Gingrich cited in Scott Smallwood, 'Ward Churchill Gets a Warm Welcome in Speech in U. Of Hawaii', *Chronicle of Higher Education* (24 February 2005), http://chronicle.com/daily/2005/02/2005022402.

Stenhouse, L. (1983), *Authority, Education and Emancipation* (London: Heinemann).

Sudbury, J. and Okazawa-Rey, M. (eds) (2009), *Activist Scholarship: Antiracism, Feminism, and Social Change* (Boulder, CO: Paradigm Publishers).

Vargas Llosa, M. (1991), '*A Fish out of Water*', in Vargas Llosa for President: a Novelist's Personal Account of his Campaign for the Presidency of Peru, *Granta 36*, June.

Younge, G. (2006), 'Silence in Class' *Guardian* 4 April. Available at http://www.guardian.co.uk/education/2006/apr/04/internationaleducationnews.highereducation (accessed 2 February 2012).

11
Contemporary Politics: Using the 'F' Word and Teaching Gender in International Relations

Christina Rowley and Laura J. Shepherd

'I don't mean to be rude, but aren't there more important issues that affect everybody?'

(Comment by a female student)

The central aim of this chapter is to explore the possibility of developing ways to teach International Relations (IR) with attention to gender as a noun, a verb and a logic, to replace 'the week on gender' (that usually, but not always, falls towards the end of the term or semester) with a more nuanced understanding of the ways in which gender (as a category of identity, an approach to academic study and as an ordering logic that pre/proscribes certain behaviours and modes of being in the world) matters in/to IR. Teaching, for us, is about engendering curiosity (pun definitely intended) and the strategies we outline in the final section of this Chapter are all aimed at facilitating the development of that curiosity in our students. We know that we will reach more students through our teaching than are likely to read our published work in any given year, and we know from student feedback that one of the most important qualities a teacher can possess is a genuine enthusiasm for their subject. Thus, we conceive of our teaching as one of the most active forms of social critique with which we are engaged.

We engage here with IR literature and textbooks, rather than Politics and IR, for two reasons: first, it is the field with which we as scholars are most familiar; and, second, the arguments we present regarding teaching in International Relations have been made elsewhere by others regarding teaching in Political Science, as we discuss briefly below. IR as a discipline has been notoriously resistant to the 'turn to culture' (see Weldes et al., 1999, pp. 2–5) – that is, to taking seriously post-positivist challenges to the dominant rationalist orthodoxy – and this resistance has also resulted in the vigourous policing of disciplinary boundaries against critical interjections. Such policing manifests in the marginalization of non-mainstream theories and methodologies within

146

IR, including feminism. '[F]eminists have written several diaries of dissidence, stories of co-option, domestication and ghettoization' (Soreanu and Hudson, 2008, p. 124); just as Soreanu and Hudson offer an alternative perspective on 'worrying about marginality' (ibid.) through their analysis of citational practices, here we do the same through critical engagement with pedagogical practices. In this chapter, we proceed in the first section to sketch out some of the possible explanations for resistance to the explicit espousal of a feminist politics. We suggest that, in part, the reasons why IR syllabuses and textbooks limit their engagement with gendered IR are rooted in wider socio-cultural debates about the relevance of feminism in the twenty-first century and about the status and character of academic social science.

A second aspect to the disavowal of gendered IR is unique to IR itself and its disciplinary historiography. Thus, in the second section we offer a corrective to the suggestion that gendered IR can only contribute to 'the week on gender', by demonstrating the wide array of materials available for citation, whatever the topic of the week. The masculinism of IR has led to a distinctive image of world politics, where issues are thought – and taught – in a peculiarly distanced and dissonant fashion; here we hope to illustrate that across the different fields of IR, from security through political economy to foreign policy analysis IR can learn 'to love' gendered scholarship (Soreanu and Hudson, 2008). Third, we analyse our disciplinary artefacts – a range of popular IR textbooks used across the UK as the basis for undergraduate engagement with the discipline – and ask whether the masculinism of research IR is present in pedagogy. Our analysis leads us to conclude that the extant materials reinforce the notion that gender *is* marginal to the discipline and, perhaps more crucially, can be incorporated without challenging the organizational schema of the discipline. Stienstra argues that 'by increasing our attention to issues of concern to women, like FGM [female genital mutilation], in International Relations classrooms and texts we begin to recognize the importance of these to the study of International Relations' (Stienstra, 2000, p. 233). In the sections that follow, we argue that such an approach is important, but ultimately of limited value, in that it reinscribes the notion that feminism is 'about women', and that gender can – and should – be fixed to corporeal forms. In the final section, therefore, we offer some strategies aimed at fostering a gendered curiosity in the minds of our students and at 'mainstreaming gender into the IR curriculum'.[1]

Using the 'F-word' – what's the problem?

All students bring cultural baggage and expectations to their learning. While by no means a representative sample, the comments and attitudes of students we have taught reveal some interesting insights into how feminists, feminism(s) and the study of gender are understood by these students. Most commonly, students have some prior awareness of the existence of *a* feminist movement, although their knowledge and understanding of feminism is filtered through positivist and liberal discourses, and popular media representations (we use the singular 'feminist movement' here as most students seem unaware of the existence of multiple feminist perspectives). A dominant theme remains that of feminists as 'nitpicking' and/or 'troublemakers', in particular with regard to 'political correctness,' and many students endorse the view that terminological issues are trivial or irrelevant (for example, making negative comments about invented neologisms such as 'personhole' or 'person-hours'). Feminism is equated with 'women's liberation' – primarily economic and reproductive – and seen as a relic of a bygone age. It is either viewed as unnecessary in a 'post-feminist' era, due to feminist 'demands' having been achieved (articulated primarily as the elimination of sexual discrimination and sexual harassment, and the recognition that domestic violence is unacceptable), or as having 'gone too far,' tipping the 'balance' towards 'favouring' women rather than 'stopping' at 'true' gender equality. Feminism is seen as synonymous with the special treatment of women (through quotas and affirmative action policies) and is argued to be antithetical to meritocratic and therefore democratic politics.

The common argument that IR is 'gender neutral' because it is about neither men nor women but about states is often articulated in tandem with the notion that, while the personal may be political, it is not *international*. Feminist focus upon 'women's issues' is understood to have relevance only in the domestic sphere; at the international level, this focus is seen to be marginal in importance, inapplicable or a distortion of the way international politics 'really' works. For many students, the conceptual leap required to view gender as a power relation is a difficult and estranging experience; only a very few students self-identify as feminist, and this is usually a liberal conceptualization of feminism, typically an understanding that unproblematically connects feminism with women, gender with (women's) bodies, and substantive feminist issues as primarily (or solely) concerned with issues of liberal democratic representation and participation in the economic and political arenas of the public sphere.

In recent years, there has been much debate within academic feminism about the vitality of feminist politics (see, for example, Halley, 2006; McRobbie, 2009; Zalewski, 2010). We do not have space to engage with this literature, save to point out that feminists are well aware that there is much resistance to – and some derision of – the overt espousal of a feminist politics in the twenty-first century. If you Google 'not a feminist but', you are offered links to over nine million pages containing this phrase. It seems that it is commonplace to quietly agree with (some) feminist principles but to disavow the identity of feminist. There are two aspects to this part of the problem: first, no scholar/educator wishes to induce apathy, or worse, antipathy in their students. We may wish to encourage students, facilitate their development, challenge them, but none of these are possible if the explicit espousal of a feminist politics has caused to disengage, and given the disidentification of contemporary undergraduate students in the UK with feminism, disengagement is a very real possibility. There is a strong heteronormative dynamic to this disengagement, with the predominant caricature of 'a feminist' strongly influenced by the stereotypical 1970s separatist feminism. Houvouras and Carater (2009, p. 234, emphasis added) suggest that '[n]onfeminists were more likely [than self-identified feminists] to define *a feminist* as one who supports female superiority, dislikes men, discriminates based on gender, has negative personal characteristics, and *is lesbian or butch*'. If even those who support some form of feminist politics feel unable or unwilling to do so in the classroom or lecture theatre, then feminism has no place to go in IR other than to 'the week on gender.'

The other side of the coin relates not to the desire to engage students but to the desire to be valued as a member of one's immediate academic community. Overt sexism, racism and homophobia in the academy is, thankfully, relatively rare in contemporary UK higher education but there is still limited discursive space to walk the talk of feminist politics through the halls of one's principal academic unit. It is unlikely that one would be formally sanctioned for mainstreaming gender into the IR syllabus, but one can easily imagine sighs, rolling of eyes and talk of 'balance' and 'neutrality.' If one were to suggest to colleagues teaching, for example, Security Studies, Theories of Development or Global Political Economy that, for the sake of 'balance' and 'neutrality', they could mainstream gender into their curricula as well – after all, such courses would likely include a realist/liberal/constructivist/critical perspective – the conversation would quite possibly grind to a halt. Dangers abound, therefore, in using the 'F' word, but use it we must.

Gendering international relations

We have seen, from our textbooks and syllabuses, which we discuss further below, that it is entirely possible to teach a version of IR without making mention of a single piece of feminist work. However, in this section we offer an overview of the wide variety of feminist work in IR, to demonstrate that there is an abundance of quality feminist scholarship available to sight and cite whatever the topic concerned. There have been a vast number of works that broadly attend to the conduct of war and armed conflict using a gendered analytical framework (see, for example, Moser and Clark (eds) 2001; Skjelsbæk and Smith (eds) 2001; Afshar and Eade (eds) 2004; Caprioli, 2005; Melander, 2005). The core analytical contribution of this selection of literature is to focus on 'the impact of gender difference in decision-making in relation to conflict and conflict resolution' (Skjelsbæk and Smith, 2001, p. 1). This not only means analysing how conflicts affect the daily lives of men and women differently, but also how gendered logics constitute and are in part constituted by the practices of conflict. There is scholarship on post-conflict reconstruction and the gendered socio-legal dimensions of post-conflict zones (see Handrahan, 2004; Kandiyoti, 2004; Rajasingham-Senanayake, 2004) and there is feminist literature on peacekeeping (see Hudson, 2000; Cockburn and Zarkov (eds) 2002; Higate and Henry, 2004; Mazurana, Parpart and Raven-Roberts (eds) 2005). Such literature skilfully interrogates the gendered myths that are influential in the very formation of a peacekeeping force – surely keeping peace is women's work, so male peacekeepers are lesser men? – and also the local and contextual gendered imaginings that help govern peacekeeping missions.

Just as in 'mainstream' IR security studies, the study of peace incorporates work on conflict resolution (Karam, 2000; Caprioli and Boyer, 2001; El-Bushra, 2007) and work on representation and domestic politics that takes gender seriously (Porter, 2003; Kardam, 2004). In addition to these facets, however, research on peace and political leadership also attends to strategies for change in a variety of institutional contexts that have an effect on policy and practice. The focus of such scholarship includes institutions such as the World Bank (see Bergeron, 2003; Griffin, 2007, 2008; Kabeer, 2003) and the United Nations (see Hill, Aboitiz and Poehlman-Doumbouya, 2003; Joachim, 2003; Shepherd, 2008); the latter is also the focus of much scholarship on the legal/political framework that supports academics and activists campaigning on the issue of human rights (see Ackerley, 2001; Bunch, 2004; Elson, 2002; Joachim, 2007). Another human rights issue that has been the subject of much feminist investigation is migration (see, for example Kofman et al., 2000; Piper, 2006: Silvey, 2006); this topic encompasses studies that explore the gendered dynamics of economic migration and the (in)security issues involved in 'voluntary' movement across borders within and between states.

It is quite clearly not the case that the lack of engagement with feminist IR is a result of a lack of relevant literature. From sovereignty to security, political economy to peacekeeping, whatever the topic there is likely to be a piece of feminist work that can offer an insightful and challenging perspective. So why is it that most IR courses that mention gender restrict the representation of feminist IR to the ways in which feminist IR has been written into and out of the discipline, to the sometimes hostile exchanges with non-feminist scholars and to the meta-theoretical pieces that, while important and interesting, are unlikely to convince a sceptical undergraduate? Why not simply teach IR as if gender matters? In the following section we analyse a range of popular textbooks and suggest that perhaps before gender can be mainstreamed into the IR curriculum, it needs to make more than a token appearance in the discipline's self-representation. 'The week on gender' is, in most cases, mirrored by the chapter on gender (and/or feminism); below we explain why we find this problematic, before offering some possible strategies for change.

Teaching 'gender and' international relations

In this section, we explore the ways in which gender is represented in six popular IR textbooks that are used to teach introductory courses on IR throughout the UK, with a view to establishing what resources are available to support teaching IR. It is important to note that we are not suggesting that the authors/editors of these textbooks deliberately or wilfully manipulate the representation of gender to reinscribe the masculinism of the discipline that we discuss above. Rather, we intend to demonstrate that the representations of gender available with which to teach are both product and productive of the disciplining of IR, and to that end we use these texts as instantiations of IR discourse. Sarah Childs and Mona Lena Krook (2006) conducted a similar analysis of British politics textbooks and found that, of their sample, only two per cent of the total pages analysed (50 of 2377) contained mention of women, gender or feminism. They conclude, and we concur, as discussed above, that this is particularly troubling, as 'it is not as if there is a dearth of research upon which to draw' (2006, p. 20). Moreover, the authors suggest that the marginalization of feminist perspectives in Politics is somewhat baffling, 'because the feminization of the British party system over the last decade is a significant transformation of formal political institutions in the UK and clearly falls within the remit of mainstream political science' (Childs and Krook, 2006, p. 20).

However, with reference to gender and politics (as distinct from gender and IR), a recent survey of research activity suggested that '[i]n the teaching of political science, gender perspectives are now commonplace' (Dahlerup, 2010, p. 9) when compared to curricula of years past. Similarly, Michael Moran argues, in response to Childs and Krook, that 'gender is an identity which now has well-organized voices in the discipline, while numerous other identities are neglected' (2006, p. 201). We do not seek to arbitrate in this disputed account of gender in politics (although if we were to venture an opinion, we would suggest that having 'well-organized voices' is not at all the same thing as having those voices heard, nor does having a voice, audible or not, necessarily translate to having authority or legitimacy); we simply want to point to research that exists that complements the arguments we present here. Through our analysis, we demonstrate that even the more recent – and more critical – IR teaching texts available retain a commitment to narrating a gender-neutral logic of the discipline, and only one of the six we surveyed treats gender as a structural logic, a verb and a noun. We argue that, given the representational practices in the textbooks, best practice for teaching gendered IR demands careful consideration of the ways in which the masculinism of the discipline organizes and limits the horizons of the discipline as we teach it.

In Table 11.1, we provide a very brief content analysis of the indexes to the six texts, summarizing the ways in which gender and/or feminism features in their narratives of IR. This is obviously a problematic way in which to proceed,

Table 11.1 Table showing content analysis of gende* and femini* in core IR textbooks

Authors/ editors	Title	Year of publication	No. of index entries gende*	No. of index entries femini*	Relative position(s) of chapters to which index entries refer
Baylis and Smith	*The Globalization of World Politics*	2005 (3rd edn)	27	25	11 and 27 of 30
Smith, Booth and Zalewski	*International Theory: Positivism and Beyond*	1996	3	25	1 and 12 of 18
Brown with Ainley	*Understanding International Relations*	2005 (3rd edn)	0	1	12 of 12
Burchill et al.	*Theories of International Relations*	2001 (2nd edn)	76	87	Introduction, and 1, 5, 6 and 9 of 10
Jackson and Sørenson	*Introduction to International Relations*	2003 (2nd edn)	2	1	10 of 10
Steans and Pettiford with Diez	*Introduction to International Relations*	2005 (2nd edn)	68	42	Introduction and all chapters

as crude quantitative measures reveal very little about the intricacies of the ways in which gender is represented in these popular texts. Also, this research design is wholly affected by the whims of indexers, who may or may not be (answerable to) the authors themselves. However, this initial analysis will give some context to the more qualitative analysis of textual representations of gender and feminism that we undertake here.

The above data suggests that we could do worse than use *Theories of International Relations* as our core text when teaching IR, as this volume provided the most mentions of gender (and/or gendered, gendering, gender variables and so on) and feminism. Similarly, those compiling an introductory course on International Relations would be advised to steer clear of the two texts that mention gender in the last ten pages of the book, if indeed it is mentioned at all. However, we contend that the utility of these texts for teachers of IR is not so easily measured. We argue that scheduling a 'week on gender' when teaching IR is problematic. Therefore, using a textbook that represents gender as an 'add on' to a predetermined field of IR – for example, through only making reference to feminist perspectives in a chapter entitled 'New Issues in IR' (Jackson and Sørenson , 2003, pp. 276–9) – is equally troublesome for IR scholars seeking to devise good pedagogical practices.

The first mention of feminism in *Theories of International Relations* is as a broad 'theoretical tradition' (Burchill, 2001, p.15), which may be accurate insofar as feminists focus on gender, but which underplays the diversity and fragmentation of feminist theorizing. It is later argued that '[f]eminists and ecologists have recently joined the debates within International Relations because of the increasingly porous state of the discipline's boundaries' (ibid., pp. 21–2). This representation of feminism, and its marker of interjection by osmosis, not only suggests that feminism came late to an already-established discipline but also that it was only the porosity of 'the discipline's boundaries' that rendered feminist critiques valuable to IR, rather than the rigour and quality of the academic research that feminist scholars were undertaking, or the issues that they identify as important to the study of IR.

In contrast, in a 'concept box' that distils complex ideas about knowledge and understanding about IR for the undergraduate readership, Steans and Pettiford note that epistemological commitments impact on our understanding of the world, including IR, and that power is intrinsically related to knowledge (Steans and Pettiford, 2005, p. 7). Importantly, feminist standpoint epistemology, which claims that 'women have very different ways of viewing the world' (ibid.) is described with the vital caveat: '*Some* feminists...' (ibid., emphasis added). The careful representation of diversity within feminist scholarship, and the recognition that poststructural theorizing of power and knowledge has been enormously influential in the discipline of IR, so early in an introductory textbook, is refreshing to say the least.

Baylis and Smith offer a similar elucidation of theory in world politics as the introduction to their textbook, arguing that '[i]t is not as if you can say that you do not want to bother with a theory, all you want to do is look at the facts. We believe that this is simply impossible' (Baylis and Smith, 2005, p. 3). However, feminist IR does not feature in their narrative until Smith and Owens's chapter on 'Alternative Approaches to International Theory'. Feminist engagement with IR is characterized as 'originally developed in work on the politics of development and in peace research' and entering into disciplinary debates in the mid-1980s (Smith and Owens, 2005, p. 281). According to the conventional narratives of disciplinary development of IR, the mid-1980s saw the inception of the 'third debate' and 1988, as mentioned above, marked the publication of the *Millennium* special issue on women in International Relations. However, in this representation of feminist International Relations, never forgetting that even the most engaged and curious students tend to read textbooks as vessels of hallowed truth, we argue that the notion that feminism as 'foreign' to IR is sustained.

As represented in Figure 11.1 below, the text by Burchill et al. (2001) mentions gender and/or feminism most frequently. However, it is the Steans and Pettiford (2005) volume that integrates gender most coherently into its representation of International Relations. Table 11.1 shows that every chapter of the Steans and Pettiford textbook mentions gender and/or feminism. While the text is organized rather conventionally, beginning with chapters entitled

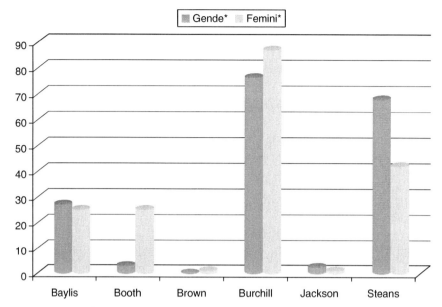

Figure 11.1   Graph illustrating content analysis of gende* and femini* in core IR textbooks

'Liberalism' and 'Realism', these are the only two chapters that can reasonably be described as 'orthodox', with chapters three to nine addressing various 'critical' perspectives. 'Feminist Perspectives', explored in chapter six, sit between 'Postmodernism' and 'Social Constructivism'. Feminist critiques of the theories of IR that Steans and Pettiford represent are skilfully interwoven throughout the text. Furthermore, their representation of feminist perspectives immediately challenges the common sense view that the study of feminism in IR is 'about women' (Steans and Pettiford, 2005, p. 155).

Our investigation of available resources was motivated by a desire to see what the IR textbooks say about gender and/ or feminism. Textbooks are an important representational practice, and we will discuss further below our conclusions regarding using textbooks to teach IR. Just as scheduling a 'week on gender' is problematic, teaching from a textbook that caricatures gendered IR or refuses to acknowledge that 'gender is not a synonym for women' (Carver, 1996) renders student resistance to taking gender seriously difficult to overcome.

En-gendering debate in international relations

Does our scholarship reinforce existing power structures and existing political, social and economic inequalities? ... We bear responsibility for constructing the framework within which our students learn to understand the world and we are accountable for how we name the world, whose voices get heard, and whose are left out.

(ISA 2007 Call for papers)[2]

Students' lack of knowledge about feminist arguments means that often, in 'the week on gender,' the feminist lecturer must explore the various schools or waves of feminism more generally before exploring gendered IR scholarship, precluding discussion that is as in-depth as in other weeks. The week on gender is problematic not only because it encourages students to compartmentalize gender, but also because it is so often relegated to the latter half (or even the final week) of the course. In this section, we explicitly reflect upon practical strategies for teaching gendered IR, although our first recommendation would always be to design courses that incorporate feminist scholarship every week.

First, we suggest that it is essential that we all (feminists and non-feminists alike) problematzse our own politics in teaching. 'To propose a pedagogy is to propose a political vision. In this perspective, we cannot talk about teaching practice without talking about politics' (Simon cited in Gore, 1993, p. 36). Commenting that research on gender 'is just not what I do,' that 'I present all theories objectively and neutrally' or 'I'm a feminist in my personal life, but I don't see what bearing it has upon my scholarship, since I don't write about women' (re)presents theoretical pluralism as apolitical, a position from which it is difficult to debate or transform extant power relations within the discipline. These are all comments that have been made to the authors regarding teaching feminist IR. That said, acknowledging that feminist research is not what one does is an important first step to explaining to students why not, and we would welcome such honesty, coupled with a willingness to teach (and write) as non-experts with regard to feminist approaches. As teachers, we explicitly state our theoretical positions to our students, so that they can better understand the weaknesses, flaws and gaps in our own thinking, and in the hope that they will be similarly self-reflexive.

Second, although it may be counterintuitive for feminists to introduce gender into IR classrooms through an exploration of masculinities (a sentiment with which we have some considerable sympathy, because of its uncomfortable resonance with studying the powerful, as opposed to the 'margins, silences and bottom rungs' that feminists such as Enloe (1996) remind us to illuminate), there are some distinct advantages to this strategy. These advantages manifest both in terms of broadening a gendered focus to include men and women, masculinities and femininities and in terms of centralizing and exposing gendered structures as always and already inherently part of the (construction of) the discipline, rather than grafting gender onto IR (syllabuses) as an afterthought, among a multitude of 'alternative' approaches to world politics. Interestingly, beginning with a discussion of masculinities in IR, of the various structures, hegemonic actors and institutions that are already accepted as central to the discipline – such as policy makers, militaries, regimes and international organizations – has proved more successful and has provoked less overt hostility from students. This also permits a transition from (multiple) masculinities to analysing the gendered (masculinist) structure of the discipline and the dominant approaches therein, and to the wealth of IR research into women and their experiences.

Third, in our own teaching we prioritize gender (and its intersectionality with other [post]structural hierarchies, as we discuss below) as a central concern from the first lecture through a critical examination of the concept of theory, within IR, within academia, and in everyday experiences, following Zalewski (1996). We ask our students for their first impressions of a photograph of the UN Security Council in session. We then juxtapose this picture with signs from public toilet doors (see Figure 11.2 below), in order to highlight that everybody has a theory of gender, whether or not they explicitly reflect upon their theorizing. Returning to the image of the UN Security Council (Figure 11.3 below),

Figure 11.2   Can you make sense of these signs? If so, you have a theory of gender... Photographs © Laura J. Shepherd

Figure 11.3   The United Nations Security Council, as pictured on the homepage at www. un.org/Docs/sc. Image © United Nations, reproduced by kind permission

Useful resources from popular cultural media include:

- *Team America: World Police* (film)
- Any films in the *James Bond* series
- Any fiction books by Tom Clancy
- *24* (television series)
- *The West Wing* (television series)
- Lyrics from contemporary popular music, for example Jessie J's 'Do it Like a Dude', Katy Perry's 'I Kissed A Girl', Eminem feat. Rihanna's 'Love the Way You Lie' and so on… (music videos all available from www.youtube.com)

Figure 11.4 Pop goes world politics? Artefacts to use to explore gender and IR

it is interesting to note how their reactions change, and how much more they have to say, not only about gender, but also about class, race and ethnicity.

The advantage of theorizing the mundane and the everyday as political and international, through, for example, the examination of popular cultural artefacts such as films and advertizements as well as signs on toilet doors (see Figure 11.4 above), is that it allows us to expose the performative and political construction of identity/ies in a way that is accessible to students, given their limited knowledge at the beginning of the course. Furthermore, it permits us to contextualize feminism as being attentive to (for example) the racial and class dimensions of gendered analyses, and to connect feminist approaches with other critical perspectives.

Finally, it is important that, in drawing attention to gender, other hierarchical structures (such as sexuality, race, class, able-bodiedness) do not remain marginalized. We acknowledge the potential for such a project to encourage students to think of subject-positions either as separate and separable categories (variables) of analysis, or alternatively as being represented by a list of identity-signifiers that closes with an 'embarrassed etc' (Butler, 1999, p. 182). However, these intersections are crucial to the understanding of globally gendered dynamics of power, just as, for example, gender is crucial to understanding racial hierarchies. Considering these intersections allows students to identify some of the valid criticisms of gendered IR scholarship, such as the implicit universalism inherent in some branches of feminist IR that has been challenged by non-white non-Western feminists (Mohanty, 1988), thereby at the same time undermining the notion that feminists are critical of everyone except themselves.

As mentioned above, these are strategies that we have found particularly useful in the development of practices that allow us to teach International Relations in a manner faithful to our politics, and our list is by no means exhaustive (see Figure 11.5). Lather suggests, and we concur, that we need

to take responsibility for transforming our own practices so that our empirical and pedagogical work can be less toward positioning our selves as masters [sic] of truth and justice and more toward creating a space where those directly involved can act and speak on their own behalf.

(1991, pp. 163–4).

To us, research-led teaching is inherently related to performing our politics on a daily basis (see also Shaw and Walker [2006, p. 156] who agree that '[i]f by 'activist' we mean to refer to a person engaged in a project of political significance, then presumably it is impossible to be an academic and not an activist'), recognizing that International Relations does not need to be (nor should be) taught as if it is

---

Fun things we have done with our students...

- From online or print media sources, find a selection of images that represent contemporary practices of global politics. In small groups of two to four, discuss the images and prepare a brief presentation for the rest of the group, focusing on the following questions:
  1. How does the image represent bodies?
  2. How does this representation of bodies fit with 'common-sense' understandings of bodies in the world?
  3. Is the image congruent with or disruptive of conventional conceptualizations of sex and gender?
  4. What does the image tell us about global politics?
- Take a trip into the town or city centre (or the centre of campus) and ask people what they think about women's role, or what women do in international politics. Consider any difficulties people might have in giving an answer. Consider the assumptions made about women and about international politics. Think how answers make you think about feminism, about women about international politics.
- Play the video game *America's Army* (www.americasarmy.com) and think about how this makes you feel in connection to militarism, violence, and war. What identity are you producing by playing a soldier at war? Are there connections between gender, soldiering and war? Does it feel masculine or feminine? Why? Do you feel powerful? Are you enjoying it? Does it make you uncomfortable? Why or why not? What do you feel about the enemy/people you are killing? What connection do you feel to the realities of war? What can you *not* think about while playing the game? Are there certain possibilities that are precluded by the parameters of the game? What are they? Do you feel a connection between the game and real practice of war? Why or why not?
- Individually, make a list of the last three things you bought. Think about your motivations for buying them – satisfy need, something to eat, wear etc. Think about how your own consumption practices are embedded in the global politics of gender inequality, and understand how this links you to the global political economy of production and consumption.

Seminar exercises from Shepherd (ed.) 2010, available at http://cw.routledge.com/textbooks/9780415453882/seminar-exercises.asp).

Figure 11.5   Seminar exercises

the sole concern of Secretaries of State, employees of the World Bank, or United Nations Ambassadors. The strategies we propose are pedagogical in focus but have implications for the study and practice of International Relations more broadly: they enable us to teach International Relations as relevant to our everyday lives – and therefore to the everyday lives of our students.

Notes

1. *ISP Pedagogy Forum* (2007), http://onlinelibrary.wiley.com/doi/10.1111/insp.2007.8.issue-3/issuetoc (accessed 10 January 2011).
2. http://www.isanet.org/meetings/call-for-papers-2007.html (accessed 10 January 2011).

References

Ackerley, B. A. (2001), 'Women's Human Rights Activists as Cross-Cultural Theorists', *International Feminist Journal of Politics*, 3 (3), 311–46.

Afshar, H. and Eade, D. (eds) (2004), *Development, Women and War: Feminist Perspectives* (Oxford: Oxfam GB).

Baylis, J. and Smith, S. (eds) (2005), *The Globalization of World Politics* (Oxford: Oxford University Press).

Bergeron, S. (2003), 'The Post-Washington Consensus and Economic Representations of Women in Development at the World Bank', *International Feminist Journal of Politics*, 5 (3), 397–419.

Brown, C. with Ainley, K. (2005), *Understanding International Relations* (Basingstoke: Palgrave Macmillan).

Burchill, S. (2001), 'Introduction' in S. Burchill, R. Devetak, A. Linklater, M. Paterson, C. Reus-Smit and J. True *Theories of International Relations* 2nd edn (Basingstoke: Palgrave Macmillan), pp. 1–28.

Burchill, S., Devetak, R., Linklater, A., Paterson, M., Reus-Smith, C. and True, J. (2001), *Theories of International Relations*, 2nd edn (Basingstoke: Palgrave Macmillan).

Bunch, C. (2004), 'A Feminist Human Rights Lens' *Peace Review*, 16 (1), 43–8.

Butler, J. (1999), *Gender Trouble* (rev. ed) (London: Routledge).

Caprioli, M. (2005), 'Primed for Violence: The Role of Gender Inequality in Predicting Internal Conflict', *International Studies Quarterly*, 49 (2), 161–78.

Caprioli, M. and Boyer, M. (2001), 'Gender, Violence and International Crisis', *Journal of Conflict Resolution*, 45 (4) 503–18.

Carver, T. (1996), *Gender is not a Synonym for Women* (London and Boulder, CO: Lynne Rienner).

Childs, S. and Krook, M. L. (2006), 'Gender and Politics: The State of the Art', *Politics*, 26 (1), 18–28.

Cockburn, C. and Zarkov, D. (eds) (2002), *The Postwar Moment: Militaries, Masculinities, and International Peacekeeping* (London: Lawrence and Wishart).

Dahlerup, D. (2010), 'The Development of Gender and Politics as a New Research Field within the Framework of the ECPR', *European Political Science*, 9, 85–98.

El-Bushra, J. (2007), 'Feminism, Gender and Women's Peace Activism' *Development and Change*, 38 (1), 131–47.

Elson, D. (2002), 'Gender Justice, Human Rights, and Neo-Liberal Economic Policies' in Molyneux, M. and Razavi, S. (eds) *Gender Justice, Development and Rights* (Oxford: Oxford Scholarship Online), 78–115.

Enloe, C. (1996), 'Margins, Silences and Bottom Rungs: How to Overcome the Underestimation of Power in International Relations' in Booth, K, Smith, S and Zalewski, M, (eds) *International Theory: Positivism and Beyond* (Cambridge: Cambridge University Press), pp. 186–202.

Gore, J. M. (1993), *The Struggle for Pedagogies: Critical and Feminist Discourses as Regimes of Truth* (London: Routledge).

Griffin, P. (2007), 'Sexing the Economy in a Neo-liberal World Order: Neo-liberal Discourse and the (Re)Production of Heteronormative Heterosexuality' *British Journal of Politics and International Relations*, 9 (2), 220–38.

Griffin, P. (2007), *Gendering the World Bank: Neoliberalism and the Gendered Foundations of Global Governance* (Basingstoke: Palgrave Macmillan).

Halley, J. (2006), *Split Decisions: How and Why to Take a Break from Feminism* (Princeton, NJ: Princeton University Press).

Handrahan, L. (2004), 'Conflict, Gender, Ethnicity and Post-Conflict Reconstruction' *Security Dialogue*, 35 (4), 429–45.

Higate, P. and Henry, M. (2004), 'Engendering (In)security in Peace Support Operations', *Security Dialogue*, 35 (4), 481–98.

Hill, F., Aboitiz, M. and Poehlman-Doumbouya, S. (2003), 'Nongovernmental Organizations' Role in the Buildup and Implementation of Security Council Resolution 1325' *Signs: Journal of Women in Culture and Society*, 28 (4), 1255–69.

Houvouras, S. and Carater, J. S. (2009), 'The F Word: College Students' Definitions of a Feminist', *Sociological Forum*, 23 (2), 234–56.

Hudson, H. (2000), 'Mainstreaming Gender in Peacekeeping Operations: Can Africa Learn from International Experience?', *African Security Review*, 9 (4), 18–33.

Jackson, R. and Sørenson, G. (2003), *Introduction to International Relations: Theories and Approaches* (Oxford: Oxford University Press).

Joachim, J. (2003), 'Framing Issues and Seizing Opportunities: The UN, NGOs and Women's Rights', *International Studies Quarterly*, 47 (2), 247–74.

Joachim, J. (2007), *Agenda Setting, the UN, and NGOs: Gender Violence and Reproductive Rights* (Georgetown, DC: Georgetown University Press).

Kabeer, N. (2003), *Gender Mainstreaming in Poverty Eradication and the Millennium Development Goals: A Handbook for Policy Makers and Other Stakeholders* (London: Commonwealth Secretariat).

Kandiyoti, D. (2004), 'Post-conflict Reconstruction, 'Democratisation' and Women's Rights', *IDS Bulletin*, 35 (4), 134–6.

Karam, A. (2000), 'Women in War and Peacebuilding: The Roads Traversed, the Challenges Ahead', *International Feminist Journal of Politics*, 3 (1), 2–25.

Kardam, N. (2004), 'The Emerging Global Gender Equality Regime from Neoliberal and Constructivist Perspectives in International Relations', *International Feminist Journal of Politics*, 6 (1), 85–109.

Kofman, E., Raghuram, P., Phizacklea, A. and Sales, R. (2000). *Gender and International Migration in Europe: Employment, Welfare and Politics* (London: Routledge).

Lather, P. (1991), *Getting Smart: Feminist Research and Pedagogy With/In the Postmodern* (London: Routledge).

Mazurana, D., Raven-Roberts, A. and Parpart, J. (eds) (2005), *Gender, Conflict and Peacekeeping* (Plymouth and Lanham MD: Rowman and Littlefield).

McRobbie, A. (2009), *The Aftermath of Feminism: Gender, Culture and Social Change* (London, SAGE).

Melander, E. (2005), 'Gender Inequality and Intra-State Armed Conflict', *International Studies Quarterly*, 49 (4), 695–714.

Mohanty, C. T. (1988), 'Under Western Eyes: Feminist Scholarship and Colonial Discourses', *Feminist Review*, 30, 61–88.

Moran, M. (2006), 'Gender, Identity and the Teaching of British Politics: A Comment', *Politics*, 26 (3), 200–2.

Moser, C. and Clark, F. (eds) (2001), *Victims, Perpetrators or Actors? Gender, Armed Conflict and Political Violence* (London: Zed Books).

Piper, N. (2006), 'Gendering the Politics of Migration', *International Migration Review*, 40 (1), 133–64.

Porter, E. (2003), 'Women, Political Decision-Making and Peace-Building', *Global Change, Peace and Security*, 15 (3), 245–62.

Rajasingham-Senanayake, D. (2004), 'Between Reality and Representation: Women's Agency in War and Post-conflict Sri Lanka', *Cultural Dynamics*, 16 (2/3), 141–68.

Shaw, K. and Walker, R. B. J. (2006), 'Situating Academic Practice: Pedagogy, Critique and Responsibility', *Millennium: Journal of International Studies*, 35 (1), 155–65.

Shepherd, L. J. (2008), *Gender, Violence and Security: Discourse as Practice* (London: Zed Books).

Shepherd, L. J. (2010) (ed.) Online Resources, Seminar Exercises Gender Matters in Global Politics: A Feminist Introduction to International Relations, London and New York: Routledge, available at http://cw.routledge.com/textbooks/9780415453882/seminar-exercises.asp (accessed 2 February 2012).

Silvey, R. (2006), 'Geographies of Gender and Migration: Spatializing Social Difference', *International Migration Review*, 40 (1), 64–81.

Skjelsbæk, I. and Smith, D. (eds) (2001), *Gender, Peace and Conflict* (London: SAGE).

Skjelsbæk, I. and Smith, D. (2001), 'Introduction' in I. Skjelsbæk and D. Smith (eds) *Gender, Peace and Conflict* (London: SAGE), pp. 1–13.

Smith, S. and Baylis, J. (2005), 'Introduction' in J. Baylis and S. Smith (eds) *The Globalization of World Politics* (Oxford: Oxford University Press), pp. 1–18.

Smith, S., Booth, K. and Zalewski, M. (eds) (1996), *International Theory: Positivism and Beyond* (Cambridge: Cambridge University Press).

Smith, S. and Owens, P. (2005), 'Alternative Approaches to International Theory' in Baylis, J. and Smith, S. (eds) (2005) *The Globalization of World Politics* (Oxford: Oxford University Press), 271–96.

Soreanu, R. and Hudson, D. (2008), 'Feminist Scholarship in International Relations and the Politics of Disciplinary Emotion', *Millennium: Journal of International Studies*, 37 (1), 123–51.

Steans, J. and Pettiford, L. with Diez, T. (2005), *Introduction to International Relations: Perspectives and Themes* (Harlow: Pearson Longman).

Stienstra, D. (2000), 'Cutting to Gender: Teaching Gender in International Relations', *International Studies Perspectives*, 1, 233–44.

Weldes, J. et al. (eds) (1999), *Cultures of Insecurity: States, Communities and the Production of Danger* (Minneapolis: University of Minnesota Press).

Zalewski, M. (1996), '"All These Theories yet the Bodies Keep Piling Up": Theories, Theorists, Theorising', in S. Smith, K. Booth and M. Zalewski (eds) *International Theory: Positivism and Beyond* (Cambridge: Cambridge University Press), 340–53

Zalewski, M. (2010), '"I Don't Even Know What Gender Is": A Discussion of the Connections Between Gender, Gender Mainstreaming and Feminist Theory', *Review of International Studies*, 38 (1), 3–27.

12
Contemporary Politics: Teaching the 'Contested Concepts' – International Terrorism Taught to Undergraduate Students in a Multicultural Environment

Knut Roder

Since September 11th, March 11th and the London bombings, global terrorism and with it perceived new realities have increased the interest among undergraduate students to enrol in courses that deal specifically with the phenomena of war, conflict, the use of force in IR and International Terrorism within the Political Science discipline. Students are naturally attracted to classes that deal with controversial topics, as they are aware of their more challenging and contested nature. Subjects such as terrorism are current, controversial, and hold the potential to touch very uncomfortable ground for teachers and students. For this reason, teaching 'sensitive topics' poses additional pedagogical challenges to teachers, in particular if students are from diverse backgrounds and have different personal belief systems. Classes call for a more carefully planned (not to mention, controlled) class structure and greater efforts need to be made to carefully and consciously optimize a positive and tolerant learning atmosphere and classroom environment.

There is no lack of teaching material on the subject; a large amount of books on terrorism in form of monographs, introductions to the subject and course readers are available. However, while there has been an avalanche of new interpretative literature on terrorism since September 11th, there appears to be a gap in pedagogical literature that aims to assist teaching practitioners to develop or apply strategies on how to teach contested concepts effectively to undergraduate students. I believe that teaching contested concepts, such as terrorism, offers great potential for enhancing and facilitating student learning and development of critical thinking skills precisely because of the controversial nature of topics, and that the specifics of teaching contested concepts are well worth being explored further.

Deal with the definitional problems of the subject

The 'concept of terrorism' itself is, of course, fiercely contested, with definitions reaching from Brian Jenkins' all inclusive 'terrorism is the use or the threatened use of force designed to bring about a political change' (Jenkins, 1984) to A. P. Schmid's classic twenty two-component long 100 word definition of the same term (Schmid, 1983) Similarly, arguments over the right to determine classifications and the right to decide who should be labelled a 'terrorist' or 'freedom fighter' or who should determine a 'just cause' creates substantial definitional problems. At the same time, the contested nature of the term involves more frequently the analysis of shades of issues and a degree of personal reflection over moral, value and personal principles that isn't that common when dealing with less contested issues. While the use of violence to bring about political change is rejected in class, the problem lies in the details and definitions that need to be assessed and studied when dealing with contested concepts of this significance. Doing so inevitably forces students to engage in deep critical thinking by reflecting on and judging political goals, examining assumptions, discerning hidden values and evaluating contextual evidence in order to reach any meaningful conclusion. Furthermore, issues of politics of conflict, violence, manipulation and intimidation cannot be studied without linking them strongly to issues of values, race, ethnicity, religion, and economic development as root causes for the continuing basis of conflict and aggression. (Merryfield and Remy, 1995, p. 9)

Deal with the media and an emotionalized public discourse

A highly emotionalized public discourse surrounds the subject of terrorism. This discourse has been strongly picked up by the media, which does not only greatly influence public perception and opinion, but also commonly mixes information with opinionated reporting, extreme generalizations, and 'information underload' (Schulze, 2004). At the same time students rely on managing to find relevant information and assess it critically in order to understand the complexities of international conflict. In the words of Ewbank, information is spread and opinions are formed by a news media that may be 'accurate and valuable as well as misleading or false, evenhanded as well as biased, straight-forward as well as highly manipulative' (Ewbank et al., 2002). When studying contested concepts, the problem of inaccurate or highly emotionalized media reporting of the topic is especially problematic. In fact, emotional attitudes are often paired with anger, and 'when political knowledge is scarce, affective attitudes, which can consist of emotion-driven feelings regarding political figures, government, country, and foreign nations, often assist policy judgment'

(Rankin, 2010, p. 258) Hence, by emphasizing and analysing the importance of the media in class, the topic of terrorism inevitably facilitates and enhances students' media literacy. Instructors should encourage students to use a wide range of media outlets, provide useful vocabulary, lesson ideas, and questions to engage students in becoming more critical consumers of information and to encourage their critical thinking and ability to analyse and draw conclusions from current media outlets. (Ewbank et al., 2002) The aim to 'de-emotionalize' the subject can be greatly enhanced by explicitly drawing on news sources from different countries; trying to distinguish between 'propaganda' and news; discussing the balance between freedom of information and the need for secrecy (for example the role of Wikileaks); and issues of media ownership, to name a few. Clearly, the 'finding *(of)* information (student research) and dealing with multiple or conflicting sources (high-level thinking) are social studies skills that are essential in understanding and making thoughtful judgments about issues in international conflict and peace' and are therefore of great educational value (Merryfield and Remy, 1995, p. 29). There are increasing numbers of publications and films available that deal in detail with the role of the media in the 'war on terror' and run up to the Iraq war and that are well worth being considered to assist teaching media literacy. An additional advantage of using footage of historic 'events' is the fact that 'media-images' are an important aspect of terrorisms' inherent need for media exposure, while the 'feel' for some of historic events of terrorism being passed on much more realistically to the students with the help of video footage.

Another aspect of the emotionalized public discourse on the subject of terrorism relates to the fact that the current 'new war' dimension of terrorism (Kegley and Charles, 2003, pp. 37–52) focus on the problem that wars are increasingly fought over ambiguous and uncertain aims such as the promotion of 'values', the endorsement of 'principles' (such as democracy and freedom), or in turn, the rejection of 'Western values' and the call for the revival of religious principles. (Gilbert, 2003, pp. 1–23) Dealing with these value issues during lectures or seminars further underlines the importance of the creation of an accommodating classroom environment that facilitates open discussion.

Creating an accommodating class room atmosphere

The study of international terrorism offers potential for controversial exchanges of ideas, in particular when students come from a wide variety of cultural, national, and religious backgrounds. Constructing a classroom environment where political debate is respectful, intellectual, productive and free of emotionalized discourse is a precondition for teaching issues that address and raise question about individual morals, values, and personal principles on a direct personal level. This stands in stark contrast to students expressing opinions on 'less emotionalized' or 'less controversial' Political Science themes, such as game theory or principles of party politics, which offer a great degree of individual 'issue detachment' and where student backgrounds don't matter. When studying a sensitive subject such as International Terrorism, the risk of offending that deters students from being open to critical argument and learning is substantial. However, when done successfully, the gains and learning outcomes are potentially huge, including such soft skills as improved critical thinking, better intercultural social skills and intelligence, a more tolerant approach to topics of study as well as fellow students, the widening of students' horizons and greater ability to educate and learn from each other, as well as enhanced communication skills.

While some instructors may choose to set out formal classroom rules in a 'student contract' to be signed by the members of class that stresses mutual respect, tolerance and rules for discussion – depending on the student body – this may not be necessary. In its place, raising student awareness early on and sensitizing them to the potential problems and pitfalls of classroom discussion of 'contested concepts' is, in my experience, sufficient to create an enabling classroom atmosphere.

In fact, sharing responsibility for the creation of a tolerant classroom environment with students should be sufficient to facilitate constructive and positive debating. Surveys recognize that successful tutorials depend on the intellectual and social climate created by instructors, which should ideally be based on a 'moral order expected by both staff and students within which students' are 'ready to express opinions and challenge each others' views' (Entwistle, 2009, p. 84). Students also appreciate a more informal nature to these kinds of classes as it encourages a greater degree of openness, with students feeling freer to contribute to class discussion without fear.

At the same time, teachers need to facilitate a dynamic and pluralistic classroom atmosphere that encourages a marketplace for the exchange of ideas that is a natural part of finding answers to public arguments and that helps students leave their intellectual 'comfort zones'. An encouraging class environment makes it far more likely that students will become active participants in democratic political discourse, as it reassures them that that their positions will be heard and taken seriously. Students need to be allowed and expected to deal with the complexity of issues, in which they are challenged to search for conclusions that require advanced explanations that they must be able to defend properly. In fact, at this stage instructors do well to stress the complexity of the issues studied, to attempt to mediate between the different aspects while remaining ambiguous and able to continue to question all arguments in order to achieve a sense of fairness that fosters a creative atmosphere. Instructor's responsibility lies in offering students knowledge, skills, examples, and opportunities to critically engage with politically charged issues instead of 'picking up and revising the right answer' for assessment.

STUDENT CONTRACT

I, _____, hereby declare that I am aware that [NAME OF COURSE], [NUMBER OF COURSE], deals with a set of strongly contested concepts, and that members of the course must exhibit extreme care in discussing these concepts, in order to foster and facilitate a supportive and productive environment in the classroom. I am aware, furthermore, that the issues and concepts studied in this course often generate sharply divergent explanations, positions and solutions, and that this is particularly likely to occur when students from a wide variety of cultural, national, and religious backgrounds take part in class discussion. By signing this contract, I commit myself to the following:

1. The creation of a classroom environment in which debate is respectful, intelligent, and consistent with University norms of conduct. Classroom debates will be rational, productive, and free of unnecessary emotion. I understand that a commitment to the aims stated above is a precondition for dealing with issues that may affect fellow students' values and moral outlook on a very personal level.
2. Tolerance with regard to the backgrounds and views of all of my fellow students. As a participant in classroom discussions, I will make every effort to formulate my own views in a rational, non-offensive, non-provocative manner.
3. The creation of an intellectual environment that encourages all students to actively take part in classroom debate and allows all of the students' views to be expressed and considered.
4. Acceptance of the ultimate authority of the course instructor in moderating classroom discussion and debate. The instructor will be available to meet with students during his office hours to discuss any special concerns relating to classroom debates or their own progress in the course.

_____   _____
Student's Signature   Instructor's Signature

NOTE: If you have reason to believe that the issues addressed in class may force you to expose too many of your personal thoughts and values, or may otherwise make you feel uncomfortable, this course may not be the best option for you and you therefore ought to consult the instructor personally before signing this contract.

Studying ideally encourages students to put themselves into someone else's position to raise awareness of the complexity of ideas, debates, and policy implications when deciding what is right or wrong. Encouraging students to become aware of their own 'lenses' when viewing problems and to be more aware of and even try those of others in order to understand issues with a different perspective is of great value. This helps encourage students to reach conclusions that are reasoned and informed and that reflect more realistically the complexity of the world around us. Part of a successful learning environment also includes the ability of the teacher to challenge students to defend their positions with intellectual arguments (moving opinion to argument) and by encouraging the systematic examination of reality (empirical reality supporting rational thought).

How to teach the contested concepts and sensitive topics

At the introductory stage of dealing with the contested concepts, instructors should aim at expanding awareness of the inherent limitations of attempts to reduce the subject to a single and simplistic account which overlooks the relationships between conclusions about terrorism's characteristics, causes, and ways to tackle the problem.

Class development should typically involve the specification of objectives followed by selection of learning experiences, and the choice of content to achieve those objectives as well as appropriate instructional methods. Sequencing could start by studying definitions and motivations of terrorism before looking at the historical perspectives of the phenomena. Aims and tactics could be as much a part of the early syllabus as well as an analysis of the causes and psychology behind this type of politically motivated violence. This could then be followed by a detailed study of the various theoretical perspectives (from Just War to Dependency, or the discussion of a clash of civilizations etc.) and their usefulness in enhancing our understanding of the phenomenon. Next in the sequencing, building on the basics of the topic could be the study of more specific and concrete contexts, aims, strategies and outcomes of various cases studies (from Russian Anarchists to Al Qaeda). Finally, the study of strategies and counter-terrorist state measures as well as state-terrorism and future trends in conflict solution and international security could be addressed. The sequencing of these kinds of courses does not require any different logic from that of any other Political Science class and leaves teachers with a great amount of flexibility over their structure of content as well as choice of methods and teaching materials.

For guidance, Merryfield and Remy suggest six factors that help teachers to choose the content and methods for teaching classes on international conflict and peace most effectively (Merryfield and Remy, 1995, pp. 7–9). First and most important is the instructors' knowledge of students' backgrounds, e.g. their nationality, religious upbringing, personal interests or experiences to help when sequencing as well as choosing methods and materials that connect them to the topic, raise their interest, and build on their previous knowledge and skills. Secondly, skills of enquiry and problem solving are taught most effectively when balanced well with the dissemination of contextual knowledge about events and root causes. Thirdly, exposing students solely to content is not sufficient to achieve a satisfying learning outcome. Instead, students should be enabled to learn by engaging in a reflective process in which they make the information their own by evaluating, applying and using the studied contents (Merryfield and Remy, 1995, p. 6). As always, a variety of teaching tools and instructional methods is of great importance.

Merry M. Merryfield and Richard C. Remy (1995, pp. 7–10) six 'assumptions about teaching and learning' that enhance classes dealing with issues of international conflict and peace:

Planning Begins with Knowledge of One's Students

Instructors' knowledge of students' backgrounds, e.g. their nationality, religious upbringing, personal interests or experiences to help when sequencing as well as choosing methods and materials that connect them to the topic, raise their interest, and build on their previous knowledge and skills.

Content is Basic

Skills of enquiry and problem solving are taught most effectively when balanced well with the dissemination of contextual knowledge about events and root causes.

Active, Reflective Learning is Essential

Solely exposing students to content is not sufficient to achieve a satisfactory learning outcome. Instead, students should be enabled to learn by engaging in a reflective process in which they make the information their own by evaluating, applying and using the studied content.

Attention to Values Is Necessary

Social studies instruction contains substantial expressions of values and deals with controversial issues. Effective instruction encourages students to understand that differences in values, gender, race, ethnicity, religion, national origin, or economic development remain the bases for conflict, discrimination, and aggression.

Instruction Must Have Variety

Employing a variety of teaching tools and methods best addresses diverse student needs and learning styles as well as stimulates learning. It also enables students to demonstrate their strengths while working on their weaknesses, and at the same time encourages teachers to improve constantly their teaching by looking for new materials and integrating new methods.

Content, Methods and Educational Goals Are Connected

Teachers should take account of the relationship between teaching content, educational goals, and the methods planned for instruction. It is useful to aim at a direct relationship between teaching methods and content, skills, and attitudinal objectives. While lecturing can be an excellent means to share a large amount of factual information with students, teachers need to be aware that educational goals are best met by employing additional teaching techniques to enhance students' thinking skills.

Teachers are well advised to teach terrorism with a detached and dispassionate critical perspective aiming at keeping their personal opinion to a minimum. This approach helps at times to play moderately the 'Devil's advocate', provoke interest, arouse controversy, and educate by demonstrating the inadequacy of simplistic theories, stereotypical images and black and white answers.

It is important to avoid leaving sensitive issues out of the syllabus. Such issues are of particular learning value when approached and dealt with in the right manner. Furthermore, students have partly chosen the class in order to be challenged and to deal with contested concepts.

For example, one such problematic and difficult issue is the study of the current discussion surrounding the use of 'torture' as linked to the 'War on Terror'. The defense of 'water boarding' by former US President George W. Bush in his 2010 memoirs, which describes it as a helpful interrogation technique that foiled further terrorist attacks, makes this discussion of the topic even more relevant (*Guardian*, 10 Nov. 2010). Contrasting arguments in favor of the use of torture as made by Alan M. Dershowitz (2002) in his book *Making Terrorism Work* with those against made by Alex Gibney in his film documentary *Taxi to the Dark Side* (2008) can be of great use. While Dershowitz defends the 'controlled' and 'regulated' use of torture in a 'safe' environment as justified and necessary when greater harm can be prevented, Gibney's film condemns 'severe' interrogation techniques as inhumane, unjustifiable and of questionable utility.

Firstly, students are requested to familiarize themselves with and attempt to understand the arguments made by Alan M. Dershowitz (2002) in his book *Making Terrorism Work*, in particular his 'case for torturing the ticking bomb terrorist'. Secondly, those points are contrasted with the less rhetorical and theoretical assessment of the use of torture on Al Qaeda suspects presented in Alex Gibney's *Taxi to the Dark Side* (2007). Here, the use of contrasting images ensures that a wide spectrum of issues that need to be considered and evaluated has been raised. Both the reading as well as the film are, of course, analysed and discussed in class, with the validity of the arguments being assessed in detail.

Lecturing

Due to the lack of formal pedagogical training provided by most Political Science (International Relations) doctoral programmes (Buehler and Marcum, 2007, pp. 21–38) instructors teaching philosophies, styles, and strategies largely reflect more than anything their personal experiences, personalities and identities. The answer to how to teach 'sensitive topics' successfully is, of course, closely related to what is required for the successful teaching of any political science and international relations subject. Here, lectures are an excellent means of conveying large amounts of factual information. However, a variety of instructional methods should be explored to help establish a relationship between the specific subject content and ways in which students are helped to engage with a variety of ideas in order to develop their own understanding. (Entwistle, 2009, p. 3)

Seminar/class room discussion

The development of a class-room atmosphere of respectful, intellectual, and productive engagement is a precondition for validating and empowering student input. Students must be reassured that all types of questions and comments are highly welcome.

In order to relate and increase the relevance of the study of wider theories, principles, and the history of current affairs, it is of great benefit to start classes with allowing students to raise news items that they judge relevant to the class. This exercise encourages students to study current affairs outside of class, as well as enabling them to introduce subjects they feel are related. In this way, issues can be successfully contextualized and explained; additional information can be provided by the instructor and issues can be linked to learning outcomes. This exercise also gives a very 'current here and now' feel to the classroom experience.

Research papers and presentations

Research papers are a great way for students to become 'specialist' on a specific area of study and to look in greater depth at one specific 'terrorist' organization's aims, motivation and strategies, and apply classroom interpretations and theory to their activities.

In my experience, case studies of a large variety of terrorist actors covering the entire spectrum of what could be, but not necessarily should be, called 'a terrorist' are a helpful teaching tool. The structure of the paper and presentation are set out in the instructions to guide students in investigating and learning about the complexity of what causes have led to the foundation of their group and in analysing its aims, strategy, and ideology.

Students learn to link the group to the international arena, look at its impact and apply studied definitions and theoretical lenses. The case study range is determined by the instructor with the aim of reflecting a balanced and wide international variety of organizations, waves, root causes, outcomes and time frames covered (for example from the activities of the Black Hand, ETA, Contras to the ALF). After having written their research papers a group presentation is a great way for them to check and reflect their own research findings. Students who have drawn the same organizations agree on key content and prepare a common classroom presentation of their research findings by synthesizing what they have learned and completing the group's assignment of presenting their key findings to the rest of the class. Group presentations help students to focus on the causation of terrorism by offering to other students an in-depth analysis of a 'wide variety of sources' (Schulze, 2004, p. 184). It also enables students to detach themselves from previous stereotypes and engage in the reasoning and multilayered issues of the previously unknown. This way a collegial class room atmosphere of learning together is being enhanced while students are able to be briefed by each other on the variety of specific organizations that could be loosely labelled as terrorist.

Students are asked to view and analyse the activities of 'their' terrorist organization and the issues surrounding it from different angles in order to help fellow students understand the activity's context, causes and actions. Instructors should encourage students to risk expressing their views and having them accepted, but also being prepared to accept critical responses (from the class or instructor).

Audio visual tools

In addition to the reading material, due to the lack of authentic research materials as well as the obvious inability to research terrorist organizations directly, an increased use of audio visual tools such as documentaries (DVDs) for teaching are well justified. For example, the four-part documentary *The Age of Terror* (Discovery Channel, 2004) enables students to come face to face with terrorist incidences, victims, former terrorists, and their interrogators explaining their motivations and sides of the story. At the same time, students appreciate the use of visual information content to experience what cannot be transmitted as easily with the help of reading or following lectures. As previously mentioned, terrorism is by default a highly media-driven phenomenon where terrorists depend on media images and choose their targets according to their symbolic or media impact value. The coverage of 'anti-colonial terrorism', 'the new left' wave, as well as 'religiously' motivated terrorism and 'state sponsored terrorism' are extremely helpful tools for students to visualize, contextualize and assess information that adds to their reading, research and classroom experience of the subject. For example, 'the Age of Terror' episode focusing on 'anti-colonial terrorism' shown early in the course has proven to be a real ice-breaker that challenges students with a different ('new') emotional logic to terrorism that usually helps them to be more open to the different textures of the problem, instead of the common mixing of all aspects of the phenomena into one 'under-differentiated' block. Helping to differentiate, even if only for a minute, to sympathize and relate to certain causes, improves the ability to think critically about the various aspects of the subject.

Documentaries, such as *The Age of Terror, Taxi to the Dark side, Buying the War*, 2007 or *Weapons of Mass Deception*, 2006, to name a few, offer crucial authentic footage of events and issues to the classroom. This justifies the more frequent use of audio-visual material for this kind of issues than would usually be advisable for political science subjects.

Researching terrorism

Although this Chapter deals with the teaching of International Terrorism to undergraduate students, the issue of research on the topic must be briefly mentioned, as some undergraduates may want to set out and write an undergraduate thesis on this topic. Students wanting to research issues linked to terrorism must be aware of two substantial problems:

Firstly, in the words of A.P Schmid,

> there are probably few areas in the social science literature in which so much is written on the basis of so little research. Perhaps as much as 80 per cent of the literature is not research-based in any rigorous sense; instead, it is too often narrative, condemnatory, and prescriptive'.
>
> (Schmid and Jongman, 1988, pp. 177–9).

> Furthermore, 'primary source material is seldom examined and cited, defying the most basic tenet of social science research. A triumvirate composed of the media, government and academic has to a great extent proscribed the course of terrorism studies.
>
> (Schulze, 2004, p. 163)

One reason for the lack of reliable research data has of course been the secretive nature of terrorist organizations.

A second problem that undergraduate researchers may face lies potentially in the field of anti-terrorist legislation. Arrests of students undertaking research on terrorist organizations have occurred in the past, in response to, for example, having downloaded 'Al Qaeda' manuals for study, which raises an entirely new spectrum of issues in regards to academic freedom in light of the 'right' to access and research terrorism materials for study and analysis (Nilson, Pupavac and Rnez, 2008). One way to avoid students downloading data that may fall under state-enforced 'prevention of terrorism acts' would be an explicit warning by class instructors for students to avoid navigating to and downloading material from 'seemingly' problematic web-pages that may be advocating the use of terrorism, or similarly joining their questionable e-mail lists. This is of course a grey, uncertain area, and an appeal to students' common sense should be sufficient. Furthermore, instructors can attempt to offer access to books that pre-summarize or contain excerpts of materials from terrorist organizations' manifestos, writings and manuals that should be sufficient for undergraduate research purposes (for example Laqueur, 2007).

Clearly, if students are conducting primary research in this area, in particular, for more advanced Masters' level courses, universities and students alike are faced with difficult ethical questions. It is unlikely that universities would give ethical approval to a Master's level student conducting research which involves interviewing ex-combatants. However, in the case of undergrad level teaching with its limited research component, the likelihood of this posing a major problem is highly unlikely.

Role of the teacher

By maintaining a degree of detachment from the material used (reading and visual) during teaching, instructors create space for intellectual exploration. As previously mentioned, teaching contested concepts requires increased awareness that class content, teaching materials and lectures may be experienced by some students as offensive as they deal, for example, with religiously-motivated violence linked to a specific faith to which students may belong. As changing class content or cutting religious violence out of the syllabus should not be an option, materials must be carefully chosen to facilitate a positive classroom environment.

At the same time, instructors are well advised to focus on their role as nonparticipant moderators to student discussion, intervening only when the class discourse becomes emotionalized or additions and corrections to stated factual information are required.

Role-modelling should be employed as a pedagogical tool, with the instructor's political views being expressed predominantly in order to teach how to construct, present and defend views in an intelligent manner. In my experience, instructors should focus on explaining how views were formed, rather than justifying them.

A moderate measure of 'Devil's advocacy' as a pedagogic tool is fully justified and adds to the attempt to remain as detached as possible from the definitions of contested concepts and ideas. A certain degree of a 'Devil's advocacy' role can actually reassure students who hold different positions from the majority of class that they are understood, respected, but also that they may be challenged (without having to fear reprisals), as instructors' positions are multiple and shifting. This helps, furthermore, to maintain the instructor's class-room credibility when challenging students to back up views that they have expressed.

Having said all that, one should avoid actively hiding or refusing to share views and opinions as an instructor when students explicitly ask for them to be shared. This refusal could be easily perceived as patronizing by some students, who do, of course, deserve an openly engaging instructor who shares his or her views when asked. At the same time, however, the teacher may feel the need to emphasize that his or her opinion does not matter and is open to be challenged.

Assessment and the grading papers

The nature of assessment tasks, questions posed, and the feedback given to students, influences significantly the approach that they adopt towards studying, and the degree to which they reach a satisfying level of personal understanding of a studied subject. In the words of Entwistle, 'the assessment procedure shapes the learning and studying process, which is why emphasis should be placed on formative assessment i.e. ongoing assessment designed specifically to encourage learning'. (Entwistle, 2009, p. 85) Although opinions vary on the arbitrariness of awarding participation marks, it is fair to remind students that their attendance and engagement in class matters greatly. As mentioned previously, a brief discussion of 'relevant current events' at the beginning of each class dealing loosely with terrorism, conflict and war contributes greatly to the students' ability to contextualize and link current news to the more historic, theoretical and analytical aspects of the class content. For this they need to be reminded, with or without participation marks, that their ability to contribute to such discussions and their effort to read up on related current affairs will be recognized.

With regard to grading research papers, student assessment grades should not reflect the evaluation of 'right' or 'wrong' conclusion statements. Instead, of greater importance is the fact that students have reached conclusions in a rational, reasonable, and empirically driven manner using a sufficient variety of research and sources. In fact, answers to research questions should contain: (a) a logical coherence to the argument, (b) employ supporting evidence and examples (c) and present clearly and understandably the issue and lines of argument. For this reason, teachers' first and foremost aim should be to correct factual errors as well as to comment on shortcomings in the above mentioned criteria.

Tackling tension in the classroom

If attempts to preempt classroom tension by creating a positive atmosphere, as previously discussed, have failed, instructors are well advised to monitor and respond swiftly to any increased tension. An immediate strategy which can be employed by the lecturer in case of problems is to shift and widen discussion from the details of a specific conflict to an enquiry about more general principles of conflict.

However, medium and long term strategies need to be employed if classroom tensions persist. Early intervention is required when student opinions and points of view are repeatedly expressed in a provocative or aggressive manner. It is important that the instructor never merely "overhear" problematic remarks. The majority of students will rightly be, looking for a response from their lecturer. One can be certain that arguments between class members that become personal are rarely a one-time occurrence, and will inevitably reoccur if not addressed early on.

Of course, every kind of class tension is different, as it depends strongly on the individuals involved. Ideally, the instructor's response turns classroom tensions into a tool to raise students' awareness of what lessons this strained classroom atmosphere can offer about the wider (and far more complex) dynamics of negative or aggressive discourse as a factor that causes conflict within society. If possible, call on students to step back from tension-creating arguments and move towards a less emotional discourse. Also, allow them to assess how opinions and views expressed consciously or unconsciously by members of the class inevitably impact upon others by provoking tension and strong reactions. If possible, encourage students to suggest procedures or rules that aim to depolarize emotional discourse and ease tensions. This way the class is empowered to enforce its own code of conduct and is enabled to move beyond the previous 'unacceptable' level of tension.

If tension rises among a group of students, it may be wise, depending as always on the specific circumstances and situation, to respond by arranging meetings with those involved on an individual basis, in order to reflect with them on their impact on the classroom dynamics and to search for solutions. Similarly, if the instructor can identify distinct groups of students who consistently express themselves in a tense and unacceptable manner which continually leads to hostile disagreements, it is best to address them after class, or in extreme cases to terminate the class, identify the individuals, and ask them to stay in order to challenge their attitude and unacceptable behavior head on.

Always remind students of the responsibility which they have to each other, which is to foster an educational environment that allows for 'neutral' academic enquiry, with everybody involved being able to express their opinions freely and without fear. Also attempt to convince students that they should aim to fully understand "the other side of the coin" in order to obtain the multiple perspectives which are sought-after and necessary in order to contextualize the causes and effects of conflict.

Without wanting to rule out more forceful means of discouraging those individuals who consistently refuse to participate in civil dialogue and perpetuate tension-creating behaviors, the instructor's priority should always lie in the attempt to discourage and ease tension through dialogue.

Conclusions

Finding the right balance in methods as well as approaches used when teaching contested concepts such as terrorism depends ultimately on the individual personalities of the students, their backgrounds, nationalities, degree of interest in the subject and previous knowledge. This is something that can be evaluated and determined only by the human factor of competent and sensitive instruction.

Overall, teaching classes on 'sensitive topics' for undergraduate students' calls for a carefully planned classroom environment. Instructors are required to make a greater effort to consciously optimize a positive and tolerant learning atmosphere in the classroom and more frequently update content and methods. And finally, teaching classes on 'contested concepts' is facilitated by teaching with a more detached and dispassionate, facilitating perspective than would usually be employed. There is no optimal way of teaching 'contested concepts', but there is real value in exchanging ideas and experiences. I hope that this Chapter has been a helpful contribution to an ongoing and needed discussion that will encourage the further sharing of ideas and experiences on how to teach these types of concepts and classes.

A guide to further reading/watching

Dershowitz, A. M. (2002), *Why Terrorism Works: Understanding the Threat – Responding to the Challenge* (New Haven: Yale University Press).
Elworthy, S. and Rifkind, G. (2006), *Making Terrorism History* (London: Rider).
Entwistle, N. (2009), *Teaching for Understanding at University: Deep Approaches and Distinctive Ways of Thinking* (Series: Universities into the 21st Century) (Basingstoke: Palgrave Macmillan).
Kegley, J. and Charles, R. (2003), *The New Global Terrorism: Characteristics, Causes, Controls* (Upper Saddle River, NJ: Prentice Hall).
Robins, R. S. and Post, J. M. (1997), *Political Paranoia: Psychopolitics of Hatred* (New Haven: Yale University Press).
Alex Gibney (dir.) (2007), *Taxi to the Dark Side* (USA: DVD).
Discovery Channel (2004), *The Age of Terror* (Lace: DVD).
Danny Schechter (dir.) (2006), *Weapons of Mass Deception* (Supersonic Films: DVD).

References

All websites cited here were last accessed on 5 September 2011.
Allen, D. I. and White, R. T. (1980), 'Learning Objectives and Teaching Strategies', *Canadian Journal of Education*, 5 (2), 23–42.
Buehler, M. J. and Marcum, A. S. (2007), 'Looking into the Teaching Crystal: Graduate Teaching and the Future of Political Science', *Journal of Political Science Education*, 3, 21–38.
Moyer, B. (2007), 'Buying the War' Bill Moyer Journal, (http://www.pbs.org/moyers/journal/btw/watch.html).
Dershowitz, A. M. (2002), *Why Terrorism Works: Understanding the Threat – Responding to the Challenge* (New Haven: Yale University Press).
Claire, H. and Holden, C. (eds) (2007), *The Challenge of Teaching Controversial Issues* (Stoke on Trent: Trentham Books Ltd).
Collins, J. and Glover, R. (eds) (2002), *Collateral Language: A User's Guide to America's New War* (New York & London: New York University Press).
Elworthy, S. and Rifkind, G. (2006), *Making Terrorism History* (London: Rider).
Entwistle, N. (2009), *Teaching for Understanding at University: Deep Approaches and Distinctive Ways of Thinking* (series: Universities into the 21st Century) (Basingstoke: Palgrave Macmillan).
Ewbank, W. (2002), 'Teaching Media Literacy through the Topic of Terrorism – Lessons and Resources on Media Literacy for the Middle and High School Classroom', Washington Commission for the Humanities, World Affairs Council, Seattle (http://www.world-affairs.org/globalclassroom/curriculum/MediaLiteracy.pdf).
Gilbert, P. (2003), *New Terror, New Wars* (Washington D.C.: Georgetown University Press).
Jenkins, B. (1984), 'The Who, What, Where, When and Why of Terrorism', (paper presented at Detroit Police Department Conference on Urban Terrorism, Detroit, MI, November 1984).

Kegley, J. and Charles, R. (2003), *The New Global Terrorism: Characteristics, Causes, Controls* (Upper Saddle River, NJ: Prentice Hall).

Laqueur, W. (ed.) (2007), Voices of Terror: Manifestos, Writings and Manuals of AL Qaeda, Hamas, and Other Terrorists from Around the World and Throughout the Ages (New York: Reed Press).

Merryfield, M. M. and Remy, R. C. (1995), *Teaching About International Conflict and Peace* (New York: State University of New York Press).

Nilsen, A. G., Pupavac, V. and Rnez, B. (2008), 'The Nottingham Two and the War on Terror: Which of us Will Be Next?' *The Times Higher Education*, 5 June 2008, (http://www.timeshighereducation.co.uk/story.asp?storycode=402258).

Rankin, D. M. (2010), 'Processing the War in Iraq While Learning About American Politics', *Journal of Political Science Education*, 6 (3), 258–73.

Robins, R. S. and Post, J. M. (1997), *Political Paranoia: Psychopolitics of Hatred* (New Haven: Yale University Press).

Rogers, P. (2005), 'A Independent Consultancy Assesses Al-Qaida's Progress and Prospects for 2005 and Beyond', (http://www.opendemocracy.net/conflict/swish_2523.jsp).

Schmid, A. P. and Jongman, A. J. (1988), *Political Terrorism: A New Guide to Actors, Concepts, Data, Bases, Theories, and Literature* (New Brunswick: Transaction Books).

Schmid, A. P. (1983), *Political Terrorism: A Research Guide to Concepts, Theories, Data Bases and Literature* (New Brunswick: Transaction Books).

Schulze, F. (2004), 'Breaking the Cycle: Empirical Research and Postgraduate Studies on Terrorism' in Silke, Andrew (ed.) *Research on Terrorism: Trends, Achievements and Failures* (London: Frank Cass), pp. 161–85.

Gibney, A. (dir.) (2007), *Taxi to the Dark Side* (USA: DVD).

Discovery Channel (2004), *The Age of Terror* (Lace: DVD).

Schechter, D. (dir.) (2006), *Weapons of Mass Deception* (Supersonic Films: DVD).

Norton-Taylor, R. and Black, I. (2010), 'British Deny George Bush's Claims that Torture Helped Foil Terror Plots, *Guardian* 10 Nov. Available at (http://www.guardian.co.uk/world/2010/nov/09/british-deny-bush-claims-foil-terror).

13

Teaching Race and Ethnicity: Towards an Engaged, Anti-Racist Pedagogy

Steve Spencer

In this chapter I will discuss the teaching of 'race' and ethnicity and make some suggestions which might assist teachers new to the issues, or seeking to enhance their practice in the classroom. 'Race'[1] and ethnicity are amongst the most complex and contentious terms in the social sciences; inherently political and contested, and raising particular challenges in the classroom. The key concern for teachers is not only the content chosen or how such knowledge is imparted (although these are significant) but about the nature of the subject as inherently personal and politically sensitive. The challenge is twofold: firstly, how to interpret the meanings of 'race' and ethnicity in ways that do not simply reproduce a narrowly ethnocentric value system, in ways which expose the mythical nature of race and move towards a position which is positive and anti-racist. Secondly, how to engage and work with students in a way which avoids delivering some worthy 'sermon on the mount' but instead fosters an atmosphere of mutual learning. To these ends I have revisited some of the strategies and suggestions outlined in *Reflections on Practice: Teaching Race and Ethnicity in Further & Higher Education* (Spencer and Todd, 2006). This was a text devoted to the question of how best to address these issues in a multi-ethnic classroom. The collective experiences of the contributors to that volume supplied some insights which are worth re-iterating and extending here. The lessons conveyed included: the importance of avoiding ones own ethnocentricity or that embedded in academic culture, learning from the dynamic issues unfolding in the classroom, and staying flexible and innovative to create greater engagement with the issues. In the spirit of these lessons, the immediate purpose of this chapter is to provide an active agenda for those wishing to engage in a reflective manner with the teaching of race and ethnicity.

When the personal is political

Intuitively, many educators in the Social Sciences feel that a programme which does not include coverage of these areas is distinctly lacking. However, for

179

teaching to reflect the reality of inequality and racism it cannot be taught 'at arms length' because members of the class (indeed sometimes the whole class) may be only too aware of the personal, family and community damage which stem from a racist value system. There are real consequences of racism which affect not only Black and Minority Ethnic (BME) groups but the white majority culture too.

Pence and Fields (1992) relate that 'resistance, paralysis and rage' are three responses from students when issues of inequality are raised. This highlights the fact that students (as well as tutors) of course come often with a good deal of emotional baggage; there can be resistance, denial and anger; at time teachers need to manage anger and ensure that individuals aren't treated as scapegoats. Having witnessed tensions in the multi-ethnic classes taught I began to realize that these feelings and reactions themselves presented opportunities (risky ones perhaps):

> ...to show that this was not mere sophistry an instrumental exercise in modular learning with its prescribed outcomes and indicators, but a power-ful and defining heartfelt force which can separate, corrode self-esteem and destroy lives.
>
> (Spencer in Spencer and Todd, 2006, p. xx).

To rely on the content of a set curriculum and adopt a *laissez faire* approach to the *process* of students' learning is clearly unacceptable. In addition, it becomes clear that students (and lecturers too) face some particular challenges in this area. First, the field of study is perceived as a potential minefield for the unwary; there is anxiety that we may infringe some barely understood bound-ary. This sense of not knowing the ground rules is one frequently commented upon by students and lecturers. Kohn suggests that

> ...we feel that the subject is covered by a taboo, but we don't know exactly what the rules of the taboo are. It seems important if not obligatory, to discuss cultural differences, but dangerous even to mention physical differences.
>
> (Kohn, 1996, p. 1 – also cited in Spencer and Todd, 2006, p. xiii)

Hence, while certain kinds of knowledge and theory might be addressed the way in which understanding is arrived at is often more dependent on working through the personal values and expressions which emerge from the classroom and its unique dynamics. The relatively privileged position of most teachers suggests that there is a duty not to side-step the hard questions, Mark Christian (2007) asked a question which goes to the roots of the issue:

> ...how do you measure someone's consciousness and her/his capacity to see through White privilege in order to make a concrete social difference in eradicating racialized discrimination in society?
>
> (Christian, 2007, p.22–3).

Thus the curriculum we inherit or construct for a course of study in this area is only one part of an often politically charged interaction, but this is not to suggest teaching race and ethnicity entails abandoning key principles of teaching and learning, making an impassioned plea for anti-racist consciousness. It proceeds like most courses with measured practices; learning outcomes and assessment criteria *etcetera*, but teachers need to recognize that this is a political subject in a different way from, for example, political constitution, it is one which affects people at the more immediate interpersonal level.

Know your history

So, a tendency to treat race and ethnicity as abstract, depersonalized concepts largely misses the point and might be alienating to members of a class who have varied experiences as members of a multi-ethnic society. These concepts are historically important; legitimating colonial exploitation from which the current world order has been shaped. In teaching, history is a vital element in forging understanding of where we are today. It often comes as a shock how little is known or how selectively the facts of even the recent past are remembered. The successive colonial 'adventures' in the Middle East are a case in point. At the time of writing this Coalition forces (with UN and Arab League agreement) have implemented a 'no fly zone' in Libya to curb Gaddafi's forces and their proclaimed intention to crush a popular rebellion which has divided the country. However, less than ten years ago Gaddafi was being lauded as a hero and Italy, France and UK along with many other European powers exported arms to the regime for many years (*Guardian* Datablog, 2011) Interestingly these three countries, which have profited by hundreds of millions of euros in arms exports, had each played a colonial or governing role in Libya in the twentieth century. But the fact is vast areas of the world were once owned by a handful of ruthlessly competitive European powers which extracted wealth from their overseas possessions, building a framework of oppression which is arguably *the* foundation of the experience of civil life in much of the world today.

> One of the most striking events in the recent history of mankind is the expansion throughout the entire world of most European peoples. It has brought about the subjugation and, in some instances, the disappearance of virtually every people regarded as backward, archaic, or primitive. The colonial movement of the nineteenth century was the most important in magnitude, the most fraught with consequences, resulting from this European expansion. It overturned in a brutal manner the history of the peoples it subjugated.
>
> (Balandier in Wallerstein, 1974, p. 34)

These events; the scramble and plunder of colonialism, have had long lasting consequences which still resonate through current world events. For this reason teaching 'race' requires an understanding of the historical context in which the experience of ethnicity and racialization was constructed:

> When we consider teaching 'race' in the social sciences, in relation to the British education scene, there needs to an understanding of how Black presence has developed since at least the post-WW II era. Without having an historical account the teacher will be bereft of a useful framework in which to develop her knowledge in the classroom.
>
> (Christian, 2007, p. 16)

Indeed (as Christian goes on to argue) teaching about 'race' needs to go further and examine the foundations of colonial powers and the use (some argue the invention) of 'race' or 'race-making' to legitimate the exploitation of most of the world by these expanding global powers. Charles Lemert has argued that 'race' is perhaps the most important and foundational structural divide of modernity, commenting:

> Race, if it can be taught at all, must be taught from within an honest recognition of the historical experiences of those affected by the violence of the capitalist world system from which most, if not all, teachers benefit.
>
> (Todd and Farrar, 2007, p.15).

So the important thing to keep in mind is that this is not a subject area dedicated solely to discussions of 'otherness'. Much teaching of 'race' issues may fall into this snare of cataloguing minority ethnic groups and their cultural mores. Ethnicity applies to all and shapes the majority culture in no small way as history shows only too well:

> Without the false doctrine of racial difference as a cultural balm to the white souls with their tepid liberal sensibilities, there would be no colonial system, no Atlantic trade, no bourgeois family, no homosexual panic.
>
> (Lemert, 2006, p.14)

In addition, it is impossible to talk accurately about the invention of 'race' without understanding it as an aspect of economics:

The British don't become slave traders and slavers because they are racists – they become racist because they use slaves for great profit in the Americas, and devise a set of attitudes about black people that justifies what they have done. The real engine behind the slave system is economics. Africans are items of trade, they are things that are bought, that are sold, that are bequeathed, that are inherited; they're like other items of trade. And once you've got that established both on the slave ships – of which there are thousands leaving British ports, and once you've got that established on the plantations, and once you've got that established as a basis for expanding British wealth, how can you argue that somehow or other the great inferiority of black people isn't built into fundamental cultural values of the British. (Prof James Walvin (2009) *Racism – A History*, part 1 The Colour of Money BBC 4)

   The series is an excellent teaching resource (Racism: a History, Executive Producer: David Okuefuna, BBC 4)

Such discussions then might examine the way in which hierarchical structuring was a feature of the first comprehensive classifications of the natural world, and that such ordering fitted well with expanding racial taxonomies, appearing to give scientific validity to degraded stereotypes and often distorted characteristics of non-Europeans, a process which tended to help legitimize the view of these outsiders as savage and threatening or inferior in intellect and morality hence a powerful discourse in the cause of economic and colonial expansion.

Recognizing 'race' as a floating signifier

Following on from this point, and the numerous lessons from history which demonstrate the use of 'race' in legitimating colonial exploitation, the concept might usefully be presented as part of a hegemonic process by which difference is *guaranteed*. It would have been very difficult to square a morally superior position with the infra-human (Gilroy, 2004) brutality of slavery, if African slaves and indigenous peoples were viewed as equals granted full humanity. As Montesquieu observed in 1748 'It is impossible for us to suppose these creatures to be men, because, allowing them to be men, a suspicion would follow, that we ourselves are not Christian". The irony implicit in this statement reflects the adoption and hardening of a process of classification which seventeenth-century naturalists like Linnaeus and Blumenbach constructed, linking mankind into a hierarchy of life on earth and attaching crude stereotypes of moral character to generalized physical types based on colour.

   In an influential video lecture Stuart Hall (1996) suggested that race is a 'floating signifier', a discursive construct, which functions like language. This construct serves to *guarantee* that difference is genuine. In the name of this expedient discourse the exploited victims of colonialism were often subject to barbarous treatment. There are many examples; the Belgian Congo was one of the most extreme cases with the impact of genocidal colonialist policies leading to the deaths of possibly ten million. (see Hochschild, 1998) The scale of these atrocities and the lack of remorse reflect the perception of the colonial 'others' as not fully human, as 'unpeople' a term Curtis (2004) uses to describe the civilian deaths in Iraq, as bodies without rights.

Hall argues that since the Renaissance race has been subject of successive discourses: religion, anthropology and finally science, each of which attempted to prove its reality. Attempts to find evidence for racial difference still arise from time to time even though there is a consensus amongst scientists that race is a spurious term with no credibility as a biological category. However, race serves an instrumental purpose as Kenan Malik (2002, p. 5) notes: 'The discourse of race emerged as a means of reconciling the conflict between the ideology of equality and the reality of the persistence of inequality.'

Furthermore, the important point is that this construct of 'race' is constantly changing to meet the political contingencies of the day. Goldberg's (1992) work has demonstrated that the concept has a long and complex history of shifting meanings '...parasitic on theoretical and social discourses for the meaning it assumes at given historical moments...' (Goldberg, 1992, p. 553) In teaching, I believe this expedient role of race is a crucial aspect to get across to students because it clearly demonstrates the illusory and pernicious nature through which race serves the interests of power; and that while it has no essential reality it rapidly shifts to capture new objects fuelling and legitimating new forms of racism. Take this example cited by the Institute for Race Relations:

In an article for the *Guardian* just before the 2010 general election, Gary Younge wrote about how Labour had left a 'more open-minded place' he argued that the connection between immigration and race in the public psyche had 'finally ruptured'. The movements of people and the colour of people were no longer routinely confused. Though xenophobia, religious intolerance and racism now bled into one another the fault lines had 'clearly shifted from colour to culture, race to religion, language and ethnicity'.[20] Our research suggests that rather than there being a clear national shift from a racism based around colour to one based around culture, it is more useful to see the UK as now witnessing an ever-expanding mosaic of different racisms based on different local conditions, including xeno-racism against foreigners who happen to be white. (Harmit Athwal, Jenny Bourne and Rebecca Wood, 2010, pp. 14–15)

This nature of 'race' which makes it elusive and mercurial can be seen in the rapid changes in the context in which race and racism are manifest. The suggestion in the above is especially interesting as it highlights the possibility that race and racism are applicable even when detached from the physical reality of skin pigmentation. The discussion of what constitutes 'race' as opposed to 'ethnicity' is commonly cited in these terms: race is... 'socially defined but on the basis of physical criteria.' While ethnicity is: '...socially defined but on the basis of cultural criteria' (Van den Berghe, 1967, p. 9). While one might assume that the language of race would be resisted by academics and those with a critical perspective, as Ratcliffe (2004, pp. 23–4) points out it can be demonstrated: 'even amongst social scientists, that contemporary African Americans are a different 'race' from whites of European origin. Differences between white Americans and those of other (non African) heritages are seen in terms of ethnicity...' But in the example above, displaced and dispossessed white European migrants are claimed to demonstrate a new form of racism:

> It is a racism, that is, that cannot be colour-coded, directed as it is at poor whites as well, and is therefore passed off as xenophobia, a 'natural' fear of strangers. But in the way it denigrates and reifies people before segregating and/or expelling them, it is a xenophobia that bears all the marks of the old racism. It is racism in substance, but 'xeno' in form. It is a racism that is meted out to impoverished strangers even if they are white. It is xeno-racism.
>
> (Sivanandan, in Fekete, 2001)

Following on from these ever-expanding and parasitic manifestations of 'race' another important issue to highlight in teaching is the concept of intersectionality which contends that understanding social divisions should be seen as multidimensional; the elaboration of oppression through complex relationships between, for example: racism, sexism and class-prejudice *etc.* (see Anthias and Yuval Davis 1992; Crenshaw, 1994/2005; Levine-Rasky, 2011) Rather than the unitary operation of class or race or gender, these and other forms of inequality are presented as inextricably combined reflecting multiple forms of discrimination. This is as true of whiteness and middle-class identity as it is for its opposites. Significantly whiteness is an unspoken identity yet one which serves as a standard against which others are measured. Close examination of whiteness can be very instructive and expose the taken-for granted privileges of white culture. Asking the question 'What does it Mean to Be White?' disturbs this unchallenged assurance of dominance. There are interesting responses to this question in a series of slides with the same title based on the work of Derald Wing Sue (also available on the excellent 'Whiteness Studies: Deconstructing (the) Race' website set up by Gregory Jay – see https://pantherfile.uwm.edu/gjay/www/Whiteness/)

> Silence about whiteness lets everyone continue to harbor prejudices and misconceptions, beginning with the notion that "white" equals normal.

'What does it Mean to Be White?'

- <u>34 year old white, female stockbroker</u>
- A: I don't know (laughing). I never thought about it
- Q: Are you white?
- A: Yes, I suppose so (seems very amused).
- Q: Why haven't you thought about it?
- A: Because it's not important to me.
- Q: Why not?
- A: it doesn't enter into my mind because it doesn't affect my life. Besides we're all individuals, color isn't important.

White Reactions to Whiteness

- White folks:
- (1) often find the question perplexing,
- (2) would rather not think about their whiteness,
- (3) are uncomfortable or react negatively to being labelled 'White'.
- (4) deny its importance in affecting their lives, and
- (5) seem to believe that they are unjustifiably accused of being bigoted by virtue of being white.

Figure 13.1 Powerpoint slides based on work of Wing Sue Derald (2004) What Does it Mean to Be White?

Whiteness oppresses when it operates as the invisible regime of normality, and thus making whiteness visible is a principal goal of anti-racist pedagogy.

(Jay, 2010)

Picture this – using the dimension of representation

The previous point highlights the need for encouraging a more critical distance to appraise ideas which are presented as natural and common-sense and hard to consider dispassionately because they run like a seam through individual and family life, drawing boundaries, they are embedded in discourses central to our cultural identity, they speak us into being.

Recognizing that such values are ingrained in language and popular culture, in the values we aspire to and the consumption system we are linked in to, suggests that those societal representations can be valuable to study as a means of exposing the dominant value system.

The diagram (Figure 13.2) below was adapted from du Gay et al. 'Circuit of Culture' (1997) it shows a matrix of processes by which cultural meanings and ideas are produced and circulated.

It is a diagram which can be adapted to discuss the central importance of identity in the ongoing process of making sense of cultural signs that are constantly being negotiated both internally within the individual and externally between the individual and others. The way ethnic identity is constructed can be seen as a complex interplay of cultural signs and meanings which are produced and consumed, reaffirming and regulating values through the media and other forms of popular representation. It has also proved to be a useful model for students to consider the construction of images and headlines in the media.

Drawing on forms of representation provides an array of readily accessible 'texts' from historical imagery (see Figure 13.1 above), to commercial materials; posters, newspapers, comic books, advertising, literature, music, television and film. I found that some older text books offered an abundance of examples from the era in which 'race-making' seemed to be overtly exposed and discussed using images like the above. This image and its chosen perspective presents two demurely posed English women between the muscular bodies of the black rowers. Interestingly, it exposes less about the reality of the people and the place (British Guiana) than it does about our fantasies. Framed within a commonsense, anthropological discourse of otherness, which is both voyeuristic and trivializing, such images offer powerful examples of the arrogance

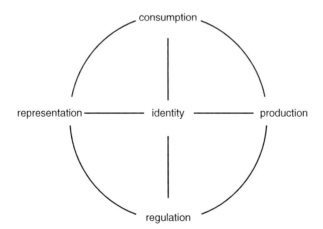

Figure 13.2 Matrix of Cultural Identity, in Spencer, S (2006) *Race & Ethnicity: Culture, Identity and Representation* (London: Routledge), p. 25

of colonial visions (the above example is *c* 1933). However, there is a marked continuity between such imagery when compared with current images from magazines like *National Geographic*, or from popular TV programmes about indigenous peoples.

Visual material operates at a deeper level and captures attention in a compelling way. Images have a seductive explicitness; photographs are said to be indexical representations of reality, but in fact have been carefully constructed; chosen, framed, cropped and at times changed beyond all semblance of the original subject or context. This is another important reason to share analyses of popular culture; to deconstruct the process by which visual or verbal texts expose the underlying values from which they are composed. Bell Hooks makes the point that one cannot avoid the avalanche of imagery and messages pouring from conduits of popular culture but it is important to don some critical amour not to perceive them as 'enlightened witnesses' (1997). In terms of race and ethnicity this is indeed important as the dominant rhetoric;

EDL stages protest in Luton

About 3,000 far-right activists in Luton for biggest demonstration in the group's history

David Cameron tells Muslim Britain: stop tolerating extremists

PM says those who don't hold 'British' values will be shunned by government

David Cameron will today signal a sea-change in the government fight against home-grown terrorism, saying the state must confront, and not consort with, the non-violent Muslim groups that are ambiguous about British values such as equality between sexes, democracy and integration.

To belong in Britain is to believe in these values, he will say. Claiming the previous government had been the victim of fear and muddled thinking by backing a state-sponsored form of multiculturalism, the prime minister will state that his government "will no longer fund or share platforms with organizations that, while non-violent, are certainly in some cases part of the problem".

In a major speech to a security conference in Munich, he will demand: "We need a lot less of the passive tolerance of recent years and much more active, muscular liberalism".

Can Top Gear laugh off its Mexican insults?

"Imagine waking up and remembering you're Mexican", said presenter Richard Hammond. Imagine if he'd said 'Pakistani'

Rodrigo Camarena

It all started with a swastika and a school project

When his seven-year-old daughter drew a swastika as a symbol of her family history, Giles Milton was shocked. He knew it was time to ask his German father-in-law about his part in the war and life under Hitler.

Figure 13.3   And now the news ... *Guardian* online headlines – 5 February 2011

for example about asylum seekers, refugees or Muslims form a constant barrage of inherently biased, negative, and sometimes wholly fabricated, stories. Using representational material; archive materials, current news stories and images from advertising gives the class a common focus. A simple method of showing the prevalence and preoccupation with discourses of race is to look at the headlines in the day's newspapers, and discuss the issues raised in terms of theories of race and ethnicity. For example the box below contains several stories extracted from the *Guardian* (online version) paper on the day I began writing this chapter.

The materials and discussions which might develop from this sample are multiple (see Figure 13.3). Students might consider the popular stereotypes of Mexicans which go unchallenged in our culture (for example the 'Western' genre, and the everyday portrayal in advertising for example for Mexican food). Cameron's assertion about multiculturalism is one of a long list of pronouncements - it might be an interesting exercise to examine collective definitions and associations with the term. Similarly the whole issue of the English Defence League (EDL) demonstration might lead to a discussion about the EDL and its links to far right politics (was it coincidental that Cameron timed these statements to coincide with their biggest public rally?)

Facilitating classroom interactions

As suggested earlier, teaching in this area is socially sensitive; these are values which are central to people's sense of self identity. One unifying strand which needs to be considered in assessing effective teaching strategies is the management of discussion and dynamics within the classroom, and the extent to which pedagogy permits a politically active role.

Our personal identity and appearance will have affects on the dynamics of teaching within a multi-ethnic classroom. It is important to remain conscious of these dynamics but not overwhelmed by them, and indeed the discussion of identity can be used to critically re-assess often ingrained and unconscious values. The exploration of anti-racist pedagogies offers teachers thought provoking ideas for re-assessing their classroom practice. Nasir's articulation of 'positionality' (in Spencer and Todd, 2006, pp. 71–98) addresses the asymmetry of the white tutor in a class of mainly BME students, or BME tutor in a predominantly white class. In the former position students might (perhaps reasonably) challenge the authority of the teacher to be able to speak authoritatively. In the latter the black tutor's analysis may be dismissed as special pleading ('well you would say that wouldn't you?') Recognizing these dynamics, and thinking 'within the frame' is clearly important and allows teachers and students to better consider how knowledge is seen as legitimate. It is significant that several of the contributors (Korner and Garrard; Housee,

Nasir and Pilkington) make reference to the Frierian conception of pedagogy (Friere, 1972) as a means for breaking down societal barriers between teacher and student and recognizing learning not as an oppressive tool for social control but as a means of greater freedom. Housee shows the implicit value in adopting hooks' concept of 'engaged pedagogy', moving away from the tradition of an instructor, this is an optimistic approach showing sensitivity, openness and respect to students, and recognizing that teachers themselves are learning from the interaction.

> To educate as the practice of freedom is a way of teaching that anyone can learn. That learning process comes easiest to those of us who teach who also believe that there is an aspect of our vocation that is sacred; who believe that our work is not merely to share information but to share in the intellectual and spiritual growth of our students. To teach in a manner that respects and cares for the souls of our students is essential if we are to provide the necessary conditions where learning can most deeply and intimately begin.
>
> (Hooks, 1994, p. 13).

In addition, Korner and Garrard (Spencer and Todd, 2006, pp. 36–7) make the point that race and ethnicity are never neutral terms which can be taught in isolation from their political and social consequences, the impact of racism and other forms of structural inequality stemming from 'race thinking', Korner argues, should be addressed before any real progress or conceptual understanding can be reached. These are issues which generate strong feelings and are at the heart of the individual's sense of identity and social being. Accounts of critical incidents in teaching race illustrate that there are substantial gains from an approach which engages students and confronts racism more directly. Secondly, effort should be taken to avoid an approach which is ethnocentric. How far does the curriculum reflect inherent biases and foreground white or Anglo-centric values? Efforts to include a broader base of literature are important and introduce students to the intercultural dimension of the debate, in the words of film maker, Josko Petkovic (1983) 'The language of the oppressed has yet to be invented.' Cumberbatch (in Spencer and Todd, 2006) and others make a plea for more heterogeneous sources to be used.

Finally, as discussed earlier, there is a need to emphasize the constructed and shifting nature of perceptions of 'the other'; social and political realities mean that the spotlight moves, highlighting different groups in different eras. In 1970s and '80s African Caribbean were under scrutiny and portrayed as muggers and rioters, today gun crime is the key focus, but while African Caribbean stereotypes are still plentiful, there is an inordinate focus on young Muslims.

Farrar makes the point that students may feel that the issues of overt racism are a thing of the past and no longer relevant so showing this constant transformation is important (Spencer and Todd, 2006, pp. 1–18). Classroom discussion often begins with a shared focus on examples from current media as a catalyst for deeper theoretical debate.

Linking research and teaching

One final suggestion is to engage in small pieces of research as a means of enriching the teaching and learning approach, and encouraging students to take part in such research themselves. Much of my work has emphasized the use of visual research methods (see Spencer, 2011) in addressing complex issues of race and ethnicity. As a recent example I asked an associate to draw a map of an area which he has had a long association with as a community worker and resident. The area has been presented in rather stigmatized terms by the mass media since a shooting took place in 2009 as a result of inter-ethnic rivalry between youth in the area. As he began to draw the map and explain the boundaries and passageways I filmed the drawing on a small portable camera. The resulting commentary and spontaneously drawn map broadened the historical and social context of the area providing a more nuanced understanding from a personal account of living in an area which has been stigmatized and misunderstood. Of course any such research requires careful permission; care about anonymity, data protection and consent based on full and transparent explanation of how the resulting recording is intended to be used. Bringing short samples of action research like this into the classroom can be a valuable catalyst for discussion of issues around a local area.

  Such uses of visual research can emphasize the tangible, open and accessible as well as the complex, critical and problematic, aspects of knowledge construction. The involvement of teachers in original research which can enrich their delivery is consistent with the concept of 'deep learning'. The key characteristics of deep learning (see Biggs, 1999; Entwistle, 1988 and Ramsden, 1992) typically include: linking course/module content to real life; to show complex connections and interrelations between subject areas and critical analytical approaches to the subject. Students develop an intrinsic interest and autonomous approach to the area rather than relying on superficial or formulaic learning with rote learning of 'answers'. However, while there is a long-standing belief that links between research and teaching are of central importance in Higher Education, being research-active does not necessarily lead to teaching that makes a difference; the measure of effective research/teaching nexus is the degree to which student learning, motivation and engagement is increased. Students may see staff research as beneficial for a number of reasons. Neumann (1994) concluded that staff research:

> ...brought tangible benefits to students, mainly because students perceived that their courses were up-to-date and that staff demonstrated interest in what they were studying. Also, staff research interests gave students "the opportunity to see their teachers as real people and to be able to glimpse what they do, how and why".
>
> (Neumann, in Jenkins et al., 2007, p. 19)

However, other findings suggest that:

> Many students did not see themselves as stakeholders in research; research was seen as quite separate from them, or in Brew's (2006, p. 52) powerful phrase, "at arm's length" from their experience of their studies. In addition many students wanted staff research to be managed better so that the negative impacts, in particular, of staff not being available to students, were minimised.
>
> (Ibid.)

In an effort to reduce this gap I chose examples from interviews and vivid visual material. These case examples brought the dynamics of ethnic identities to life using current examples in people's own words. This tended to make theoretical ideas more accessible and tangible and less obscure or daunting, and hence more able to engage students in the research. By choosing local and international examples, students' understanding of theory and their ability to integrate and apply knowledge were visibly strengthened. These visual case studies were also a way of introducing reading which is often theoretically challenging to students. Because case examples provide the everyday context, the theory is perceived as less abstract and easier to assimilate and criticize.

Over the years I have used interviews with staff and students from African-Caribbean, Mexican, Malaysian and Chinese, backgrounds. I have also included short video examples of the difficult conditions faced by indigenous Australians, debates around multiculturalism in the UK; and in several cases included video interviews with academics, community members and policy advisors.

Moreover, by observing the open and ongoing nature of research in the area of race and ethnicity, some students have been encouraged to take part in original research themselves; an essential part of developing scholarship. The examples of research, presented were exploratory and open to critical scrutiny, rather than demonstrating finished or polished research approaches they illustrate a reflexive spectrum of approaches and interpretations. This accessibility seems to be important if research is going to be assimilated effectively:

> '...staff who see their research as tentative and as part of a wider debate in the discipline, and see their teaching as supporting student conceptual change, are more likely to bring their teaching and research together.
> (Prosser et al. in Jenkins, Healey and Zetter, 2007, p. 18).

Conveying a sense of the excitement of discovery in examining and exploring the social world counters the student perception of an academic gulf by which tutors and students are separated; instead the system is open and students are therefore more able to engage with research. It is therefore important that students recognize knowledge as created, uncertain and contested, rather than controlled and directed by unassailable figures of authority.

> We suggest the way forward is to hold on to von Humboldt's view that "universities should treat learning as not yet wholly solved problems and hence always in research mode".
> (Elton, in Jenkins, Healey and Zetter, 2007, p. 45).

An approach which includes current research and connects with local as well as global communities is likely to maintain a more dynamic and questioning teaching approach, rather than one which presents a theoretical terrain which is abstractly complex. The use of these small interpersonal research explorations was managed within a teaching-focused institution, and for the most part without extensive funding or competitive bidding. In some cases using a series of case studies derived from mixed methods has provided sustaining examples for teaching, and facilitated the development of materials, videos and text books.

In conclusion, this short discussion has highlighted just a few of the key theoretical and pedagogical aspects raised by the challenge of teaching race and ethnicity. I have argued that the following concerns are important in the development of a serious and inclusive teaching practice:

- Recognize that this is a subject area with real consequences which cannot be approached as an abstract, theoretical subject in a detached way.
- Be sensitive to the classroom dynamics and draw from these to examine the real affects and shared implications of differences; taking care to set up 'house rules' to set standards of respect and protect vulnerable members.
- Examine the history of race and racism and its elusive and expedient movement which is frequently linked directly to economic and social power.

- Be aware of the reality of racism and the changing rhetoric about modes of 'incorporation' of differences in society. Especially significant are the meanings which cluster around terms like 'multiculturalism', assimilation, 'the integration agenda', 'community cohesion' and 'anti-racism' in both informal rhetoric and policy pronouncements.
- Draw on current popular culture as a valuable array of materials reflecting the movement of ideas, showing the primacy and persistence of 'race' and racism its different guises and the subtlety of forms parasitic on the political context of the time.
- Examine 'whiteness' a category which is inherently normalized, rather than focusing on BME groups. Some of the strands of theory which have emerged from Critical Race Theory offer a progressive standpoint which recognizes the inherent racism at the heart of institutions and in our daily lives.
- Finally, teaching in the area can benefit from some small pockets of action research, which might enliven and enrich the teaching experience and further involve both staff and students.

The intention is to reduce the distance between students and academics allowing 'engaged pedagogy' to develop fostering a more critical appraisal of the social and historical construction of race and the reasons for pursuing an anti-racist approach.

Note

1. These terms are recognized as contested and frequently carry scare quotes – but from here on I will take this as given and dispense with them.

References

Please note that the sections on 'Facilitating classroom interactions and 'Linking research and teaching' are adapted from an unpublished PhD thesis Spencer, S. (2008), 'Developing Research-informed Strategies for Teaching "Race" and Ethnicity in Higher Education', July, 2008, Sheffield Hallam University.

Anthias, F. (2002), 'Beyond Feminism and Multiculturalism: Locating Difference and the Politics of Location', *Women's Studies International Forum*, 25(3), 275–86

Anthias, F. and Yuval-Davis, N. (1992), *Racialized Boundaries: Race, Nation, Gender, Colour and Class and the Anti-Racist Struggle* (London: Routledge).

Athwal, H., Bourne, J. and Wood, R. (2010), Racial Violence: The Buried Issue', IRR briefing paper no.6. [online document] http://www.irr.org.uk/pdf2/IRR_Briefing_No.6.pdf (date accessed 28 march 2011).

Balandier, G. (1974), 'The Colonial Situation: A Theoretical Approach (1951)' in I. Wallerstein, *The Modern World System: Capitalist Agriculture and the Origins of the European World Economy in the Sixteenth Century* (London & New York: Academic Press), pp. 34–61.

Biggs, J. (1999), *Teaching for Quality Learning at University* (Buckingham: OUP) and SRHE, p. 18.

Brew, A. (2006), *Research and Teaching: Beyond the Divide* (Basingstoke: Palgrave Macmillan).

Christian, M. (2007), 'Reflections on Teaching "Race" and British Racism: Employing C. Wright Mills' Biography/history Perspective', in Todd, M and Farrar, M (eds) *Teaching Race in H.E. Social Sciences – What Next?* C-SAPhttp://www.teachingrace.bham.ac.uk/media/document/June_06_event.pdf (accessed 21 June 2011).

Crenshaw, K. W. (1994/2005), 'Mapping the Margins: Intersectionality, Identity Politics, and Violence Against Women of Color', in M. A. Fineman and R. Mykitiuk (eds) *The Public Nature of Private Violence* (New York: Routledge), pp. 93–118.

Curtis, M. (2004), *Unpeople: Britain's Secret Human Rights Abuses* (London: Vintage).

du Gay, P., Hall, S., Janes, L., Mackay, H. and Negus, K. (1997), *Doing Cultural Studies*. London: Sage.

Elton, L. (2008), 'Scholarship of Teaching and Learning' Keynote Speech at Sheffield Hallam University Conference – Integrating Teaching and Research, June 9th 2008.

Entwistle, N. (1988), *Styles of Learning and Teaching* (London: David Fulton).

EU arms exports to Libya: who armed Gaddafi? *Guardian Datablog* posted by Simon Rogers Tuesday 1 March 2011 14.08 GMT [Online] http://www.guardian.co.uk/news/datablog/2011/mar/01/eu-arms-exports-libya (date accessed 28 March 2011).

Farrar, M. (2006), 'Thirty Years of the Changing Same: Four Lessons in Teaching "Race"' in S. Spencer and M. Todd (2006) *Reflecting on Practice: Teaching and Learning Issues in Race and Ethnicity*, (C-SAP Monograph, University of Birmingham), pp. 1–18.

Friere, P. (1972), *The Pedagogy of the Oppressed* (Harmondsworth: Penguin).

Fekete, L. (2001), 'The Emergence of Xeno-Racism', 28 September 2001 in IRR News Independent Race and Refugee News Network 2001 http://www.irr.org.uk/2001/september/ak000001.html (date accessed 28 March 2011).

Gillborn, D. (2006), 'Critical Race Theory and Education: Racism and Antiracism in Educational Theory and Praxis', in *Discourse: Studies in The Cultural Politics of Education*, 27 (1), 11–32.

Gilroy, P. (2004), *After Empire: Multiculture or Postcolonial Melancholia* (London: Routledge)

Goldberg, D. T. (1992), 'The Semantics of Race', *Ethnic & Racial Studies*, 15 (4), 543–69.

Hall, S. (c.1996), *Race, the Floating Signifier*, film, Director – Sut Jhally Hall, (videotape lecture), Northampton, MA, Media Education Foundation.

Hochschild, A. (1998), *King Leopold's Ghost A Story of Greed, Terror, and Heroism in Colonial Africa* (Boston: Houghton Mifflin Company).

Hooks, bell (1994), *Teaching to Transgress. Education as the Practice of Freedom* (London: Routledge).

Hooks, bell (1997), *Cultural Criticism & Transformation* Video Produced and Directed by Sut Jhally Media Education Foundation.

Housee, S. (2006). 'Battlefields of Knowing: Facilitating Controversial Classroom Debates' in S. Spencer, and M. Todd, *Reflecting on Practice: Teaching and Learning Issues in Race and Ethnicity*, (C-SAP Monograph: University of Birmingham), pp. 54–71.

Jay, G. (2010), 'Teaching About Whiteness (Whiteness Studies: Deconstructing (the) Race' [online] https://pantherfile.uwm.edu/gjay/www/Whiteness/index.html (date accessed 28 March 2011).

Jenkins, A., Healey, M. and Zetter, R. (2007), 'Linking Teaching and Research in Disciplines and Departments, Higher Education Academy', April [Online doc.] http://www.heacademy.ac.uk/assets/York/documents/LinkingTeachingAndResearch_April07.pdf (date accessed 28 March 2011).

Kohn, M. (1996), *The Race Gallery* (London: Verso).

Korner, B. and Garrard, D. (2006), '"Is It Wrong to Be Racist?" Dealing With Emotion and Discomfort in Classroom Discussions of "Race" and Ethnicity' in S. Spencer and M. Todd, *Reflecting On Practice: Teaching and Learning Issues In Race and Ethnicity*, (C-SAP Monograph: University of Birmingham), pp. 18–54.

Lemert, C. (2006), 'Racism and Atlantic Violence', in Todd, Malcolm and Farrar, Max (eds) (2007) *Teaching Race in H.E. Social Sciences – What Next?*, C-SAP, 6, pp. 14–16.

Levine-Rasky, C. (2011), 'Intersectionality Theory Applied to Whiteness and Middle-Classness', in *Social Identities*, 17, (2), 239–53

Malik, K. (2002), *Race, Pluralism and the Meaning of Difference, New Formations*, 33 (Spring 1998) Available online at: http://www.kenanmalik.com/papers/new_formations.html (date accessed 28 March 2011).

Nasir, S. (2006), '"Well You Would Say That Wouldn't You?" Subject Positions and Relationships Between Knowledge and Commonsense' in S. Spencer and M. Todd (2006) *Reflecting On Practice: Teaching And Learning Issues in Race and Ethnicity* (C-SAP Monograph: University of Birmingham), pp. 71–99.

Neumann, R. (1994), 'The Teaching-Research Nexus: Applying a Framework to University Students' Learning Experiences', *European Journal of Education*, 29(3), 323–39.

Pence, D. J. and Arthur Fields, J. (1992), 'Teaching about Race and Ethnicity: Trying to Uncover White Privilege for a White Audience', *Teaching Sociology* (Washington, D.C.: American Sociological Association) 27 (2), 150–8.

Petkovic, J. (1983), Director, *Frame on Dreaming* (Edith Cowan University: Western Australia).

Pilkington, A. and Acroyd, J. (2006) 'Sins of the Fathers: Using Drama in Teaching the Sociology of "Race" and Ethnicity' in S. Spencer and M. Todd (2006) *Reflecting on Practice: Teaching and Learning Issues in Race And Ethnicity*, (C-SAP Monograph: University Of Birmingham), pp. 162–81.

Prosser, M., Martin, E., Trigwell, K., Ramsden, P. and Middleton, H. (2004), 'Research Active Academic Staff Experiences of Teaching, Understanding Subject Matter And Research', paper presented at *Research and Teaching: Closing the Divide?* An International Colloquium, Marwell, Winchester, UK, 18–19 March 2004. Available at: www.solent.ac.uk/externalup/318/michael_prosser_s_paper.doc. (date accessed 28 March 2011].

Prosser, M., Martin, E., Trigwell, K., Ramsden, P. and Lueckenhausen, G. (2005), Academics' Experiences of Understanding of Their Subject Matter and The Relationship of This to Their Experience of Teaching and Learning', *Instructional Science*, 33, 137–57.

Ramsden, P. (1992), *Learning to Teach in Higher Education* (London: Routledge).

Ratcliffe, P. (2004), *'Race', Ethnicity and Difference: Imagining the Inclusive Society* (Buckingham: OUP).

Spencer, S. (2011), *Visual Methods in the Social Sciences: Awakening Visions* (London: Routledge).

Spencer, S. (2010), Visual Methods in the Social Sciences: Awakening Vision, Companion Website, Routledge http://cw.routledge.com/textbooks/9780415483858/

Spencer, S. and Todd, M. (2006), *Reflecting on Practice: Teaching and Learning Issues in Race and Ethnicity*, (C-SAP Monograph: University of Birmingham).

Spencer, S. (2006), *Race & Ethnicity: Culture, Identity and Representation* (London: Routledge).

Spivak, G. C. (1994), 'Can the Subaltern Speak' in P. Williams and L. Chrisman (eds) 1994, *Colonial Discourse & Postcolonial Theory: A Reader* (New York: Columbia University Press), pp. 66–111.

Todd, M. and M. Farrar, M. (eds) (2007), *Teaching Race in H.E. Social Sciences – What Next?*, C-SAP Conference Proceedings 27–8 June 2006, C-SAP.

Van den Berghe, P. (1967), *Race and Racism: A Comparative Perspective* (New York: John Wiley).

James Walvin BBC 4 *Racism – A History*, part 1 The Colour of Money.

Derald, W. S. (2004), 'What Does it Mean to Be White?: The Invisible Whiteness of Being' DVD video, (Framingham, Mass : Microtraining Associates).

14
Developing Research Literacy in Students

Simon Lightfoot

Recent research highlighted the perception amongst academics that A-levels are not preparing students for the research demands of university study (Bassett et al., 2009), whilst a recent House of Commons Select Committee report found that the oft cited evidence for a clear link between research and teaching in UK universities was not wholly convincing (House of Commons, 2009). Given that after administration, teaching and research make up the majority of an academic's time and given that to some extent they can pull academics in opposite directions, there is a need to better align the two activities, especially in the minds of the students. It is, therefore, unsurprising that the national strategic priorities for learning and teaching in HE (HEFCE 2006/11) called on institutions to ensure that 'teaching is informed and enriched by research' and that 'students experience research, and develop research skills'.

The current body of knowledge has tended to focus on specific institutions (Hughes, 2005), disciplines (Brew, 2006) or in interdisciplinary areas that can more easily foreground research-led teaching. A review of Jenkins, Healey, and Zetter (2007) shows that whilst there are examples of good practice in the social sciences, they are nowhere nearly as developed as those of the natural or earth sciences. The literature in Politics and International Relations (IR) is very limited. A common problem is how can we get students to engage with our research when there are no labs, few experiments and a predominance of desk-based research? One colleague jokingly said 'we can all read the same book in the library!'. However, it is clear that whilst the ways to engage students in Politics and IR research are less obvious, it also means that we can develop our own models within the discipline or adapt models in use elsewhere.

The need for Politics and IR academics to engage students with our research is increasing. A major driver is that there is a common negative connection between research and teaching for students, with many students not really understanding what academics do (Zamorski, 2002; Robertson and Blackler, 2006; Turner et al., 2008; Willison and O'Regan 2007; Healey and Jenkins

2006). Surveys of students reveal a lack of awareness of the nature of the academic work model, especially in research intensive universities at a national level within the Higher Education sector. This chapter argues for the need to manage the transition from school/college to university (Wingate, 2007) and therefore calls for Politics and IR courses to develop their students as researchers (see Jenkins, 2004; Jenkins et al., 2007; Elsen et al., 2008). Having an early sense of proximity to and/or participation in a research community is vital in ensuring students recognize the links between research and teaching (Healey, 2005; Robertson and Blackler, 2006). Therefore it is vital that we 'decode the research process' by making the student experience of research more equitable and more visible. We also have to be clear about the integration of research in our own minds. Often we link scholarship with teaching and not research (see Nicholls, 2005). By heightening student awareness of research-led teaching and developing their research skills, this chapter outlines ways in which students can gain more explicit exposure to, and learn more directly from, the research that energizes the teaching they receive.

Student perceptions of teaching and research

There is a clear need to close the perception gap in student minds between teaching and research. In the National Student Survey (NSS) for every comment like 'enjoyed being taught by experts in the field, some currently doing research', you get three that complain that 'You really get the feeling sometimes that the lecturers are there for the sole purpose of research and do not care for the teaching' or 'any of the lecturers seem more concerned with their research than engaging with the students and their teaching'. Yet it is clear that few graduates use the detailed subject knowledge they obtain in their degree in their jobs. We therefore must be honest and accept that it is the research skills we taught them at university that are invaluable for employability and personal development (see Box 14.1). We also have to accept that whilst research is crucial for our career development, many of our students do not understand what we do.

We must therefore work hard to develop an understanding of the research process in students. This works from day one. Research and independent learning is the biggest difference from A-level not contact time and so ensuring research awareness is crucial to ensuring successful induction to higher education. Some of this is also driven by the need to recruit both PGT and PGR students and so introducing them to research early may inspire students to consider further study. However, it is also about general employability. The House of Commons report highlighted the link between developing students' research skills, and the development of their 'employability' skills (House of Commons, 2009). Many of the research skills we wish to develop in our students are transferable to a wide range of professions and fit many of the

Box 14.1   Why is research literacy crucial in students?

1. Important for employability (see Brew, 2006)
2. Important to understand what university is about
3. Important to understand what their lecturers actually do
4. Important to understand how the research feeds into the classroom
5. Important to understand that research is the basis of their university experience – other people's research and their own research collectively make up the scholarship which defines a university

'top ten things employers want from graduates' lists (see CBI/NUS, 2011 for example). Finally, the hardest angle to quantify is the sheer enjoyment and excitement felt by students when they get the opportunity to become involved in staff research projects. Some students have a clear focus on their own learning, whilst some only seem to care about the social side of university life but many are really engaged with what university is about and want to experience research. This is visible even at open days where some students name staff members and their research as the main reason for choosing a particular university. Whilst this sounds trite, we were all undergraduates once and something must have happened during our degree that sparked our interest in the subject. Probably though we never got an opportunity to experience "research" until we started a PhD, with the probable exception of a dissertation. To overcome the perceived gap between teaching and research we need to ensure our students become research literate.

This chapter highlights a variety of projects that have attempted to overcome this perception gap by making the student experience of research more visible. Three key projects are outlined: using podcasts to 're-attend' research seminars; students as scholars; students as researchers. Other models including induction and Level 1 frameworks for showcasing School/Faculty research to new students and publishing opportunities for undergraduate students will also be examined. It should be noted that the last two schemes are still very much in their infancy so only initial thoughts and impressions will be possible at this stage.

Background

There are a number of differing definitions in use concerning research and teaching (see Griffiths, 2004). The first is perhaps the most often cited: that of *research-led teaching*. This is a common model in Politics and IR where the curriculum is structured around the subject content that reflects the research interests of the member of staff leading the module. This model is commonly found at MA or Level 3 where the wide range of module choices reflects the particular research interests of staff in a given department. These modules are therefore informed by staff research 'rather than research processes' (Griffiths, 2004, p. 722). The other models include: res*earch-oriented teaching* which places emphasis on understanding the research process and therefore exposes students to the whole research experiences of teaching staff from the difficulties of undertaking fieldwork through to the problems associated with coding data etc; *research-based teaching* where the students are encouraged to undertake research through inquiry-based learning. This model places much less emphasis on the content of the module. Finally, Griffiths identifies *research-informed teaching* where the emphasis is on applying pedagogic research (Griffiths, 2004, p. 772).

What is Research Literacy?

This chapter acknowledges the usefulness of these terms but argues that these terms carry baggage, so takes as its core premise the need to develop research literacy in students (Butcher, 2009). By this we mean producing graduates who have an appreciation and experience of carrying out research in their discipline: they understand what the big questions in their disciplines are and how academics are trying to resolve them; they understand who is doing what and where the major work is taking place, and they have heard cutting-edge information from their lecturers. Crucially, for Politics and IR, they have the ability to deal with the greys in academic research rather than always looking for the black and white. Research literacy therefore not only prepares students for university level research, it also trains students to translate research findings in domains of public impact and employment. Therefore, linking research and teaching is much more than just being a researcher and then teaching the same topic. Personal expertise and interest are vital, but we need to be able to engage students with the whole research process.

Part of the driver for this, as Zamorski (2002) found, is that the most visible sign of the research process is the completion of the final year project or dissertation, yet even then many students needed prompting to recognise this research/teaching link. There is a need introduce research-based learning into the whole undergraduate experience and to involve students in this learning (Blackmore and Cousin, 2003; Robertson and Blackler, 2006; Brew, 2006; Healey and Jenkins, 2006). Blackmore and Fraser (2003) highlight the need to emphasize process, and argue that students who acquire higher level technical skills in sourcing and consolidating new knowledge and who develop critical thinking and questioning skills help create a better research culture. Needless to say these are also the types of skills highly prized by employers.

At the University of Leeds a number of excellent examples of research literacy can be identified in the Social Sciences (broadly defined). In Earth and Environment, introducing staff research is a key element of the induction process. In Psychology, a level one module psychology@leeds showcases the research strengths of the school to new students, focusing on the key research groups and the uniqueness of the degree at Leeds. There are other key examples from History that *explicitly* integrate the lecturer's research findings & process into the module as the students work through research problems with the lecturer at the same time he is working on them his research timetable directs the topics and issues covered in his course. Within Politics and IR the Scholarship of Engagement for Politics gives students excellent opportunities to collaborate in research with selected local NGOs/businesses/government agencies, with each student given a research topic to work on for the organisation (see Moon and Schokman, 2000; Sherrington et al., 2008). These types of placement opportunities are relatively common place in Politics and IR but what marks these projects out is the explicit links to research projects and research skills.

Pilot projects

Before examining a selected group of pilot projects, it is worth giving a little more detail as to why there was a need for pilot projects. The biggest reason was that very little work has been done on integrating research and teaching into undergraduate Politics and IR teaching, beyond the research modules. Therefore it was not always clear what would work and what would not, hence the need for small scale pilot studies. The other reason was the fact that this research is an example of action learning, where by the participant reflects on their own action and activities. For me to be able to manage them on top of my normal workload meant they needed to be relatively small.

Virtual research seminars

This pilot aimed to embed current research activity in the curriculum content of core modules and re-focus skills modules with an explicit research focus. We planned to engage level one students with research that is being conducted in both the school and the wider profession at all levels (PhD student to professor) *via* the creation of new materials such a recordings of school research seminars (where papers are presented by staff or external speakers) and/or a library of existing external resources (iTunes U) that could be used to allow virtual integration to research communities alongside physical ones. Our plan had two clear aims: the first was to allow students to re-attend research papers in the same way that they could re-attend lectures through the podcasts described earlier (of course this would also allow students who had missed the paper access to the material). Secondly, by listening and critically engaging with the papers, we hoped it would demystify the process of a staff research seminar and encourage more undergraduate students to attend. We recorded the regular research seminars from October 2008 and planned to integrate these recordings into the student curriculum from February 2009. In order to fully utilize these resources, and to maximize their potential as a teaching aid, our pedagogic research suggested it was better to merge the audio (MP3) recording into the PowerPoint slide using software known as Articulate. However, our findings also point to the fact that if students feel the benefits of attending research seminars is opaque, then getting them to listen to them is also hard. Student feedback was very firmly of the opinion that these recordings needed to be integrated into a particular module. Engaging students with the research process is an increasingly important aspect of curriculum design (Healey and Jenkins, 2006) and in this area we need to do more work. A key aspect is the linkage at level one between modules and the research process. In the current HE sector, some students argue there is little incentive/encouragement to engage with non credit bearing extra curricula activities as they need to concentrate all their energy into obtaining the highest marks possible for each separate assignment. This problem can be exacerbated by the modular system in use in many universities as students tend to see modules as stand alone units and fail to understand the links between the modules on a particular programme of study. Ensuring students have research literacy will in part expose students to different research projects and research methods/methodologies and allow them to make the links between modules.

Research studentships

Opportunities were provided that allowed level two students the opportunity to work with active researchers on clearly defined research projects (see Brew, 2006, p. 90). In 2009/10 the Faculty of Education, Social Science and Law (ESSL) offered an Undergraduate Research Scholarship Scheme which gave successful student applicants, in their second year of study, the opportunity to working with a research team in a supervised research environment on an individual research project related to their degree subject and interests. The scholarships and projects were undertaken in June-July 2010 and ran for between 4 and 6 weeks. Research scholars were supervised throughout by an academic tutor (see Box 14.2). In POLIS we ran five different schemes; one where students mainly engaged in literature & policy review, the other where we asked students to undertake specific pieces of research for the School. Similar schemes exist in an increasing number of other universities. A quick Google search highlighted projects in Warwick, Cardiff, Oxford Brookes, Reading, St. Andrews, Sheffield, University of East London and University of Central Lancashire. There is also a National Teaching fellowship project on 'students as producers' being co-ordinated by the University of Lincoln, which has innovated in this area (see http://studentasproducer.lincoln.ac.uk/).

There have been a number of issues raised thus far. It was important to clarify that the data and any outputs of the research project could not be used

Box 14.2   The student voice

I feel that undertaking the research project has really assisted me with my course. Over the summer months it is often the case that students lose focus on their degrees and subsequently find it hard to return to study the following September. Instead I felt the project kept me motivated and engaged over the five weeks and keen to start research on my dissertation. The project was useful as it allowed me to complete an extended piece of research without the pressure of looming deadlines as it often the case at university.

The assistantship was at a very appropriate time for me as it was a perfect step from being a student to getting a job or thinking about post-graduate options. It gave me an idea of what working life would be like without it being a huge step from being a student as I was still in university and the atmosphere was very relaxed. It also meant that I got experience in research which I am sure will help if I apply to those kinds of jobs.

as part of the student's dissertation although this could inform the work they subsequently undertake for their dissertation, as it was felt that those students would be receiving an unfair advantage through in effect more personalised dissertation supervision. Making sure the student experience is equitable is crucial. All students may have the opportunity to apply for the scholarship but clearly places are limited. Allowing the successful student then to obtain an advantage in credit bearing modules is a different matter. At first, it appeared that students were wary of this new initiative, although with the deadline just passed we had 12 very good applications for projects in the School. Those students who applied were highly motivated and had clearly spent time thinking about the development of their research skills, as their *cvs* were almost all of a very high quality. There are obvious issues related to the work-load of academic staff and the lack of reward structures. Staff may get a research assistant but they still need to be managed and if the work is 'on top' of existing workloads it could damage the experience for both students and staff (see Brew, 2006, p. 91). In the midst of a financial crisis spending money on providing an intensive research experience for one student in a cohort of over 200 is also a major concern. There have also been concerns about students being exploited and their contribution not being recognized, but the scheme has very clear management structures and a clear policy on citation.

Students as scholars programme

A key aspect of academic research is the presentation of your early thoughts/ initial findings at conferences or as research papers. Hundreds of these events are taking place every week in universities across the UK, yet attendance at these events by students can be patchy. However, the opportunity for students to be exposed to cutting-edge research being conducted both by academic staff members in their own department but also by academic staff in other academic departments or universities is an under-exploited resource in teaching terms. The ability to observe how we as academics start our research journeys, overcome problems and, crucially, deal with criticism of our ideas encourages students to realize that in Politics and IR there are lots of greys! Evidence from the Italian Department in Leeds highlighted the significant differences between research seminars on the one hand, and undergraduate lectures, classes and seminars on the other. In particular, the crucial difference was that the learning outcomes for students from the research seminar risk being opaque, and the experience risks being intimidating for undergraduates. To try and overcome these issues they created a 'Students as Scholars' programme. In 2010 I opened up the scheme in POLIS to my MA class 'EU and the Developing World' on a voluntary basis. Four of the 16 students signed up for the scheme. In part the decision to opt for an MA class was purely practical- it was the only class I taught that semester! However, I was also keen to see how it worked with students who were potentially at the beginning of their research journey.

We meet briefly before and after the research seminar and students are asked to complete a brief form with three sections: one for before the event, one during and one after. The first section encourages students to engage with the research field of the seminar and investigate what the speaker has published previously. Clearly asking students to prepare before the seminar makes them more likely to be aware of the issues under discussion. During the seminar the students are asked to discuss what the argument of the research paper is, whether it is an advance on existing work by the presenter or the canon and also to think about methodological questions. In the de-brief students are asked to reflect on the event and identify links between the paper and their modules of study.

I have been able to undertake one full event with the four students. Student feedback was favourable. The opportunity to discuss the seminar before the event was highlighted as a key benefit. In part students acknowledged that they could have done the reading before any seminar but the scheme gave them added incentive. It also allowed them to ask questions related to the paper abstract in a safe environment. The de-brief was also popular as it allowed them to make explicit links with my modules. It also provided a nice space to debate and discuss the ideas raised and to show that despite being an academic member of staff I too learned new things. As a staff member it was interesting to have a vehicle to discuss seminars with students and to highlight my thoughts. In the teaching timetable you do not always have space to do this, especially if only four students have been to the seminar. Issues such as the timeliness of the initial meetings and de-brief are crucial. The pressures on MA students to prepare for class, and in many cases work, mean that projects like this can become sidelined. It is a time commitment on behalf of the staff member and again this commitment is not necessarily rewarded or visible.

Conclusions

In terms of the debate in the UK, there is a tension between improving the student experience (especially since the introduction of tuition fees) and ensuring a good return in the Research Assessment Exercise/Research Excellence Framework (see Breen and Jenkins, 2002 for a fuller discussion). Breen and Jenkins (2002) argue that greater student understanding of the research process encourages a more positive attitude to staff engagement in research. There is also the need to demonstrate the links between research and teaching to a wider audience, one that is increasingly interested in assessing the impact of publically funded academic research (see Box 14.3). It is vital for maximizing the impact of research on teaching and of teaching on research.

This chapter has highlighted a variety of ways in which the research experience can be made more explicit to undergraduate and postgraduate students. Whilst the projects are still in their infancy and there are some teething troubles to overcome, what has struck me is the enthusiasm for engaging in research amongst the students. Our experience at Leeds shows that if you provide opportunities for students a willing minority will really get involved. It is also clear that the more opportunities we provide the more demand there is. The crucial thing is to ensure students obtain the skills they need from us early in their undergraduate career. We need to help students become university learners by not only providing the knowledge within the discipline but by helping students 'learning to learn' and thereby become independent learners (see Wingate, 2007; Christie et al., 2008). A relatively simple way to do this is by decoding the research process and making the connections between research and the student experience, especially in terms of teaching, more explicit. We need to show how we carry out research, how we struggle with difficult aspects of research questions and perhaps crucially how there are numerous interpretations of political events that all have validity.

Traditional teaching methods are ideal for this-challenges faced by us all can be discussed in lectures and seminars with students. Huston's (2009) book highlights that as staff we can admit to not knowing everything or having uncertainty, without damaging our authority in the classroom. We also need to have more faith in our students it is vital to remember that these are individuals at the very start of their academic journey so we need to judge them against that criteria not against what we can produce now.

We need to identify the key skills involved in research and how these are applicable beyond university. The vast majority of undergraduate Politics and

Box 14.3   Integrating Research into Teaching

1. Be enthusiastic about your research enthusiasm can be infectious!
2. To do this you need to talk about your research to students! This sounds very obvious but many students do not know what we do
3. Linked to the above, use examples from your research in class. In particular, give students an opportunity to realise that we don't know all the answers, hence the need for further research
4. Allow students to read and critique early drafts of conference papers and/or articles
5. Discuss methodological, theoretical or just practical issues that you have encountered in your research and how you have or have not overcome them
6. Create an expectation that students will attend research group seminars and offer support, even if it is just "Prof X is coming to talk next week at a research seminar. You should try and attend because her work is crucial for our understanding of the European Commission (week 6!). Before the seminar, try and read one of her articles that I posted links to on the vle (virtual learning environment)".
7. Find ways to involve students in the research process. Can they undertake literature reviews as part of their assessment? Can they read interview transcripts? Can they have access to your raw data?
8. Make space in the curriculum for the above. Do you need all that content? Korosteleva (2010) talks about threshold concepts-what exactly do you need your students to know? Making sure your student have deep knowledge about the subject and the skills to study that subject may be more beneficial than us telling them more content.
9. Praise and reward top quality work. At times we appear to "review" first class work highlighting any flaws with the engagement with the theoretical literature in the same way we would when reviewing an article. We must remember that these are undergraduate students and therefore we need to recognise their work as commensurate to their age and stage of academic career

IR graduates do not go into academia, so we need to show how the research skills they obtain in a Politics/IR degree (critical analysis, research, ability to construct an argument, use of evidence) are applicable in a variety of employment fields. Few graduates use the detailed knowledge they obtain in their degree in their jobs, but the research skills we taught them at university are invaluable. This is a crucial aspect of research literacy. The added advantage is that it allows academic staff to stay in a relative comfort zone. Academics can sometimes feel that they are being pulled in numerous, often contradictory, ways with the increased tasks assigned to our roles (research, teaching scholarship, pastoral support, careers advice and personal development to name a few). Advising students about employability is an increasing part of our jobs, yet this is not a role we necessarily have expertise in. Discussing research and the research skills we share with the students and ensuring the students explicitly acknowledge the skills they have obtained from their Politics/IR degree and how these have developed over the years is something that is more familiar. Making the link visible between research skills and say employability is crucial as the student needs to be fully aware of, and be able to articulate, the skills they acquire at university and to understand how these can be applied in the workplace/further study. In the current financial climate and with the advent of £9000 fees, if we do not then there is a very real risk that student satisfaction surveys will continue to highlight the disconnect between academics engaging in research and 'my' student experience. Ensuring students are research literate is an important step in reducing this disconnect.

References

Bassett, D., Cawston, T., Thraves, L. and Truss, E. (2009), *A New Level*, Reform, June.

Brew, A. (2006), *Research and Teaching: Beyond the Divide* (Basingstoke: Palgrave Macmillan).

Breen, L. and Jenkins, A. (2002), 'Academic Research and Teaching Quality: The Views of Undergraduate and Postgraduate Students', *Studies in Higher Education*, 27 (3), 309–27.

Blackmore, P. and Fraser, M. (2003), 'Research and Teaching: Making the Link', in R. Blackwell and P. Blackmore (eds) *Towards Strategic Staff Development* (Buckingham, Open University Press), 131–41.

Blackmore, P. and Cousin, G. (2003), 'Linking Teaching and Research Through Research-Based Learning', *Educational Developments*, 4 (4), 24–7.

Butcher, C. (2009), Personal communication to author.

CBI/NUS (2011), *Working towards your future* (CBI/NUS: London).

Christie, H., Tett, L., Cree, V., Hounsell, J and McCune, V. (2008), '"A Real Rollercoaster of confidence and Emotions": Learning to be a University Student', *Studies in Higher Education*, 33 (5), 567–81.

Elsen, M., Visser-Wijnveen, G. R., van der Rijst, G. and van Driel, J. (2009), 'How to Strengthen the Connection between Research and Teaching in Undergraduate University Education', *Higher Education Quarterly*, 63 (1), 63–85.

Griffiths, R. (2004), 'Knowledge Production and the Research-Teaching Nexus: The Case of The Built Environment Disciplines', *Studies in Higher Education*, 29(6), 709–26.

Healey, M. (2005), 'Linking Research and Teaching to Benefit Student Learning', *Journal of Geography in Higher Education*, 29 (2), 183–201.

Healey, M. and Jenkins, A. (2006), 'Strengthening the Teaching-Research Linkage in Undergraduate Courses and Programs', *New Directions for Teaching and Learning*, 107, Autumn/Fall, 45–55.

HEFCE (2006/11), HEFCE strategic plan 2006-11, www.npc.org.uk/.../npc0601bhefce strategicplan200611consultation (accessed 9 May 2011).

House of Commons (2009), Innovation, Universities, Science and Skills Committee – Eleventh Report Students and Universities, *Report* 20 July. http://www.publications.parliament.uk/pa/cm200809/cmselect/cmdius/170/170i.pdf

Hughes, C. (2005), 'Linking Teaching and Research in a Research Orientated Department of Sociology', C-SAP Project. http://www.c-sap.bham.ac.uk/media/com_projectlog/docs/13_S_03.pdf

Huston, T. (2009), *Teaching what you don't know* (Boston: Harvard University Press).

Jenkins, A., Breen, R., Lindsay, R. and Brew, A (2003), *Reshaping Teaching in Higher Education: Linking Teaching with Research* (London: Kogan Page).

Jenkins, A. (2004), 'Linking Teaching and Research' The Higher Education Academy. http://www-new2.heacademy.ac.uk/assets/York/documents/ourwork/research/id383_guide_to_research_evidence_on_teaching_research_relations.pdf

Jenkins, A., Healey, M. and Zetter, R. (2007), 'Linking Teaching and Research in Disciplines and Departments' The Higher Education Academy http://www.heacademy.ac.uk/assets/York/documents/LinkingTeachingAndResearch_April07.pdf

Jenkins, A. and Healey, M. (2009), 'Developing The Student as a Researcher Through the Curriculum' in C. Rust (ed) *Improving Student Learning Through the Curriculum* (Oxford: Oxford Centre for Staff and Learning Development, Oxford Brookes University).

Korosteleva, E. (2010), 'Threshold Concepts Through Enactive Learning: How Effective Are They in the Study of European Politics?' *International Studies Perspectives* 11 (1), 37–50.

Moon, J. and Schokman, W. (2000), 'Political Science Research Internships and Political Science Education', *Politics* 20 (3), 169–75.

Nicholls, G. (2005), The *Challenge to Scholarship: Rethinking Learning, Teaching, and Research* (Routledge: London).

Robertson, J. and Blackler, G. (2006), 'Students' Experiences of Learning in a Research Environment', *Higher Education Research & Development*, 25 (3), 215–29.

Sherrington, P., Axford, B., Blair, A., Curtis, S., Huggins, R. and Gibson, C. (2008), 'Research-Led Placements in Politics: A New Approach?', *European Political Science* 7 (2), 175–85.

Turner, N., Wuetherick, B. and Healy, M. (2008), 'International Perspectives on Student Awareness, Experiences and Perceptions of Research: Implications for Academic Developers in Implementing Research-Based Teaching and LEARNING' *International Journal for Academic Development*, 13 (3), 199–211.

Willison, J. and O'Regan, K. (2007), 'Commonly Known, Commonly Not Known, Totally Unknown: A Framework for Students Becoming Researchers', *Higher Education Research & Development*, 26 (4), 393–409.

Wingate, U. (2007), 'A Framework for Transition: Supporting "Learning to Learn" in Higher Education', *Higher Education Quarterly*, 61 (3), 391–405.

Zamorski, B. (2002), 'Research-led Teaching and Learning in Higher Education: a Case', *Teaching in Higher Education*, 7 (4), 411–27.

15

Supervising a Doctoral Student

Carmel Roulston

> We know that the supervisor can make or break a PhD
> student.
>
> (Lee, 2008, p. 267)

> Tales of PhD woe are ten-a-penny among graduate students – and
> the vast majority of these involve problems with supervisors.
>
> (Lynch, 2008)

Supervising a doctoral student will most often be exciting, satisfying and enjoyable, but, particularly for those who have come across – in newspaper articles and elsewhere – accounts of bad or problematic experiences of doctoral supervision, the prospect of commencing supervision can be daunting. The majority of recently appointed lecturers in Politics will have themselves completed a doctorate; their experience of that process may well have considerable influence on their expectations of how they will manage in this important academic role. Increasingly, all lecturers are likely to be required to undertake research supervision and examination at some stage in their careers; successful supervision is certainly one of the elements of appraisal and promotions criteria. In this chapter, I will set out the (changing) contexts for PhD supervision, the steps which make supervision more likely to be successful and the tricky questions and dilemmas which arise as a normal part of 'the demanding intellectual and personal task of overseeing the development of graduate students' (Delamont et al., 2004, p. 12).

You will not be entirely and solely responsible for your students' futures. There will be training and support available in every academic department, and points at which input and advice from colleagues can be drawn in. There is still, however, an element of 'learning by doing' associated with this important area of teaching and learning. This branch of academic life involves a close – in many cases on-to-one – relationship between mature individuals, so in many respects each supervision experience will have its own unique qualities and dynamics. There are however important commonalities – including common risks and possible pitfalls – which I will attempt to outline. Both the doctoral student and the new lecturer require clear structures for support and development; I will outline the support you will require at various stages of the process.

What follows is written for the most part with a relatively inexperienced lecturer in mind. As such, you are in a relatively subordinate position, constrained by hierarchies and subject to conflicting demands and pressures. The doctoral student is, however, (as the case studies in Delamont et al., 2004, Eley and Jennings, 2005 and Wakeford, 2004 and elsewhere indicate) in a more vulnerable position. The underpinning principle of all supervision has to be a focus on achieving outcomes that are in the best interests of the student (which is of course not necessarily the same as achieving the outcome that the student wants).

Contexts

Doctoral students and supervisors are all individual and the relationships between each student and their supervisor distinctive in many ways, but there are increasingly standardised structures and frameworks within which students are selected and managed which can impact on the processes of supervision. The spectre of the REF looms over this aspect of academic life (with beneficial as well as problematic effects). A higher number of completed doctoral dissertations will improve a department's REF rating, so there are incentives to increased recruitment of doctoral students. Most departments will have some Research Council (or other publicly) fully-funded full-time students, some self-financing full- and part-time students, some overseas students sponsored by governments, charitable funders or universities. In almost all cases, there will be pressure to achieve completion of the thesis within a clearly defined time period (no longer than four years – sometimes even within three years full-time or seven years part-time). Since the 1980s, amid concerns about the high numbers of doctoral students never submitting a thesis, or doing so after ten years or more, we have seen increasing monitoring and regulation of PhD study. Departments which do not achieve a satisfactory percentage of completions by full-time funded students within the four year period are not only harshly judged in league tables (and generally in the press: see for example, Corbyn, 2007) but also punished by the application of 'sanctions' – refusal of access to funding for new students for a defined period - by the various funding bodies. This can be particularly serious for smaller departments, as, up until the time of writing, funders such as the Department of Employment and Learning (DEL) in Northern Ireland have proven resistant to claims that crude percentages should not apply to cases where one student out of an intake of three or four has required extension or withdrawn for reasons not connected with the quality of supervision or support.

The scrutiny of completion rates has resulted in pressure on Universities to comply with various codes of practice (most particularly from the QAA) for the management of doctoral students (or 'candidates' (QAA, 2011, p. 4).

The standard expectation is that there will be clear criteria and processes for selection and admission of postgraduate research students, and clear criteria and processes for examination of the finished thesis. In between, there will be a structured training programme (whether as part of an integrated one-year taught Masters programme followed by progression to the thesis stage or provided throughout a three-year registration with a specified number of training credits which each student is required to attain) and monitoring and review processes which result in approval to continue with doctoral research, or lead to transfer to an MPhil or withdrawal. The continued consensus that the quality of supervision is the most significant factor on the success or failure of a PhD means that there must now be training for supervisors and an expectation that each student will be allocated at least two supervisors. This emphasis on regulation and training (for students and supervisors) as the answer to problems of late or non-completion has been received with scepticism or even hostility by many academics, particularly those in the Social Sciences and Humanities (see Wright, 2000), who argue that there are many factors involved in non-completion, that the proliferating codes of practice do not address the most common dilemmas for supervisors (Cryer, 1998) and that the consequence of all this regulation may be to reduce the PhD to a formulaic exercise in research training.

Certainly, we have moved from the minimal definition of a PhD provided in the 1980s (ESRC, 1984) to the current attempts to create programme specifications and standard descriptors for doctorates (QAA, 2011). This process has not yet resulted in complete standardisation.

> Doctoral qualification descriptors promote a high level of consistency while affording universities the autonomy they are entitled to as research degree awarding bodies. This allows institutions to augment the generic requirements in the descriptors with detailed assessment criteria that are appropriate for different subjects and qualifications.
>
> (QAA, 2011, pp. 6–7).

In the Social Sciences and Humanities, the PhD is still defined in fairly generic terms as a substantial piece of work on a defined topic based on independent (supervised) research which makes an original contribution to knowledge in the given discipline or area. In political studies in the UK, there still prevails an eclectic – or 'anything goes' – approach to research in general, which can be viewed as beneficial or problematic depending on the context (Burnham et al., 2008, pp. 29–30). This open-endedness can, at various stages, increase the weight of responsibility upon the supervisor.

Tip one

In theory, before you have been appointed as a supervisor you should have received training in effective supervision. In the best case, you will be given the opportunity to shadow or assist a more experienced supervisor so that you have an opportunity to experience the process. In practice, crises happen and you may find yourself asked to take on a supervisory role without much preparation. Any lecturer taking up a new post (even those who have supervised in a previous lecturing position) should locate the policies and processes that apply in their current University. There should be a code of practice, a research student handbook or resource area and some guidelines on frequency of meetings, arrangements for progress reviews and examining the thesis. If in doubt, identify the administrative department, which manages registration and assessment for research students. Staff there will certainly make you aware of regulations, standard procedures, practices to avoid and where to locate support for you and the student. Ideally, there will be a Research Graduate School with a Director (76% of universities now have at least one according to QAA, 2011), or at least a key member of academic staff in your Faculty or Department with responsibility for ensuring good practice in supervision. Get to know that person quickly!

There are many online resources which provide guidance and information. Look at and consider registering with, for example, Vitae on the Research Information Network website; look at the information for doctoral students on there as well.

The stages of the supervision process

Selecting the right students

Supervisors can face dilemmas before they even begin to supervise. Given that funding is not unlimited, it is likely that there will be more applicants than studentships, so difficult choices will have to be made during the selection process. Most universities now have formal and transparent arrangements for the selection of research students. These have emerged as one of the measures to improve completion rates, though it is still widely accepted that there is no foolproof way of determining at the outset which applicants will turn out to be successful doctoral students. Nevertheless, increasing clarity and formality has been beneficial to both applicants and supervisors. Firstly, the process of submitting an application, which for the most part now involves submission of a structured outline of the proposed topic with a mini-literature review helps to 'induct' candidates into the disciplinary area that they are proposing to study and provides an incentive to invest some effort into preparing for higher degree study. Secondly, the submitted proposal and the selection interview allow departments not only to assess whether the candidate is a 'good prospect', but also to identify at an early stage what training or development he or she will require. One of the most agonizing choices relates to deciding whether to accept an outstanding applicant who has proposed to research a topic in which the department has no supervisory expertise. It can be tempting to admit the student with the expectation that he or she will change the focus to one that fits departmental priorities or expertise, or that supervisors will adapt to the interests of the student. Both of those courses of action have enormous risks attached and should be followed only after considerable consultation.

Tip two

Selecting part-time or other self-funding students should be conducted with the same formality and attention as that given to full-time funded students. While six or seven years may seem a long time, in reality, a part-time student who is in full-time employment with family commitments will have less time in total to devote to his or her research than the funded student who has to finish in three/four years. (See Murphy, 2007, and Frank Wareing's Diary, Missenden Centre).

You have been appointed as a supervisor: what happens next?

There are two important processes to initiate right way: clarifying expectations and creating good communications. As the selection section above suggests, lecturers cannot always rely on the expectation that there will be a perfect match between their interests and expertise and the proposed research area of their research students. However, due to the growing body of evidence that a very poor match is likely to lead to poor outcomes (see particularly the examples and case studies in Delamont, et al., 2004 and Eley and Jennings, 2005), universities have become more aware of the need to ensure that this does not happen. This is one of the reasons for appointing at least two supervisors for each student. Lecturers are unlikely to be appointed as principal or co-supervisor until one of their supervisees has successfully completed a doctorate. However, this is no guarantee that they will not be asked to take on most of the responsibility. So, the first relationship where expectations and communications must be clarified is that between co-supervisors. In my experience, in the initial stages of a PhD, supervisors should discuss the student's written work and progress together before any feedback is provided to the student. Supervising and researching a PhD are dynamic processes, during which the student gradually becomes more autonomous, so at a certain point, supervisors can relate separately to the student. At the beginning, however, the supervisory team should reach agreement among themselves about important issues such as frequency and location of meetings, how formal and informal interactions will be structured, how to clarify and refine the project and who will communicate feedback to the student, when and how. If you have concerns about whether the proposed topic is realistic or requires revision, and/or whether you are the right supervisor, this is a good point at which to express them.

The next duty is to begin to build the relationship with your student. Notwithstanding all the codes and precepts around joint supervision, at some point you will be the person who carries most of the responsibility for supervision. 'The candidate's relationship with his/her supervisor is key to a successful research degree programme' (QAA, 2011, p. 9). The student is new to research, perhaps to the university and may even be new to the country, so he or she may be unsure, intimidated, and anxious or even have unrealistic expectations about how much or little input they can expect from a supervisor. It is up to you to 'set the scene' by finding out from them what their expectations are and reaching agreement with them about what you expect from each other. Do you need a 'learning contract' at this stage? I tend to think that as long as there is some record of your discussion (perhaps by using a tool such as described in Box 15.1 and summarising your subsequent discussion), no more formal agreement is required.

Box 15.1   The Supervisor-Student Questionaire

Many universities now recommend that supervisors and new students each complete a questionnaire in which they each identify and then discuss/negotiate their understanding of the tasks and roles expected of each other. This should include practical questions such as whose role it is to ensure that the student is aware of all the facilities and resources available, and issues such as who is responsible for deciding on the methodology. It might well include questions relating to responsibility for presentation and proof-reading.

This is the point at which to discuss and agree a programme for the first few months, to set ground rules for meetings (including how many formal meetings and how students should prepare for them, what kinds of informal contact you will have and how you will give feedback on written work submitted). Recording formal meetings is vital; the records create a useful log of progress for students and provide a record for supervisors (particularly if you have more than one student). There is a growing consensus that the student should draft a summary of what was discussed and what tasks they must complete before the next meeting, then send it to the supervisor(s) who either confirm or edit.

Remember that communication must be a two-way process; you should be reflecting on your expectations and reviewing them in the light of what you are hearing from the student. Has your own experience of supervision influenced your ideas about what is required? (Lee, 2008). If so, are you sure that your experiences are relevant to your new student? However competent you may feel, it is essential to seek some staff development training in supervision and to scan the available guides to good supervision (Delamont et al., Thompson, Wisker for example) to find one which best fits with the type of research you will be supervising. I recommend also reading guides to writing a PhD aimed at students (most notably, Dunleavy 2003, which your student should also read).

In these initial weeks, supervisors and students have to spend some time identifying the student's training needs and working out how they can access any essential training (if it is not available within the university). Part-time students are often disadvantaged in respect of access to research training, as work or family commitments mean that they cannot attend in-house training programmes and departments may not have the funds to procure external training. Murphy (2007) also points out that mature part-time students may have different training needs from students coming straight from an undergraduate or taught postgraduate course. They may well have, for example, excellent time- and project-management skills but need support to develop, for example, their academic writing skills.

Beginning the research work: clarifying the topic, selecting the literature, deciding on paradigms and methods

Research is a dynamic process and your relationship with students you are supervising must change over time. One of the objectives for the supervisor is to guide the student towards becoming an independent researcher who can manage his or her own research project. One of the dilemmas for supervisors is deciding the point at which the student is now 'launched'; you have to begin preparing your student to become an independent researcher from the first meetings.

Your communication style is important throughout the research period, but it is critical in these early meetings as the impression you give the student at this stage may impact on their ability to relate to you in the future. If you are too negative you may destroy their confidence in their ability, too positive and you will give them false confidence, too prescriptive and they stay too dependent on you, too hands-off and you may leave them with insufficient guidance. Can the supervisor ever get it right? If you think of the doctoral research project as a collaborative endeavor involving partners who are equally but differently important to its success then you will build a sound relationship. As the 'senior' partner, you have an important guiding and directing role (see Wisker, 2006, pp. 120–33, for a very thought-provoking and insightful discussion of supervisory dialogues).

The early meetings in which you discuss refinements to the topic, the relevant literature and the choice of methods all require you to give guidance without taking over control of the thesis. Critical questions arise with each student. How do you lead them to defining and limiting (or expanding) the scope of the proposed topic so that it is both clear and realistic without in effecting giving them a topic to work on? Do they need you to give them a 'starter' bibliography or simply to outline what the literature review should contain, locate some training in literature searching and send them away to do it for themselves. Who decides on methods? Politics is a relatively eclectic discipline, but there can be quite deep-seated disputes over paradigms and methods. You may well find it difficult to supervise a student who wants to deploy methods you consider unreliable in certain aspects, or who wants to frame their research in ways you do not regard as valid, but you should be prepared to be somewhat open-minded. The student has the right to academic freedom; you are however fully entitled to make clear your reservations and the consequences which may follow from deploying methods or frameworks you have doubts about (including, importantly, the impact this may have on the eventual examination and publication of the thesis).

There are practical considerations to take into account in relation to these initial meetings: within a couple of years, you may have as many as six research students to supervise, or you may have a heavy teaching load or your own research to manage: your time for intensive one-to-one feedback will be limited. This is where good record keeping pays off. If you begin to notice that you keep having to give the same advice and feedback to students, then there is a potential problem somewhere. You are not communicating well, they have not understood, their confidence is low, or they are resisting your advice for reasons to do with their commitment to an approach, paradigm or methodology which you are sure will not be appropriate or effective. The sooner you identify this problem the better; sort it out through reviewing your practice, being open with the student about your concerns and calling on the advice of colleagues.

Tip three

You do not have unlimited time and so you cannot time after time correct errors in students written work. Your rules for this should be clear and accepted by the student from the start: it is their responsibility to improve their work on the basis of feedback. One method is to correct their first draft piece of work by pointing out presentational, typographical and referencing errors; if they recur in subsequent work, comment on this in general and perhaps recommend training in writing skills. If it continues, you may have to refuse to read a chapter until the student has corrected errors.

Finally, you should set a time limit for this preliminary work. If your university has formal processes for monitoring progress, then the student will have to submit after (usually) three – four months a revised outline of the topic, with a rationale, a preliminary literature review, and indication of methods and a plan of work. A panel including senior academics discusses the submission, after which it is either approved (sometimes with recommendations for amendments to the proposal or the plan) or the student is required to resubmit within a specified time. Even if your department does not have such formal processes, you should invent them, perhaps with the help of colleagues.

Making and monitoring progress

Supervisors have to decide whether students are making sufficient progress with their research, and are responsible for recommending whether they can continue to be registered (and in some cases to receive funding). This is a serious and difficult part of your role.

Increasingly, universities are moving towards requiring a review of students' progress at key points: the beginning of the second term, the end of the first year, perhaps during second year and certainly towards the end of second year of registration. At all of these points, academics not involved in the supervision review written work submitted by students and, often, discuss an oral presentation by the student. Such panels can allow the student to progress (perhaps with some instructions or advice), can require the student to rethink and resubmit within a specified period or even recommend withdrawal or transfer to a Masters thesis.

There are clear benefits to such progress reviews: at the most simple, they remind students that their work on the thesis is time-limited and they have to develop the work at a reasonable rate. They encourage the students to write and re-draft; it should not be possible for students to leave all the 'serious' writing to the final six months. They are good training for conference paper drafting and presentation, and can be in the later stages a first preparation for the viva. They remind the student that the thesis must be convincing to a wider audience (including of course the examiners). Presenting their ideas and findings to a wider audience can help identify writing problems: the student may have wonderful ideas and excellent research findings but have difficulty expressing them clearly in formal academic writing. Finally, but not least, a critical review by experienced researchers will almost certainly result in useful feedback which can help the student to improve in some areas (or encourage them to go on with confidence).

There are certainly valid objections to some of these processes: some students may seem them as an end in themselves, work frantically to win approval for progress then slacken off afterwards. They are no guarantees that a student who progresses into final year with a panel's approval will not lose confidence or motivation or even simply find writing up too difficult. More serious is the possibility that criticisms might arise from academics defending their preferred paradigms or approaches rather than from any 'failure' by the student. Where such panels are properly structured with clear criteria for approval or otherwise, criticisms which arise from epistemological or methodological differences can be noted but not delay progress. There is no denying, however, that this can be a tricky situation for an inexperienced supervisor or a recently-appointed lecturer. You may have to defend your student's approach and negotiate with senior colleagues over the appropriate feedback and any changes that should be required; this is where the constructive advice from the faculty director of research or head of research graduate school should be sought.

Even if your university or department does not have formal structured progress panels, there will no doubt be progress review points where the supervisors are required to indicate whether the student has made sufficient progress. This is another point where you are being asked to make a serious professional judgement which will have consequences for student. This is where you have to consider – with advice from colleagues if necessary – what is genuinely in the interest of the student. Would extra time/ a leave of absence help? Are they progressing more slowly than you hoped, or have they such a limited grasp of the essentials that improvement is unlikely? You will certainly worry that recommending withdrawal or transfer to a Masters thesis will be devastating for your student. However, recommending continued registration for a student who, for whatever reason, has not fulfilled agreed targets will be worse for them. In any case, you should make sure that your students are aware of your concerns before such critical points have been reached.

Dealing with personal problems

There are three key questions covered in this section: how friendly can or should you be with your students; how much responsibility do you have for solving their personal problems and what do you do about complaints by students about you or one of your colleagues?

The answer to the first question depends on several variables. You may like to socialise extensively with colleagues or you may be someone who keeps work and social life very separate. You may have a general rule about not ever socialising with students or you may see some social interaction as part of your mentoring role. You will find yourself liking or empathising with some students more than others. There are few hard and fast rules but I would suggest two. Firstly, if you socialise at all with students, try to ensure that there is a rough parity of treatment among all your students. You may for example think it is obvious why you would invite an overseas student living alone in a foreign country to dinner while seeing no need to do the same for your local student who has a family and well-established friendship network. This may not be apparent to the lonely local student now living two hundred miles from his or her family. You do not have to have all your students to dinner at your home, but you should be prepared to have some social contact with all your students if you socialise with one. Secondly, if you fall in love with one of your students and commence an intimate relationship, you have to stop being his or her supervisor. Within limits, I would recommend being friendly and approachable. At the very least have a coffee with your students from time to time so that they can feel comfortable discussing issues that go beyond the strict confines of matters related to their thesis; this may help you to anticipate and respond to the next set of issues.

As noted above, doctoral students may be unable to complete in time for several reasons which have nothing to do with quality of supervision. Students may become extremely poor or ill, may have emotional problems or have to deal with family crises. They may fall behind and become demotivated because of poor working habits. How much pastoral care or remedial support is the over-worked academic required to provide? If you discover de-motivation, you could intervene by providing (or directing them to) intensive coaching in the relevant skill. If they are depressed, ill or experiencing emotional crises, your university will have specialist departments who can provide the necessary support. If students have run out of money for some reasons, then clearly you cannot give them cash (though you can pay for occasional meals) but you can locate resources that might reduce their costs (such as access to a comfortable place to work) and direct them to the student welfare officers. There is, however, a potential downside to knowing about all these problems: you may consider that for the sake of the student and for the department's completion rates the student should take a leave of absence, which may in the short term lead to a suspension of funding. You should only take decisions such as that after consulting colleagues and your university's student health and counselling department.

Finally, how should you deal with students who have complained about you (or possibly worse, who are complaining to you about your co-supervisor)? Fortunately, malicious and completely unfounded complaints by students against supervisors are very exceptional; in fact, students may feel too vulnerable to lodge justified complaints. You can anticipate problems and avoid complaints by being aware of how your students are responding to you. Keep good records of all communications and ask for advice if you begin to be aware of problems. You can 'train' yourself to understand why students might complain by looking at some research student forums (for example, the 'thesis whisperer' http://thethesiswhisperer.wordpress.com/). Complaints are upsetting, but you can limit the impact by co-operating with the processes for handling student complaints and being prepared to be flexible: accepting that the relationship has not worked and allowing the student to change supervisors with good grace may be hard but can be the best solution. It is much more difficult to deal with students complaining to you about a colleague. You have to listen to your student and explore the nature of the problem; a student who has the impression that a supervisor does not take their research sufficiently seriously may be due to miscommunication; a student who can demonstrate that a colleague has not responded to them or missed appointments is clearly not misinterpreting poorly phrased remarks. In these cases, you can assist the student by taking responsibility for feedback and arranging meetings for a time. If a student comes to you to discuss harassment of any kind by a colleague, you should not try to handle this yourself; bring in the Head of Research Graduate School or equivalent in your university.

The final stages: finishing and preparing for the examination of the thesis

> These concluding weeks are an emotional cocktail of exhaustion, frustration, fright and exhilaration. Supervisors correct errors we thought had been removed a year ago. The paragraph that seemed good enough in the first draft now seems to drag down a chapter. My postgraduates cannot understand why I am so picky. They want to submit and move on with the rest of their lives.
>
> (Brabazon, 2010a)

As the above extract indicates, there are two aspects to the final stages: supporting the student in completing the writing, and making arrangements for the examination. By the beginning of the final year of registration, the student should already have drafted a considerable proportion of the thesis. Some, ideally most, of this can be incorporated into the final version but the final write-up requires a different approach. Wisker (2005, p. 283) makes the important point that a PhD thesis 'is not a diary of work done'. In the final months, all those drafts have to be turned into a well-structured coherent argument which presents clear conclusions which are strongly related to the literature and the research methods. It will almost certainly feel as if time is going to run out; your student will either want to finish at all costs and submit a thesis that is at best lacking polish and at worst is unfinished, or they will want to keep revising until unattainable perfection has been achieved. You have to ensure that they have a realistic set of targets, taking into account possible mishaps and setbacks; you may have to give explicit direction as to how much time to spend on each chapter, and to indicate the relative importance of each section. Students may not be aware of how important the concluding chapter is and how it must be integrated into the thesis as a whole. You may even have to remind them of your university's regulations for presentation of a draft thesis.

Ultimately, at this stage, the student takes responsibility to submit the thesis; students are required to sign an intention to submit. If you have created a good relationship where you can be responsive to their needs and concerns and they trust your judgements then you will not have to deal with the student submitting a thesis that you consider unsatisfactory; if they are adamant in the face of your good advice, then you should make your reservations clear and provide remedial advice to improve the thesis as much as possible before submission.

As the writing up progresses, you (and your co-supervisors) should be identifying the External Examiner. The notification to submit is provided two to four months before actual submission; the External Examiner should be identified by then, so that you can make arrangements for a viva voce within a reasonable time after submission (a time limit for the examination is usually prescribed by regulation). This requires a great deal of care. Ideally, you should find an expert in the area who is likely to have broad sympathy with the student's paradigm or methodology, and who, if possible, is able to comment on most of the content. You obviously will not choose someone whose work the student has strongly critiqued in the thesis, but it is a good idea to choose someone whose work is referred to in the thesis. 'Mismatches between the research paradigms of the student and the examiner can lead to disagreement about the quality of a thesis' (Leonard et al., 2006). If you are going outside your own network, then you may have to do some research on prospective examiners' personal qualities. You want to select someone who is 'generous-minded' rather than proud of his or her exacting standards, or who has very fixed ideas about what a thesis must be. The External Examiner you choose may make a contribution beyond the examination process: they may be able to write references or reports on the thesis for publishers. Most universities now expect there to be an internal Examiner, an academic colleague not involved in the production of the thesis. Many of the same considerations apply to the choice of internal Examiner. In both cases it is a delicate balance; you want someone you can trust to give the thesis a fair reading, but not so close to you that the student suffers from any suspicion that you have somehow 'fixed' the outcome of the examination.

One further consideration may affect your choice of internal Examiner. Despite the moves towards standard practices, there are still some differences in how the viva voce is managed in different universities. Some, like mine, have an independent chair who is responsible – among other things – for ensuring that the viva is conducted fairly and that the criteria for assessing a thesis are applied consistently. The chair produces a report of the proceedings. In other universities, it is the internal Examiner who is responsible for managing the viva and producing a clear report; if that is your system, you should choose an internal Examiner who is experienced, trained and takes the regulations seriously.

With the thesis safely in the hands of the Examiners, you now have to prepare for the *viva voce*. The student should go in to the viva voce calmly confident that he or she has produced a coherent work which makes a valuable contribution the knowledge in the area. They should be confident but not arrogant; they should be able to defend the work without being overly 'defensive'. In most cases, they will have had some experience of being asked tough questions and receiving constructive criticism. However, what they have read and heard may make them feel panicky rather than healthily nervous.

> There is a lack of clarity on the part of examiners, supervisors and candidates about the purposes of the viva. The viva is perceived by both supervisors and candidates as an unpredictable process and difficult to prepare for.
>
> (Leonard et al., 2006).

How can you help them prepare? You and your student should know exactly how the viva is managed in your institution, including the criteria for assessing a thesis. They should read a reassuring guide such as Murray (2003) or even a guide for examiners such as Peace (2005) – you should certainly read both of those. In some places, a practice viva is obligatory. If that applies in your university, then you should ensure that it includes some serious questions about the work as well as generic questions. So, you should either find a colleague or colleagues who will read all or key sections of the thesis (you will have to reciprocate) or you will have to provide colleagues with a script. If you are not required to arrange a mock viva, you should certainly make sure that students see a video of a viva such as that on the PORT website (although that site is for Language rather than Politics doctoral students). Brabazon (2010b) provides a useful checklist of how to prepare.

Finally, your work is not finished when the examination is over. If your student has been successful you may have to ensure that they are aware of the regulations for final submission. They may want your advice and support in achieving publications based on their thesis, as well as advice and support in securing employment. If they have been asked to make corrections – or to resubmit – then you should be prepared to clarify what they are required to do, advise on deadlines and read a draft of their revised sections to ensure that they complete the tasks set by the examiners.

Conclusion

There is a lot to worry about when you embark upon doctoral supervision; however, in my experience few achievements give as much satisfaction as guiding a new researcher through a thesis. When it is over you will have, if not a friend for life, then certainly a new colleague in your discipline who is entirely likely to be a member of your growing network of research colleagues and collaborators. Your future students are likely to benefit from contact with your former students (if only to learn how to manage you) and you will learn something about supervising from each doctoral student. Finally, look at all the books and training manuals for supervisors. The titles and introductory headings include the words 'good', 'effective', 'successful' or even 'excellent'. None of them include the word 'perfect'.

Further reading

The seminars and training provided by John Wakeford from the Missenden Centre (http://www.missendencentre.co.uk/index.htm) have been warmly received by many academics. A selection of articles on issues in higher education research is available at that website at http://www.missendencentre.co.uk/johnwakeford.htm. Of enormous value on the same site are a series of diaries from doctoral students; for social science supervisors, Carol's PhD Diary is of particular relevance. Happily, it includes a 'good supervisor' and ends with a good outcome, but you can easily identify the points at which everything might have fallen apart. (http://www.missendencentre.co.uk/docs/ Carol%20stewart%27s%20full%20story2006.pdf) Julie's and Peter's stories, covered in Wakeford, 2004, make more salutary reading.

References

All websites cited here were last accessed on 9 September 2011.

Brabazon, T. (2010a), 'How Not to Write a PhD Thesis', *Times Higher Education Supplement*, 28 January, available at http://www.timeshighereducation.co.uk/story. asp?storycode=410208.

Brabazon, T. (2010b), 'Take the Heat Out of Trial by Fire', *Times Higher Education Supplement*, 21 April, available at http://www.timeshighereducation.co.uk/story.asp?sectioncode=26 &storycode=411311&c=1.

Burnham, P., Gillan Lutz, K., Grant, W. and Layton-Henry, Z. (2008), *Research Methods in Politics*, Basingstoke, Palgrave Macmillan.

Corbyn, Z. (2007), 'PhD Failure Rates Revealed', *Times Higher Education Supplement*, 5 October, available at http://www.timeshighereducation.co.uk/story.asp?storycode= 310709.

Cryer, P. (1998), 'Beyond Codes of Practice: Dilemmas in Supervising Postgraduate Research Students', *Quality in Higher Education*, 4 (3), 229–34.

Delamont, S., Atkinson, P. and Parry, O. (2004), *Supervising the Doctorate: A Guide to Success*. Maidenhead, Open University Press and McGraw-Hill Education.

Dunleavy, P. (2003), *Authoring a PhD: How to Plan, Draft, Write and Finish a Doctoral Thesis or Dissertation*, Basingstoke, Palgrave Macmillan.

Eley, A. and Jennings, R. (2005), *Effective Postgraduate Supervision: Improving the Student/ Supervisor Relationship*, Maidenhead, Open University Press.

Eley, A. and Murray, R. (2009), *How to be an Effective Supervisor: Best Practice in Research Student Supervision*, Maidenhead, Open University Press and McGraw-Hill Education.

Economic and Social Research Council (1984), *The Preparation and Supervision of Research Theses in the Social Sciences. Swindon*, ESRC.

Lee, A. (2008), 'How are Doctoral Students Supervised? Concepts of Doctoral Research Supervision', *Studies in Higher Education*, 322 (3), 267–81.

Leonard, D., Becker, R. and Evans, J. (2006), *Review of Literature on the Impact of Working Context and Support on the Postgraduate Research Student Learning Experience*, Higher Education Academy, available at http://www.npc.org.uk/whatiswherecanifindhowdoi/ Useful_Documents/DoctoralExperienceReview.pdf.

S. Lynch (2008), 'Happy Days: Why PhD Students Need a Helping Hand from Their Supervisors', *Independent*, 14 February, available at http://www.independent.co.uk/ news/education/higher/happy-days-why-phd-students-need-a-helping-hand-from-their-supervisors-781842.html.

Murphy, E. (2007), 'Part-Time Doctoral Students: What the Research Says', Paper presented to a seminar of the UK Council for Graduate Education, 11 October, available at http://as.exeter.ac.uk/media/level1/academicserviceswebsite/academicpolicyand studentadministration/documents/graduateresearchfaculty/supervisorhandbook/part-time_doctoral_research_students.pdf.

Murray, R. (2003), *How to Survive Your Viva : Defending a Thesis in an Oral Examination*, Maidenhead, Open University Press and McGraw-Hill.

Pearce, L. (2005), *How to Examine a Thesis*. Maidenhead, Open University Press and SRHE.

Postgraduate Online Research Training 'The Viva as an Experience', available at: http:// port.igrs.sas.ac.uk/videos/vivaexperience.

Quality Assurance Agency for Higher Education (QAA) (2004), *Code of Practice for the Assurance of Academic Quality and Standards in Higher Education*.

Quality Assurance Agency for Higher Education (QAA) (2011), *Doctoral Degree Characteristics*, available at http://www.qaa.ac.uk/Publications/InformationAndGuidance/ Documents/Doctoral_Characteristics.pdf.

Thompson, P. and Warner, M. (eds) (2010), *The Routledge Doctoral Supervisor's Companion: Supporting Effective Research in Education and the Social Sciences*, London, Routledge and Taylor and Francis.

Vitae, http://www.vitae.ac.uk/policy-practice/1389/Supervisors–managers.html.

Wakeford, J. (2004), 'The Missing Links', *The Guardian*, 16 March, accessible online at http://www.guardian.co.uk/education/2004/mar/16/postgraduate.highereducation? INTCMP=ILCNETTXT3487.

Wareing, F. (no date), 'A PhD in Just Over a Year and a Half …'m The Missenden Centre, available at http://www.missendencentre.co.uk/PhD1.pdf.

Wisker, G. (2005), *The Good Supervisor: Supervising Postgraduate and Undergraduate Research for Doctoral Theses and Dissertations*, Basingstoke, Palgrave Macmillan.

Wright, T. and Cochrane, R. (2000), 'Factors Influencing Successful Submission of PhD Theses', *Studies in Higher Education*, 25 (2), 181–95; available at http://www.cs.ucl.ac.uk/ staff/M.Sewell/faq/publishing-research/WrCo00.pdf.

16
The Loneliness of the Long-Distance Student: Supervising Students You Rarely See

Dave Middleton

There is little denying that higher education in the UK has changed dramatically over the past few years. The number of full-time students in part-time employment rose by 54 per cent over the 10 years to 2006 (TUC, 2006). Since that report it is likely that the numbers have increased as public subsidy has decreased. Being full-time, for many students, no longer means having nothing to do but study. Education is something that students now have to fit in around the rest of their lives. Accompanying this has been a structural shift in modes of study. Part-time students are now 43 per cent of the total student population (Million+, 2010). In 2009/10 there were 770,000 part-time students in the UK (HESA, 2011). Changes to funding mean that students now consider themselves as consumers and lecturers as service providers. If they cannot find the time to meet with us then, in this increasingly service orientated industry, we have to find the means to provide them with viable alternatives. In effect, the future for many higher education institutions is very similar to the present in my own – The Open University.

So, what does all this mean for those of us engaged in supervising students? The expectation that students can and will attend lectures, seminars and all the extra-curricular activities on offer will no longer hold for a large proportion of students. Let me be clear, however. These changes will not apply to all students: full-time will still be the major mode of study for most students. Not all part-time students will become distant learners, most will attend lectures and seminars and will build their studies into their lives in creative ways. But, as the proportion of students studying either at a distance, or on a part-time basis grows the ways in which we deliver the educational experience must adapt.

In this chapter what I want to do is suggest some ways in which academic staff might create more flexible learning methods better suited to this new type of student. In drawing upon work carried out on the HEFCE funded project PARLE (see Middleton and Bridge, 2008 for an overview, and Middleton, 2009 for some examples of the teaching), I want to suggest that e-learning far from being a threat (see for example Lambeir and Ramaekin, 2006), or a nirvana (see for example, Salmon, 2005) provides a set of tools which can supplement the more tried and tested methods of supervision. Indeed, most of these tools can be used, with a little imagination, to supplement lectures and seminars too.

Supervising students

While most part-time and distant students can arrange their lives to accommodate structured teaching opportunities, the more 'ad hoc' relationships associated with supervising dissertations and theses may present more of a challenge. There is considerable evidence that students who develop a good working relationship with their supervisors tend to achieve better results (see, for example, Holmberg, 1986; McMann, 1994; Sewart, 1993; Keegan, 1986) It is clear that the student-supervisor relationship is usually envisaged in terms of a one on one engagement taking place in the supervisor's study. For example, Chris Hart gives the following advice to Masters students:

> Use your supervisor as much as possible throughout your dissertation research. They have the experience of supervising many previous students and therefore have a knowledge you do not have. They will be able to help you to formulate your ideas on a topic, direct you to reading and may even suggest a topic they know can be done.
>
> (Hart, 2005, p. 78)

Now it may well be the case that there are supervisors who fulfil these criteria. But a number of supervisors, particularly inexperienced newer colleagues may have little previous experience and don't possess the encyclopaedic knowledge necessary to deal with every students dream project. Moreover, and perhaps more importantly, many students will not be in a position to use their supervisor as much as they might like. Work, family and personal commitments are increasingly likely to intervene in the relationship, particularly with the growth of part-time and distant students.

The kind of activities which promote independence of thought and scholarly skills are often undertaken in supervision circumstances arranged to coincide with a particular crisis point. Part-time/distant students can feel further marginalised as they lack the opportunity for ad hoc meetings to which they assume, rightly or wrongly, that full-time on-campus students have ready access. As a part-time PhD student myself I remember feeling that there was a whole on-campus world of which I was an outsider. Other PhD students seemed far more integrated into the academic community than I was able to be. In this context failure and drop-out become a more likely outcome of those whose need for support, guidance and care outweighs their desire for independence.

Box 16.1   Key areas in supervision

What question is the student trying to answer with their dissertation/ thesis? Is the question sensible and manageable? Is the question too narrow, or too wide? Does it require resources (for example, time) that the student is unlikely to have?

What knowledge are they building on? Is their topic related to their undergraduate studies or a previous dissertation? Are they attempting a PhD when they should be doing an undergraduate dissertation? How do you limit their ambitions?

How much reading do they need to do? How much new material do they need to read? What sources should they be encouraged to look at (Wikipedia)? When should they stop reading?

Is their study empirical, theoretical or a mixture of both? How do you help them to develop a theory? What empirical methods are appropriate for their research question? How important are epistemological considerations?

What is an appropriate academic writing style? How do they avoid 'inadvertent' plagiarism? How much of what they write should be in the final product?

The student-supervisor relationship is complex being simultaneously, subject and skills driven. The subject is the pivot on which the skills element turns. But, without developing the necessary skills, the student's interest in the subject will never extend beyond repetition of existing sources. Lisa Harrison notes that in doing a dissertation attention must be paid to both *generic* and *specific* skills.

> Generic skills apply equally to all dissertations: it is the ability to present a clear, structured argument which demonstrates an appreciation of the relevant information and appropriate writing skills. Specific skills should reflect the nature of the dissertation: being able to apply appropriate political theory(ies), operationalising appropriate methodological skills and developing knowledge in a particular research area.
>
> (Harrison, 2001, p. 143)

From a supervisors point of view there are 5 key areas which the student needs to address. See Box 16.1.

E-learning

E-learning as a term has existed since at least the mid-1980's (Middleton, 2009) and can mean anything from posting lecture notes on a server to fully integrated online courses.[1] What follows are brief discussions of four relatively easy to use web-based applications – blogs, wikis, podcasts and screencasts – which could be used to deliver supervision to part-time/distant students.

Clearly different students require different types of support. Some are self-managing and require only the occasional meeting (or email) to keep them on target. Others need a more hands-on approach. A range of e-tools could be used to assist in this work. While there is no real replacement for face to face interactions, it is possible to do some of the work via the use of online tools – aimed either at individual students or groups of students.

Blogging

There are around 60 million blogs on the Internet, and it is estimated that a blog is created every second. The term was coined in the 1990's as a way to describe online diaries. Blogs can be either public (anybody, anywhere can see them) or private, so that you can share your thoughts with just your students. There are a number of free, easy to use, blog systems including Google's Blog spot. It took me precisely 10 minutes to create a blog using their blog creation wizard.[2] You could also use the free system at www.posterous.com or your own institutional website (For example, see Jim Newell's politics blog at http://jlnewell.com/blog/).

Blogging does require some commitment on your part. Very often people start a blog, make one or two entries, and then run out of enthusiasm. This can be because they were unsure what their blog was trying to do from the outset. Like most educational endeavours a little planning goes a long way. See Box 16.2.

Each blog entry should be no more than 1,000 words. It should be written in an accessible style, it is not an academic paper or textbook chapter. It should pose questions and encourage readers to comment and respond. A really good blog will have comments on your text, plus comments on comments. But, clearly, if your audience is limited then the chances are that commentary will be rare, so don't necessarily judge your blog by the debate it creates, but rather by how you can point students to what you have written rather than have them camping outside your door needing your advice.

Do not underestimate how much time it takes to write 5–600 words on a regular basis. Many bloggers tend to produce random streams of consciousness, the best blogs – unless, they happen to be extremely witty (very few bloggers

Box 16.2   Some topics for your blog

Does the bibliography count in the word count?
How many quotations are permissible before it becomes plagiarism?
What's the difference between a research question and a research topic?

Box 16.3   Top blogging tips

Keep them short
Keep them regular
Ask questions that invite comments

are as witty as they think they are – a bit like lecturers, then) – are subject specific. Of the 60 million blogs on the Internet, I would wager that at least half have no entries from the past six months. It is important if you blog to your students to ensure that you put aside a set time each week to do so. Make Thursday afternoon, for example, blogging day. That way, your students will come to expect the blog on a Thursday afternoon and will set aside Thursday evening to read and comment on it (hopefully). See Box 16.3.

Wikis

The word wiki derives from the Hawaiian term meaning 'quick'. Wiki's have been around since 1994 when they were 'invented' by web designer Ward Cunningham and the most famous, some might say infamous, example is Wikipedia, which launched in 2001. This is not the place to have a debate about the pro's (yes, there are some) or cons of Wikipedia. Your institutional Virtual Learning Environment (VLE) – usually Blackboard or Moodle – will include the capacity to create a wiki. The question is: how useful could it be in supervising students?

What follows then is one example from the Open University Masters Foundation Degree Module on a way in which we used a wiki to create an interactive exercise to assist students in sifting through potential sources.[3] The teaching objectives of the module were to encourage students to use a variety of sources, but to privilege academic sources. So, in effect we were using a wiki in an attempt to undermine Wikipedia. This involved setting up a number of linked pages, the first of which was a simple instructions page.

Each page is linked to another page via a hyperlink. These are very easy to set up, usually requiring you to click on a link called hyperlinks. At the top of the instructions page we put in bold: **Please don't edit this page.** This was put in following previous iterations of the module where the wiki pages became a jumble of student entries and the instructions of what to do were lost in the middle somewhere. At the bottom, following the introductory text are a series of hyperlinks to three 'case studies', each containing a research question and a list of sources.

Most students carried out the exercise and the wiki page for comments became very long indeed. This module contained over 200 students, all

Box 16.4   Uses for a wiki

Create communities of learners
Create a repository for students own data
Set up interactive exercises for assessing sources, referencing etc.

studying at a distance. Every student in the last cohort tackled the exercise and the vast majority reached the correct (in my view) conclusions.

There could be a number of uses of wikis in the supervision process. For example, it would be possible to set up a wiki with sub-sections for different topic clusters, allowing students with an interest in feminism, Marxism or Italian politics to create their own community of scholars. A place where they could discuss what they have in common as well as how they differ. Or, you might use a wiki as a repository for any original research asking students to upload datasets that they have created, interview transcripts, research notes or draft chapters for others to share and comment on. See Box 16.4.

Podcasting

A podcast is an audio file available for downloading via an RSS feed. Creating a podcast is fairly easy. All you require is a microphone and recording software. A number of academics are already using podcasts, some of which are professionally made.[4] Of the more home made variety, many are done using the free software programme Audacity, available for download at www.audacity.com.

There has been a considerable literature on podcasting, although to be honest most of it espouses the benefits without any great evidence to back up the claims (Booth, 2007). There is also a wealth of free advice on the internet about how to make a podcast. From my own experience with the medium let me pass on what little I have learned. My inclination on making my first ever podcast was to simply speak into a microphone on a topic which I felt students were struggling with. When I played it back I quickly realised how incoherent I was. There were a lot of mm's and ah's which was bad enough but a couple of times I also lost my way. Quickly abandoning my pretensions to be the new A. J. P. Taylor, I decided to type a script. I duly typed out my script and then read it into a microphone. Pleased with the result I played it back and surprise, surprise, I sounded like a person reading a script. The joke, not that funny to begin with, was entirely flat. The whole thing was a very dreary 15 minutes worth of recorded boredom. Inadvertently, I may have found a cure for insomnia. Sounding natural is not as easy as professional broadcasters make it seem. However, after recording and playing back the same script 4 or 5 times the results improved both because I became more relaxed and I had learned the script off by heart.

232 Supervising Students You Rarely See

Box 16.5   Podcasting – some tips

Use a script, but try not to read it
To sound natural, do a number of retakes
Avoid copyright complications by downloading royalty free music

Based on these early experiences I realise that it is incredibly difficult to speak for 5–10 minutes (and the average podcast, if it is to be listened to, should be no more than that) without stumbling over the words. It was at this point that I realised something I had learned in making audios at the Open University with professionals at the helm. Actors also stumble over their words, but rather than collapse into a fit of giggles (although some do) or give up, they simply pause go back and read it again. The pause is important as it allows the editor to delete the parts that didn't work so well. But, given that I was to be the editor, I thought it might be good to practice on a smaller section first. I therefore recorded precisely one minutes worth of material. With pauses and mistakes this took about five minutes. The pauses allowed me to delete out all the mistakes and hey presto, there it was – one minutes worth of seamless audio ready to be unleashed upon an unsuspecting student audience.

Of course, I still had to do this a further nine times before I had the 10 one-minute sections that would be made up into the whole thing. Altogether this 10 minute sequence took me about a day to complete. Although this included creating a transcript, which I did by transcribing the completed tape. I have since progressed to a point where the process is quicker and easier. I now write a script, in about 5 two-minute slots. I don't read the script, anymore than I would read my lecture notes, but they provide a structure. When I am happy with the section I then edit it, which is usually a question of simply taking out all the mistakes, and then listen to it and amend the transcript.

This file can then be uploaded onto a server, a process that will probably require you to liaise with your technical department. It is possible to add music and sound effects to your podcast. But if you are thinking of doing so remember that copyright restrictions in the UK are very strict. There are websites where you can download copyright free music.[5] If all you want is an opening piece of mood music then this avoids any copyright complications. On the other hand, you might be able to persuade your institution that £3000 for that clip from Pavarotti is a good use of their money. See Box 16.5.

Screencasting

The final e-tool which is easy to use and free is screencasting. Technically a screencast is a tool which captures what is happening on your screen as a video file.

Screencasting has been fairly extensively used by software companies to create simple online tutorials. Many of us will be familiar with the Microsoft screencasts used to support their Microsoft Office suite of programmes. Their use in higher education is less well documented, with Petersen (2007) claiming that it remains a relatively new idea. Falconer et al. (2009) used screencasts to supplement their chemistry classes claiming that these simple to create 'videos' are 'quite similar to what could be presented in class, but students can go through them at their own pace'. While Loch (2011) used screencasts to support a maths course 'to explain topics students usually find difficult to understand'. Screencasts require detailed planning to coordinate the script with what is happening on screen. The free software for doing this is fairly limited and I would suggest the free programme Jing (www.techsmith.com/jing) for a tool that sits on your desktop and is easy to use.

The technical ability to make a screencast is no more than the ability to download and install this piece of software. It is then simply a question of clicking the record button and using the five minutes which you are allowed to say something useful over the screen. You will have already seen the potential problem, however. While Jing does allow you to pause a recording while you are making it, you do need to plan how you intend to use your five minutes of fame. As with podcasting, I would advise splitting the time into discrete sessions. So utilizing five lots of one minute sessions allows you to get your breath back and change your screen if necessary. The other major problem with Jing is the inability to edit after the event. This requires specialist software such as Camtasia, which while not prohibitively expensive will cost upwards of £140 for a single user licence. If you are intending to use screencasts on a regular basis then well worth the investment in my opinion. However, once you have created your screencast you can upload it to www.screencast.com and circulate the URL to your students, who can then access it from their computer.

The advantage of a video file is obvious. If you want to show students how to interpret a table of data, or discuss an image then the ability to be able to see as well as hear brings a new dimension to e-learning scenarios. A screencast does not have to resemble a professional video (actually, it's unlikely to) to be effective. You may want to create a screencast that shows students how to write an abstract or illustrates how to reference their work. If you want to encourage the use of RefWorks or similar programmes then a single screencast will allow your students to follow your instructions at their own pace. Moreover, students could be encouraged to present their research as a screencast which other students could then comment on. See Box 16.6.

Conclusion

E-learning is here to stay. While it is true that many e-learning tools have been introduced in what Booth (2007) called an 'evaluation bypass', the

Box 16.6   Screencasting – some tips

Plan ahead thinking about what images complement your script
Use PowerPoint animations to create dynamic movement on the screen
Record in short sections (one minute at a time)

'early adopters' (Rogers, 1995) will continue to experiment with new software and the rest of us will struggle to keep up. E-learning is being driven by what I would call 'the 3 E's' – economics, experimentation and expectations. Universities in the UK have been forced to become leaner and more cost effective. One place Vice Chancellors look to make savings has been in the area of e-learning. But, at the same time, lecturers with an interest in teaching have always experimented with new methods of delivery (Middleton, 2010), and will continue to do so. But, what is really driving the e-learning boom is that the expectations of students are changing. Students are switched on; they possess smart phones, i-pads, laptops. They now expect free wi-fi connections, course websites, and instant access to their tutors via email and text. This is a massive shift in educational expectations in a single generation. Lecturers who refuse to be online or who do not engage with e-learning will in Lambeir and Ramaeken's pithy rephrasing of Shakespeare face 'the choice *to be* online *or not to be*' (2006, p. 545).

The four tools discussed in this chapter are not groundbreaking; neither do they require a sophisticated knowledge of computing. They adapt the skills most lecturers already possess to the challenges facing us today. They are what I like to think of as a set of survival tools equipping you for the e-learning present. They each have their advantages and disadvantages but anybody with a computer and internet connection should be able to begin experimenting with these tools, and in doing so should be able to find creative uses for e-learning that rather than threatening their identity as educators will enhance it.

Final word: e-learning is about sharing. Let me know if you feel inspired to experiment as a result of this chapter or if you have any further questions visit the blog at http://helearn.blogspot.com/2011/09/supervising-students-using-e-learning.html

Notes

1. Examples of e-courses can be seen at The Open University's OpenLearn website (www.open.ac.uk/openlearn). In addition, I have placed a number of resources which I have been involved in developing over the past 5 years at: http://labspace.open.ac.uk/course/view.php?id=7515 which are you are free to experiment with.
2. You can view it here: http://helearn.blogspot.com/2011/09/supervising-students-using-e-learning.html

3. You can see the full wiki on my labspace, at the address above.
4. You can see some examples of professionally created podcasts at the Open University Open Politics site: http://www.open.ac.uk/openlearn/whats-on/open-politics
5. Try http://www.seabreezecomputers.com/tips/freemusic.htm for a list of free music that you can use

References

Booth, A. (2007), 'Blogs, Wikis and Podcasts: The Evaluation Bypass', *Health Information and Libraries Journal*, 24, 298–302.

Falconer, L., deGrazia, J., Medlin, J. W. and Holmberg, M. P. (2009). 'Using Screencasts in Che Courses', *Chemical Engineering 286 Education*, 43 (4), Fall 2009, vol. 43 (available at: http://cache.org/site/news_stand/summer10/summer10%20Using%20Screencasts.pdf, accessed 2 February 2012).

Harrison, L. (2001), *Political Research: An Introduction* (London: Routledge).

Hart, C. (2005), *Doing Your Masters Dissertation* (London: Sage).

HESA (2011), Statistics available from http://www.hesa.ac.uk/index.php?option=com_content&task=view&id=1897&Itemid=239.

Holmberg, B. (1986), 'A Discipline of Distance Education' *Journal of Distance Education*, 1(1), 20–40.

Keegan, D. (1986), 'Interaction and Communication' (Chapter 6, pp. 89–107), in D. Keegan (ed.) *The Foundations of Distance Education*, Kent UK, C room Helm, (available at: http://www.c3l.uni-oldenburg.de/cde/support/readings/keegan86.pdf.

TUC (2006) *All Work and Low Pay* London, TUC.

Lambeir, B. and Ramaeken, S. (2006), 'The Limits of Blackboard are the Limits of My World: On the Changing Concepts of the University and its Students', *E-learning* 3 (4): 544–51.

Loch, B. (2011), 'Screencasting for Mathematics Online Learning – A Case Study of a First Year Operations Research Course at a Dual Mode Australian University', available at: http://stan.cc.swin.edu.au/~lochb/download/Loch2011.pdf.

McMann, G. W. (1994), 'The Changing Role of Moderation in Computer Mediated Conferencing', in *Proceedings of the Distance Learning Research Conference*, San Antonio, TX, April 27–9, pp. 159–66.

Middleton, D. and Bridge, K. (2008), 'Multimedia Learning: Lessons from the PARLE Project', *European Political Science* (7), 144–52.

Middleton, D. (2009), 'When Eric Met Sally: Putting the Drama into Ethics Teaching', *Enhanced Learning in the Social Sciences*, 1 (3), (available at: http://www.heacademy.ac.uk/resources/detail/subjects/csap/eliss/1-3-Middleton, accessed on 9 September 2011).

Middleton, D. (2010), 'Putting the "e" into E-learning', *European Political Science*, 9 (1), 5–12.

Million+ (2010) *Fair Funding For All* London, London Economics Limited.

Petersen, E. (2007), 'Incorporating Screencasts in Online Teaching', *The International Review of Research in Open and Distant Learning*, November 2007, (available at http://www.irrodl.org/index.php/irrodl/article/viewArticle/495/935)

Rogers, E. M. (1995), *Diffusion of Innovations*, 4th edn (New York: The Free Press).

Salmon, G. (2005) 'Flying not flapping: a strategic framework for e-learning and pedagogical innovation in higher education institutions', *ALT-J: Research in Learning Technology* 13 (3), pp. 201–18.

Sewart, D. (1993), 'Student Support Systems in Distance Education', *Open Learning*, 8 (3), pp. 3–12.

17

From Politics Past to Politics Future: Addressing the Employability Agenda through a Professional Politics Curriculum

Matthew Wyman, Jennifer Lees-Marshment and Jon Herbert

> I am not satisfied with the quality of undergraduate education in the University... the pressures on universities mean that they have been fighting I think a long defeat to maintain standards in undergraduate learning... [the undergraduate experience] is too impersonal, it's not sufficiently interactive... the curriculum is being developed a little incrementally and it's not profoundly thought through.
>
> (Professor Alan Gilbert, President,
> Manchester University, August 2009)

Recent studies of political education in UK universities largely focus on teaching methods, and advocate various admirable changes in approach. These can be summed up as more deep learning, more focus on what students do rather than what teachers do, and assessment diversification for skills development (for example, Stammers, Dittmar and Henney, 1999; Sloam, 2008). It is striking, though, that curriculum content as a whole has received little attention. Facing rising student numbers and falling units of resource, a deafening silence has settled around an unsatisfactory *status quo*. Most, although not all, UK curricula look today much like they did two or three decades ago. For understandable reasons, the Politics and International Relations benchmark statement (QAA, 2007) is primarily a codification of existing practice rather than a challenge to development. This Chapter suggests that there is an important opportunity to reform curricula to reflect a new set of priorities. A combination of Political Science research and professionalization literature could be used more systematically to prepare our students for a range of government, public sector, media and third sector jobs. At the very least a more practically-oriented degree could support student interest in topical and applied politics, thereby capturing student interest when it is most passionate. At best it might help society by developing appropriately trained professionals who can engage at the level of applying academic research. Drawing on our own teaching experiences, this article explains the rationale for change, makes suggestions for underlying principles, and then proposes ideas about how the twenty-first-century Politics degree might look if it were designed from scratch, with the hope of opening a new debate on what Politics we teach as well as how we teach it.

Current curricula

The traditional driver for curriculum content is the academic perspective. Above all, the academic approach has generated a system of self-reproduction, asking undergraduate students to pursue an academic apprenticeship, even as most scholars and the research councils have recognized that an undergraduate degree can only play a limited part in preparing students for a research career. While acknowledging that the crude generalizations below cover a wide variety of actual practice, we characterize the traditional academic approach as rewarding the skills associated with scholarship, as measured by

- breadth, extent and strategic selection of reading.
- critical and analytical faculties, represented by the ability to develop a clear and well-constructed written argument for an audience of subject specialists.
- appropriate use of evidence.
- an appreciation of research in the field.
- intellectual honesty, measured in part by accurate citation practices.
- exam performance, often reflecting the capacity to reproduce rote learning.

There is limited consensus on the actual substance of the curriculum, except regarding introductory political theory; the main determinants of what is taught are sometimes the internal politics of institutions for staff and administrative convenience. As suggested by the opening quote, most curricula appear to have evolved through incrementalism rather than design. Public choice scholars of a certain vintage would have a field day explaining the design of Politics curricula.

The academic approach has long been dominant in curriculum design. However, as many lecturers recognize, a series of challenges to this *status quo* are emerging. Curriculum design is being exposed to two distinct sets of interests and concerns that traditionally have been marginalized in the process: those of Politics students and of wider society.

The challenges posed by the student universe

We would contend that the academic-driver is now at odds with the current demands of Politics students. Teachers of Politics are being asked to take greater account of student concerns. With the National Student Survey and other attempts to increase the amount of information available to future students to inform their choice of degree, the rise of staff-student liaison bodies and surveys of students' views on individual modules under Quality Assurance procedures, student opinions are more widely articulated and their consideration more institutionalized than ever before.

To us, the interests expressed by Politics students suggest three principles to underpin curriculum design: a greater focus on public policy, addressing the employability agenda through professionalization and greater training in active citizenship.

Young people who come to study Politics are, very often, motivated by their political commitments. They want to understand the issues. What is painfully obvious is that there is frequently a lack of meeting points between current affairs and Politics degrees. We wonder whether colleagues share our bemusement concerning the almost incidental value attributed to Politics students' knowledge and understanding of current controversies? It is impossible to watch students reflecting on their experience and not conclude that they are entitled to the opportunity to learn more about the issues that motivated many of them to come and study Politics in the first place. Students put a premium on issues, and therefore public policy should have a higher place in the curriculum.

Experience shows that many students also want to learn how to act on their beliefs, in political life or in public service employment. University study already delivers some understanding of issues but rarely has anything to say about what to do with such an understanding. There is usually a detachment from the practical which frustrates many who are motivated to engineer change. To address these student interests, a Politics degree should include developing the qualities of the active citizen.

Students are also more concerned with their degrees as a preparation for employment. The introduction, and subsequent rise, in tuition fees has changed the context for all UK universities. While such a perception understandably disturbs many academics, most students see the delivery of degree programmes as an implicit contract, where the costs of the degree programme legitimize questions as to what the outputs are, particularly in financial or career development terms. As most Politics staff who have faced an open day audience will testify, students and parents want to know how their studies, and the costs incurred during them, will improve career prospects. A Politics degree is conceived by its students in far more instrumental terms than in the past, which highlights a new need to address the employability agenda.

The degree based on an academic apprenticeship is convincing students less; the value of the predominant approach is far from self-evident to young people arriving at university and often, our worries about method and evidence, while recognized as part of the degree experience, are seen as crowding out the topics students most want to study. Such instrumentality suggests a need for systematic consideration of how Politics degrees can be made more practical and vocational without sacrificing the value of disciplinary content.

The challenges posed by the social universe

This rather instrumental understanding of a degree's purpose is also the primary pressure exerted by the social universe. Whether one conceives the social universe as expressed through the views of politicians of the day or even the perceptions of the man on the street, the role of graduates in the economy is at the forefront of discussion.

Politicians' unnerving tendency to conceive universities' role primarily as sustaining the economy is difficult to accept. Discussion of degrees as a means to produce economically productive agents is seen by many members of the profession as a betrayal of traditional virtues of higher education in challenging conventional wisdom. Few academics see their role as preparing students to earn an extra star on a McDonald's name tag; we offer our suggestions precisely to avoid such an outcome, instead intending to give students both control over their own destinies and the ability to make a difference through active citizenship. With both students and politicians asking awkward questions about the return on their investment in higher education, particularly of degrees as a preparation for employment, the discipline of Politics faces a challenge. The challenge is heightened by the diversity of employment destinations adopted by our graduates. It is becoming increasingly difficult to justify our existence in terms that fit with the employability agenda. Without internal reform there is a real possibility of our discipline ending up ornamental in the view of policymakers.

Of course, this challenge is not the only one to be confronted. Diminishing resources, increased administration driven by demands for greater accountability, expanded assessment and management of research all sap time and effort that might be spent on refreshing the curriculum. It is easy, and widespread practice, to conceive these challenges as threats to the profession. We are confronted by a series of encroachments produced by incremental reforms. Quality assurance, in the absence of strong structural incentives to attend to it, is handled as paperwork to be shuffled at the expense of valuable time. Student concerns over employability are dismissed as a failure to understand tutors' aspirations and the very nature of education itself. The result has been a tendency to go for lowest common denominator answers: we tinker at the fringes of the curriculum and devote effort to minimizing the impact of QA. Teleological (and tedious) processes of justification for the *status quo* ensue.

Responding to the challenges

In responding to the challenges, one option is to man the barricades in defence of the 'pure' Politics education. This battle is being lost in Westminster and has rarely registered beyond the Radio 4-listening public. Such a defence would be challenging and would rely upon a faith in the political power and organizational capacities of the academic community that is without recent historical precedent.

Alternatively, Politics teachers will continue to face these challenges. We contend that, as the institutionalization of these alternative conceptions of higher education develops, the interactions between the sets of interests offer interesting lines of investigation for future curriculum design. Underlying these challenges and frustrations are opportunities for new syntheses. Scholars of Politics need to take control of this agenda, rather than accepting a crude re-characterization of our work as producing thousands of economically productive agents each year. We should aspire to translate this agenda into something comprehensible to those that deliver the education and that reflects our teaching capacities and expertise. We argue that our discipline has much to offer, but currently, much of that potential is unrealized.

Our understanding is that there is enormous opportunity to be derived from the concepts of 'professionalization' and 'graduateness', as long as they are properly applied to our discipline. At the core of our approach is the concept of active citizenship. This phrase is firstly important as it represents, to us, a preferred understanding of the role of a Politics education. Rather than the economic driver often underlying employability discussions, we see the opportunity for a Politics degree to prepare participants to know how to make a difference to the community. A training in active citizenship should equip its graduates with practical capacities to operate in, including winning jobs in, the political environment. This characterization, we hope, can capture both students' interest in issues and their aspiration to participate in politics.

Professionalization

Society has embarked upon an extensive process of professionalizing careers. Government, parents, students, and even the man in the street increasingly perceive a degree as a route to a profession. It is this impulse which provides the discipline of Politics with an extraordinary opportunity. The answer to us seems quite similar to expectations of any professional education – say in medicine, law or social work.

While the language of professionalization may appear distant from our current curricula, that impression is misplaced. Most degree programmes have already adopted a relatively narrow approach to professionalization: the widespread conception of undergraduate degrees as research training, or as the first phase in an academic apprenticeship, does much to explain the shape of current Politics curricula. Particularly with the growth in avowedly Political Science curricula which place emphasis on methodology, Politics degrees often aim to develop a tranche of professional researchers equipped with the skills required to research in our discipline. Here, a lot of the thinking about directions of change has already been done; any university teacher who is unfamiliar with the Boyer Commission report (1998) on *Educating Undergraduates in the Research University* will find it a stimulating and challenging read. The main thrust is that inquiry-led learning should be standard from the start of degree programmes. Therefore, there needs to be much greater use of enquiry or problem-based learning in curricula than is currently the case. The recent Politics FDTL project led by the University of Huddersfield on Case Based Learning in Politics was of course philosophically inspired by this approach, and represents an excellent example of the application of the principles to one area of political studies (Craig and Hale, 2008). Nevertheless, evidence of this approach's limitations is to be found in graduate career destinations data, which demonstrate that we are preparing people for a career that the overwhelming majority choose not to pursue. Furthermore, given research council criteria for the approval of Master's programmes, there is some question as to whether we are able to deliver that preparation appropriately. For these reasons, there is a good argument to be made that this route will only prove appropriate for a limited number of institutions.

Instead, we argue that the emphasis on potential destinations should change to a more realistic and relevant target for most of our students: Politics degrees should produce politics professionals working in the political sphere, broadly understood. There has been a rise in professional politically-related jobs, due to the professionalization of government and political parties. As a result there is a broad range of politics-related work that we could consider preparing our students for. This includes, for example, work as an elected politician, member of politician's staff, staff of national and devolved parliaments, local councillor, civil servant, local government officer, think tank employee, political journalist, political party worker, public affairs officer, non-governmental organization worker, charity worker, diplomatic service officer, employee of a range of international organizations, teacher of politics or citizenship. If we consider the extraordinary range of subjects that we research as academics, the knowledge we hold has great potential here. We have an industry to serve where the knowledge and analytical capacities we teach are very relevant.

This approach is also useful because it captures the aspirations of students. Many students talk with enthusiasm about these forms of employment and want their degree to help them to develop the knowledge and skills which will support them in these kinds of work. Others have a broader, if vaguer, concept of wishing to be politically active. A professionalized Politics degree would directly address the need to justify Politics degrees in terms of employability, and it would also co-opt student enthusiasm.

How could the politics curriculum be professionalized?

Professionalization would involve a decision to deliver vocational training to our students. We would seek to develop the range of skills required in students' potential areas of employment. It would, of course, demand changes in Politics curricula. However, those changes, rather than arbitrary or *ad hoc* responses to the employability agenda, could become an exercise in capturing the insights of our discipline to equip professional practitioners. Some will interpret discussion of employability and skill sets as an alien discourse and a formula for launching an assault upon all that we hold dear within the discipline of Politics, but we do not accept this interpretation. On the contrary, among the humanities and social sciences, Politics is an extraordinarily good position to apply its research expertise in forms that equip students to work in the political environment. The match between our academic interests and relevant skill sets is an opportunity to be exploited.

Such an approach does not have to occur at the expense of work commonly conceived as being more cerebral. Instead, it is a case of demonstrating the application of our research in a practical and vocational manner. Beyond its capacity to generate Political Science researchers, Political Science can contribute a great deal to the enhancement of the skills of active Politics students. We are not suggesting academics change what they research, or stop teaching some topics. This isn't a case of throwing out Political Science literature; there is a wealth of potentially applicable research being conducted, but it is a case of using it in a different way. We are suggesting that if we change the way we teach we can make both new and established areas of investigation and study more relevant. Our proposal comes from a serious respect for the merits of academic research, but an understanding that the way we currently teach fails to draw out the practical lessons of such research. We tend to teach theories and models of what happened; we often neglect to project from this what works or what should be avoided. It is a natural outgrowth of our discipline's greater emphasis on theory that we should examine theory's potential applications. Just as importantly, a professionalized Politics programme needs to explain why certain approaches work, as we need to equip our graduates with the analytical capacity to apply their learning effectively and adjust in response to changing circumstances.

Those building such a degree programme would need to comb the discipline's knowledge base to identify the practical political knowledge we could usefully impart. For example, in relation to political cognition we can ask what an understanding of how people think about politics has to tell the practitioner.

For political participation, can an understanding of non-engagement in politics help find solutions to the problem? What can membership studies tell us about how to recruit members to parties and interest groups? Can studies of political communication help train our students in how to convey and gain support for new policy initiatives? These are just examples: it is hard to imagine such a combing of the discipline failing to embrace any particular sub-field if colleagues are willing to pursue this reinvention. Could the true 'active citizen' function without an understanding of democracy, a proper conception of power, a grasp of the public policy process or expertise on institutions?

Here we present a series of roles in the profession which we might prepare our students for, alongside existing academic fields that could support that preparation (see Table 17.1).

Our discipline can enrich these professions if we focus more on how we apply our expertise.

Having established that we have a remarkably diverse and relevant knowledge base at our disposal, the other aspect of building a programme would be the identification of the relevant skill set. While 'skill sets' tend to feature within the language of the general employability agenda, we aspire to a more subject-specific approach, so instead of *transferable* skills, our approach is about *political* skills.

Table 17.1   Examples of political jobs and relevant academic field

Role	Relevant academic field
Advisor to a politician	Research methods, public policy
Diplomat	International relations
Parliamentary staff	Institutions and parliaments, research methods, public policy
Communications advisor	Media, political communication
Strategist	Political marketing, public choice
Media advisor	Media, political communication
Pollster	Voting behaviour, political marketing, public opinion, quantitative methods
Social marketer	Political behaviour
Press Officer	Media, political communication, political behaviour
Journalist	Media, political communication, political behaviour
Charity work	Media, political communication, political behaviour, campaigns
Activist	Campaigns and campaigning
Consultation Manager	Deliberative democracy, consultation, political marketing, engagement, participation
Politics teaching	All fields
Citizenship teaching	Citizenship, democratic theory
Elected politician – MP, local councillor, mayor	All fields but esp. communication, campaigning

In our discussions of skills, it has become clear that enabling skilled participation within the political environment depends upon generating a confluence of forces. First, there is the opportunity to borrow frameworks from existing professionalized degrees. We have much to learn from our colleagues in other disciplines. Professionalism is a contested concept, but most definitions, and the frameworks of most existing professional degrees, contain the dimensions of interpersonal, public and intrapersonal professionalism (van de Camp et al., 2004). These ideas offer an opportunity for innovative thinking about the teaching of Politics. Second, the development of a permanent discourse with the relevant professions would have to become an integral part of curriculum design, placing greater emphasis on alumni networks as a means to hone the curriculum and develop placement opportunities. Indeed, such a skill set could only be developed in discussion with potential employers of our graduates. Third, just as we have an existing knowledge base, we have an existing set of assumptions about skills that, although challenged by the forces above, still have much to contribute to the development of politics professionals.

Our challenge would be to establish a new discourse on the teaching of professionalized politics. Such an approach would demand a number of stages. First, we would need to identify the particular professions that this new form of Politics degree could support. We have offered some ideas on this subject above. Second, we would need to establish a further, but related, debate to establish the relevant materials such a degree would aspire to teach. As explained below, these debates can be approached in terms of both the knowledge base we already possess and skills we already teach, but in combination with skills sets derived from professionalization and engagement with the relevant professions. Finally, these debates would feed into the proper development of a teaching programme with assessment designed to capture students' achievement, or failure to achieve, both understanding of the practical political knowledge and the relevant skill set. Such a strategy would sit comfortably alongside the emerging emphasis on the identification and teaching of graduate skills.

The recent trend towards developing statements of graduate attributes, which began in Australia, is becoming influential in the UK. Concepts of 'graduateness' include all of the qualities of a professional but are broader. Unlike narrow definitions of employability, statements of graduate attributes represent progress because they introduce balance into the debate over curriculum content. They recognize the virtue of traditional academic skills associated with university education such as; intellectual development, analysis, clear written communication and the ability to make sense of a large amount of conflicting material. Statements of graduate attributes also, though, identify a number of other desirable qualities, such as personal skills and social capabilities which could include effective public speaking, a sense of ethics or personal integrity. Such statements acknowledge that these qualities do not arise automatically, and that to inculcate them requires conscious design.

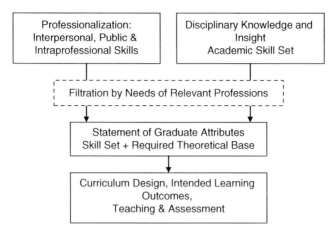

Figure 17.1   Designing the professionalized politics degree

They also acknowledge that the skills, knowledge and capabilities needed to secure, maintain and change employment do not automatically grow but need to be nurtured and practiced. Hence an effective statement of graduate attributes would be a key stepping stone to developing a curriculum for pro-fessionalized Politics degrees. This curriculum design process is represented in Figure 17.1 above.

Throughout this development process, we would need to establish the capacities we have as a discipline to deliver such a programme, what weaknesses might stand in our way, and how we achieve this change without compromising the integrity of the discipline we wish to teach and our students wish to study.

The professionalized politics skill set: a sketch

While acknowledging that a lengthy process of debate is required to identify the relevant skill set, concepts of the professionalized degree do offer initial directions for investigation. We suggest the following dimensions of political professionalism:

- **Interpersonal – meeting the demands for political practice:** honesty, integrity, altruism, leadership, respect, compassion, empathy, people-skills, clear and effective communication, listening
- **Public – meeting the demands placed by the public on public servants:** accountability, excellence, self-regulation, negotiation, sense of justice
- **Intraprofessional – meeting the demands to function as an individual in public life:** lifelong learning, self-awareness, morality, aspiration for excellence or impeccability in relation to professional skills and knowledge, ability to deal with uncertainty.

If you asked a well-informed non-specialist about the problems of democratic political systems in the twenty-first century, the majority of responses would, we suggest, argue that several of the interpersonal qualities above were in short supply.[1] They should be taught. In response to the anticipated criticism that these are personal qualities that cannot be taught, we respond that many medical degrees aspire to precisely this. In part it is a matter of demonstration; that you practice what you preach. So for example, medical education enforces much higher standards in relation to attendance and engagement than do many political educators. Similar points would apply to other qualities: mutual respect and interest, encouragement of self-regulation, taking a reflective approach to practice. All of these are simply part of a professional educational culture. It is also a matter of observation: the Objective Structured Clinical Examination that is common practice on most health programmes requires the student to demonstrate their professional skills in a variety of simulated clinical situations, and this is just as much part of the goals of the degree as subject knowledge.

One can go further into a profound exploration of what these qualities mean in a political context, taking politics in its widest sense, including interpersonal relationships in which one person is trying to influence another. For example, in the student representative training we conduct at Keele University, we explore scenarios of personal conflict with which students are familiar. A favourite is the example of the untidy flat-mate. We analyse the scenario in terms of the judgements which are being made, the implicit 'shoulds', 'oughts' and fixed beliefs about the situation, with a view to demonstrating that these fixed ways of thinking create a structure for the problem which make a mutually satisfactory resolution impossible. We also analyse the benefits that both parties gain from maintenance of the conflict, and also the costs that result. We then explore possible solutions, all of which involve in some way one party changing their mind about what the other's behaviour means. In so doing, we are both exploring the deep issues about interpersonal skills, and simultaneously fostering understanding of the structure of intractable political conflict. It is 'the personal is political' in practice.

Professionalism in the public sphere involves dimensions of accountability, excellence and self-regulation. These are rich issues for us to explore in the context of any number of recent public policy *causes celebres*, which can be taught depending on local expertise.

We describe intraprofessional skills as involving issues of lifelong learning and aspiration to excellence in terms of professional skills and knowledge, as well as morality and self-awareness. Politics students, like any others, need to be able to articulate the skills they have developed over their lives, reflect on personal values and motivations, research the graduate labour market, and make some kind of match between these.

Each of these dimensions of professionalism can be connected to relevant political materials or teaching methods. A sketch of how this might work is summarized in Table 17.2.

Beyond this broad framework, it is possible to develop specific ideas on the skills required to function in the political environment effectively. We suspect that professional graduates should demonstrate their aptitude for communication, leadership and influence, organization, research, negotiation and arbitration, teamwork, strategy, ethical/moral conduct, representation and campaigning. Clearly this is neither a polished nor comprehensive description of the skill set required, but as emphasized above, what is required is a starting point for discussion among colleagues and current participants in the political environment.

Delivering the professionalized programme

The broad discussion above offers a starting point on the skill set required for a professionalized Politics degree. The process of using our existing expertise to deliver this skill set deserves more investigation. Looking at the specific skills we suggest, the examples below demonstrate the potential syntheses between our existing expertise as a discipline and a skills-oriented approach.

Political communication would need to be a core skill for anyone graduating from a professionalized programme. Almost every occupation within the political environment depends on an interaction with other participants. Politics provides perfect vehicles for the practical teaching of communication, yet it remains a poorly exploited opportunity. While we teach political communication, we rarely teach it on an individual level such as effective public speaking. Instead, public speaking is taught in other contexts, such as business training and law-mooting, therefore leaving the training bereft of the political dimension. Public speaking and debate skills can and should be a mainstream parts of Politics degrees. Rhetoric was part of the core curriculum in the original academy, and for good reason. The teaching can be sustained by intelligent use of political communications research, as already pursued in programmes at the Masters' level such as LSE's MA in Political Communication.

Representation is another field that cries out for emphasis in a professionalized degree. Our knowledge base is extensive and the opportunities to provide practical experience are manifold. The training of student representatives on course committees and other forms of university politics is one interesting vehicle for teaching this material, giving students the opportunity to try out such ideas in a relatively safe environment. We have tried this out at Keele in the form of an interdisciplinary first year module on 'Representing Students'.

Leadership and community building are both subjects that have generated much discussion in other fields of study, but relatively little in terms of political

Table 17.2 Connecting dimensions of professionalism to political materials

Professional Qualities	Sub-Categories[2]	Relevant Political Materials or Teaching Methods
Interpersonal: meeting the demands for political practice	honesty, integrity, reliability altruism, service respect, tolerance compassion, empathy people skills communication skills leadership, avoiding misuse of power listening	Political Scandals Political biography (in particular the modern-day 'secular saints' such as Gandhi, Mandela, Martin Luther King etc) Coalition theory, internationalization of education Peer assessment (giving and receiving feedback develops these qualities) Decision-making studies, small group work, team-based assessment Political communication, political marketing Leadership theory Negotiation, also peer assessment
Public: meeting the demands the public places on public servants	accountability excellence, expertise self-regulation negotiation sense of justice	Representation, political communication Public policy, policy evaluation Public and campaign finance, Problem based learning sets International relations, coalition theory Political ideologies
Intraprofessional: meeting the demands to function as an individual in public life	Critical analysis lifelong learning: aspiration for excellence or impeccability in relation to professional skills and knowledge self-awareness morality ability to deal with uncertainty	All academic writing Implicit in the degree experience Self-assessments and reflective writing Political Philosophy Implicit in studying current events

practice (see Block, 2008; Kouzes and Pousner, 2007; Wheatley and Kellner-Rogers, 1996; Wheatley, 2002 and 2005; although of course see Putnam, 2000 and 2003). Similarly there are lively debates about ways of achieving genuine and lasting change which seem to be happening outside of the corridors of UK Politics departments (for example, Block, 2008; Kahane, 2004; Senge et al., 2004).

Numerous areas seem ripe for the application of such an approach. Politics graduates trained in negotiation and arbitration would be at a premium in the political environment. There are many remarkable studies of seemingly intractable political conflicts that have been resolved creatively. Political campaigning also deserves exploration. Students want to know how to act on their commitments; the opportunity to explore the whole process of planning, conducting and evaluating campaigns should be available to many more politics students. The study of political biography and leadership are both superb vehicles for exploring interpersonal skills. A special word is also warranted for public policy. There is every reason to promote public policy to the forefront of the curriculum, both as study of the issues and as an understanding of the policy process. Standard institutions-based and nation-based curricula have tended to tiptoe around this field in the last 30 years.

The above suggests potential in a handful of specific areas, but we speculate that the potential for further synergies between academic expertise and practical application abound. These are not all new ideas: courses are taught that pick up on these synergies, particularly at Masters' level. However, the application of these ideas to undergraduate curricula largely remains under-investigated.

Sketching the twenty-first-century politics degree

In its fullest form, compensating for that under-investigation suggests a complete re-orienting of Politics teaching. Using the principles advocated, we offer a suggestion of different modules that could be part of a new Politics degree. This is a rough draft, but we hope an imaginative and exciting one. It is particularly worth noting the potentials that lie in the translation of our knowledge at the mass level to an understanding of what we believe works in the political arena if used at the individual level. For example, teaching of political communication at the mass level translates to the individual level, such as effective public speaking. Campaigning is another area taught at macro level but can also be taught from the student viewpoint in terms of how to act on commitments. This mass/individual translation is highlighted in Table 17.3 below.

Table 17.3 A model new Politics degree

Module title	Content
Listening	Listening skills on an individual level; market research, consultation on a mass level
Communicating	Individual level: effective public speaking, assertiveness, negotiation, dealing with difficult people, written skills
	Mass level: Press releases, political communication, media
Leading	Individual level: leading, ethics, management of others
	Mass level: leadership studies, character
Researching	Individual: research skills; could be a 'research apprenticeship' course where students are trained by doing a project for academics; would then support both teaching and research
	Mass: political science methods
Organizing	Individual: time management, team work
	Mass: membership, participation, engagement and party organizational and institutional studies
Watching/ commenting	Individual: debating skills, researching a moving target, observational skills
	Mass: topical, current day issues; to include debates, election watching parties, media reporting, budgets and other relevant events
Influencing	Individual level: negotiating, debating, persuading, respecting
	Mass level: Social marketing, voting behaviour, public opinion, advertising, campaigning
Advising	Individual: being a mentor, providing support, empathy, offering critique, reviewing, developing rapport and trust
	Mass: advisor and consultant studies
Campaigning	Individual level: gaining support for your ideas, team work, networking
	Mass level: single issue, election campaigns, interest groups
Professionalizing	Individual: stress management, life-learning, reflectiveness, non-linear learning, philosophy
	Mass: professionalization of political parties, party staff, party funding, civil service/bureaucracy
Advancement	Individual: Networking, careers, work-life balance, negotiating, strategizing
	Mass: career politicians, leadership selection
Behaving ethically	Individual: values, integrity, making positive interventions
	Mass: ideology, values, ethics, scandal, political theory, democratic principles, equity laws, minority representation/exclusion; pragmatism versus principle; goals

(continued)

Table 17.3 Continued

Module title	Content
Designing	Individual:
	Mass: Institutional theory, political theory, democracy
Representing	Individual: advocacy, listening, student rep roles
	Mass: representative theory and assessment, democratic theory, electoral system design, justice

Placements, career development and assessment

Delivering a genuinely professionalized programme also demands a revised attitude to placements' role in curricula. Practical experience is routine on professional degrees in health but not in social sciences. Graduates would need the opportunity to use and hone their skills in a practical environment. Placement learning for Politics has been addressed in detail in the FDTL project on the scholarship of engagement for Politics, and in the forthcoming edited collection of detailed and practical advice on ways of developing this aspect of political education (Curtis and Blair, 2010). One important issue is about the ways in which the workplace experience can be made to dialogue with curriculum content. This is easier in some subject areas than others: local government, political marketing, campaigning and media studies offer natural linkage with practical politics, but with a bit of creativity, even political theory modules could be integrated in this way. There are also a range of organizational and practical issues, but a lot of the groundwork on these has been completed by the FDTL team, and we suggest that it is entirely legitimate for students to wonder why this sort of experience is routine on professional degrees in health but not in social sciences. Another opportunity to make the degree more practical is through the use of *alumni* as visiting speakers from the start and throughout.

A related need is for career development education to support students' ambitions. Politics students, like any others, need to be able to articulate the skills they have developed over their lives, reflect on personal values and motivations and research the graduate labour market, in light of their personal development. They also require transition skills to do with self-presentation, such as completing effective application forms and *CVs*, performing well at interview, dealing with assessment centres and psychometric testing, as well as a realistic understanding of the nature of work, and the serendipitous way careers often develop. Simply put, this is the agenda represented by the process of personal development planning (PDP); to develop a professionalized degree course, the community of political educators would have to take PDP seriously.

Education along these lines should be an entitlement not a bonus. Relying on informal processes and serendipity in this area may have been good enough for many universities in an era of elite higher education where most students had access to social networks which supported transition to the workplace. However it is clear that these networks do not exist for many in the era of mass higher education and widening participation. The world outside academia may be unfamiliar and the profession may doubt it has the resources to take this on, but we must ask ourselves what is our responsibility by our students (for further discussion of means for this, see Wyman and Longwell, 2010)

Consideration of placement learning and career development education are integral parts of the re-thinking of assessment that would be required for a professionalized degree. Assessment would need to focus upon students' demonstration of the ability to apply appropriate skills practically. Of course, in many cases it would not be easy to assess these sorts of soft skills. Reflective portfolios are excellent for demonstrating a process, demonstrating that learning is happening. There are more objective approaches possible too. For example why not adapt the Objective Structured Clinical Examination for political purposes? Let's see whether participants can demonstrate the political equivalent of 'bedside manner'...

On the occasions that our students meet this kind of approach, they appreciate it. Practically-oriented reports received positive comments from students with direct links made to post-graduation possibilities:

> Really enjoyed the process of writing a report. Very applicable and practical, link between theory and the real world showed how my Politics degree could be used after university
>
> Reports encompass theoretical understanding and analysis but more importantly they have an overall practical utility which the department has overlooked in papers I have previously conducted
>
> My best work was the political marketing report I did on the ACT party... your class inspired me to consider politics as a career instead of as just an interest

A rethinking of assessment practices would allow qualification in a professionalized Politics degree to demonstrate the capacity to pursue a job in the professional political arena.

Conclusions

The teaching of Politics as a discipline confronts an environment that is changing rapidly. Over the last decade, interests that have been traditionally less well represented have begun to gain a foothold in shaping the delivery of Politics programmes. We have presented a view of how the challenges we discuss might be met through curriculum reform. The 'research professional' model may suit certain institutions but for many, we believe that a professionalized Politics degree offers the best way to respond to these pressures effectively, serve student needs and retain the academic and intellectual integrity of our programmes. There is also the intriguing prospect of teaching the two in parallel, perhaps as 'Politics' and 'Applied Politics'.

We have offered a series of ideas on how existing expertise within our discipline could be approached to deliver a professionalized degree that would equip our graduates to deal with the kind of challenges they would confront in the arena of practical politics. Our choices of area are particular, but only because we believe there is extraordinary scope for creative thinking and teaching in so many areas of the discipline that no comprehensive approach could be offered by a small handful of authors. We hope others will see further potentials that lie in their particular specialism. Education in politics can be extended into many new areas to become more relevant to students and to the outside world.

Notes

1. The use of 'political skills' and 'professionalism' in politics have connotations of 'black arts' of manipulation and spin. It often functions as an antonym for virtue in political practice. Here, however, we attempt to differentiate 'professionalism' from the term 'professionalization' to emphasize the latter term's denoting of approaches used by academic disciplines which stress professional training.
2. All these categories are adapted from van de Camp et al. (2004), p. 699.

References

Block, P. (2008), *Community: The Structure of Belonging* (San Francisco: Berrett Koehler).

Boyer Commission (1998), *Reinventing Undergraduate Education: a blueprint for America's Research Universities* http://naples.cc.sunysb.edu/pres/boyer.nsf/673918d46fbf653e85 2565ec0056ff3e/d955b61ffddd590a852565ec005717ae/$FILE/boyer.pdf (accessed 20 March 2011).

van de Camp, K., Vernooij-Dassen, M. J. F. J., Grol, R. P. T. M. and Bottema, B. J. A. M. (2004), 'How to Conceptualize Professionalism: A Qualitative Study', *Medical Teacher*, 26 (8), 696–702.

Craig, J. and Hale, S. (2008), 'Implementing Problem-based Learning in Politics', *European Political Science*, 7 (2), 165–74.

Curtis, S., Blair, A., Sherrington, P., Axford, B., Gibson, A., Huggins, R. and Marsh, C. (2009), 'Making Short Placements Work', *Politics*, 1, 62–70.

Curtis, S. and Blair, A. (eds) (2010), *The Scholarship of Engagement for Politics: Placement Learning, Citizenship and Employability* (Birmingham: C-SAP) http://www.lulu.com/product/file-download/the-scholarship-of-engagement-for-politics/6427740 (accessed 2 February 2012).

Gilbert, A. (2009), Comment made during interview on BBC Radio 4, *Beyond Westminster*, broadcast 15 August 2009, available at http://www.bbc.co.uk/programmes/b00m0gr2#synopsis

(accessed 24 August 2009); reported at http://news.bbc.co.uk/1/hi/education/8198318.stm (accessed 1 September 2009).

Kahane, A. (2004), *Solving Tough Problems* (San Francisco: Berrett Koehler).

Kouzes, J. M. and Pousner, B. Z. (2007), *The Leadership Challenge* (San Francisco, CA: John Wiley & Sons).

Putnam, R. (2000), *Bowling Alone: The Collapse and Revival of American Community* (New York: Simon & Schuster).

Putnam, R. and Feldstein, L; with Cohen, D. (2003) *Better Together: Restoring the American Community* (New York: Simon & Schuster). Quality Assurance Agency for Higher Education (QAA) (2007), *Politics and International Relations Subject Benchmark Statement*, http://www.qaa.ac.uk/academicinfrastructure/benchmark/statements/Politics.pdf (accessed 20 March 2010).

Senge, P., Otto Scharmer, C., Jaworski, J. and Flowers, B. (2005), *Presence: Exploring Profound Change in People, Organisations and Society* (London: Nicholas Brearley).

Stammers, N., Dittmar, H. and Henney, J. (1999), 'Teaching and Learning Politics: a Survey of Practices and Change in UK Universities', *Political Studies*, 47 (1), 114–26.

Sloam, J. (2008), 'Teaching Democracy: The Role of Political Science Education', *The British Journal of Politics & International Relations*, 10 (3), 509–24.

Wheatley, M. J. (2002), *Turning to One Another: Simple Conversations to Restore Hope to the Future* (San Francisco: Berrett Koehler).

Wheatley, M. J. (2005), *Finding Our Way: Leadership for an Uncertain Time* (San Francisco: Berrett Koehler).

Wheatley, M.J. and Kellner-Rogers, M. (1996), *A Simpler Way* (San Francisco: Berrett Koehler).

Wyman, M. and Longwell, S. (2010), 'Teaching the Practice of Politics' in Curtis, S. and Blair, A. (eds) *The Scholarship of Engagement for Politics: Placement Learning, Citizenship And Employability* (Birmingham: C-SAP) http://www.lulu.com/product/file-download/the-scholarship-of-engagement-for-politics/6427740 (accessed 4 April 2011).

Index